WORKING-CLASS
ANTI-SEMITE

WORKING-CLASS
ANTI-SEMITE

A Psychological Study in a London Borough

JAMES H. ROBB

M.A., Ph.D.

TAVISTOCK PUBLICATIONS LTD.

First published 1954
by Tavistock Publications Limited
2 Beaumont Street, London, W. 1
and printed in Great Britain
in 12 pt. Bembo by
The Pitman Press, Bath

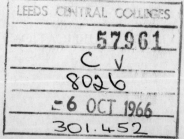

FOREWORD

THE problem of anti-Semitism, to which Dr. Robb has addressed himself, has prompted an enormous amount of research and speculation. It is, of course, only part of the more general topic of ethnic prejudice, but the long and dramatic history of the Jews and the mass persecutions of which they have been the victims have given special prominence to the hostility so widely directed against them.

There are two lines of attack, and it is to the credit of Dr. Robb that he has made use of both of them. On the one hand there is the sociological approach, which is concerned with the existence of minority groups, the history of their relations with the larger society in which they are incorporated, and the study of the cultural characteristics of both parties, a matter which is relevant to the tensions which may develop between them. On the other hand there is the psychological approach. After all, the ascription of general qualities to groups, irrespective of—and, indeed, often in defiance of—manifest differences between one member and another, and the direction of hostility in varying degrees towards such groups, frequently irrespective of personal friendship towards individual members, are done by persons. The question then arises: are there any other characteristics of personality which go with these marks of prejudice? Obviously both approaches are necessary. If you find, as Dr. Robb has found and as other investigators have found, that certain personal maladjustments make people prone to prejudices of this kind, you still have to consider the target against which their prejudice is aimed. There is some evidence, it is true, that people who are prejudiced against one group are likely to be prejudiced against another, and even against groups that do not exist at all. Such evidence, however, should not lead us to suppose that prejudice is simply a "psychological" matter. The groups themselves are in some sense "collective representations". From a purely theoretical point of view any set of qualities can be used for grouping, hair colour, height, sex, religion, language, and so on, or any combination of these, and a person may very well have an irrational dislike for the presence of any quality you choose to name. The fact, however, is that certain groupings are selected, and members of such groups are collectively represented as possible targets of abuse. Which characteristics are chosen for what one might call "collective representational" grouping will vary from culture to culture, and will depend on historical circumstances. Furthermore, not all "collectively agreed" groupings will be deemed appropriate targets. The Quakers, for example, grouped according to the criteria of religious beliefs and practices, have not, so far as I know, been the targets of prejudice in recent years, and yet they, like the Jews, have the reputation of marked efficiency in business. The laws which govern these collectively agreed groupings, and determine which shall be accepted targets, have never been worked out, perhaps because the existence of such groups is taken for granted, but it is clear that such an enquiry should be part of the sociological approach to the problem of prejudice.

When, however, we have our groups, it is clear enough that, although they are *possible* targets of prejudice, not every member of the host cultures feels antagonism towards them. Many, indeed, scarcely recognise their existence, except in a purely formal way. Some treat then as a joke, while a few feel violently ill-disposed towards them. It is this fact that has given rise to the greater bulk of the research into ethnic prejudice; and it is this that particularly interests Dr. Robb. His principal contribution to the study of ethnic-prejudice, in the form of anti-Semitism, lies in this method of enquiry. Nearly all his predecessors have relied on some form of questionnaire method, supplemented by other forms of testing, in which they have made use of subjects detached from their normal habitat. Dr. Robb approached his subjects in their homes. Realising that prejudices develop in a social context, and appreciating the significance of sub-cultural differences, he advanced upon Bethnal Green with the intention of finding our what life was like to its inhabitants, and how this affected those who had pronounced anti-Semitism attitudes. Now it is the easiest thing in the world to give a questionnaire to groups of students, but it is a very different matter to try to turn oneself into a fly on the wall in Bethnal Green. He started off by turning himself into a bar-man. Then he made use of the fact that he was a New Zealander, and styled himself as a student of demography, studying problems of housing and mobility. Some oblique approach had to be made. He could not just stop every other person he met and say: "do you like or dislike the Jews?" What he had to do was to carry on a conversation about housing, making it as engaging as possible, until the Jews "cropped up." The result of these techniques—barman-ship and chat-manship, as one might say—is that his description of life in Bethnal Green is what is sometimes contemptuously called "impressionistic", and that the number of quasi-formal interviews is small, though the subjects were chosen with due regard to sampling requirements. There does not seem to me to be anything inherently wrong about this. He had to fit his methods to his problems. The proof of the pudding he presents us lies, as with any scientific research, in its eating. His results are valuable if they give rise to verifiable expectations. The issues are: (1) If anyone else goes to Bethnal Green, will the expectations evinced by Dr. Robb's account of the salient features of child-rearing and its consequences be confirmed? (2) Is it true that anyone upon whom the pressure of the culture he has to absorb bears extra heavily will be more prejudiced against the local variant of ethnic target than in the case with those whose passage has been easier? The first hypothesis can be tested in Bethnal Green, the second can be tested anywhere. Every hypothesis has its own range of verifiability and Dr. Robb's hypotheses are no exception.

Dr. Robb is mainly interested, as I have said, in the relation between personal adjustment and prejudice. His work will therefore take its place with that of Frenkel-Brunswick, Adorno, Allport, and other social psychologists, interested in the same problem. He has, however, rightly seen that personal adjustment is a function of the culture to which persons have to adjust. This is why he starts off with a description of life in Bethnal Green. In doing so he has made a secondary contribution to social psychology. It is all too often assumed that English culture is homogeneous. There are, it is true, pervasive features, but it is of vital importance to the understanding of social behaviour that we should realise that sub-cultures exist in this country which differ in significant ways from the "official" culture of the middle classes. If I may speak personally on this subject I would say that in his findings on the issue of personality characteristics making for prejudice Dr. Robb has "merely" confirmed the findings of other social psychologists, but in his analysis of Bethnal Green life he has made a major contribution to the study

of English society. I do not, of course, wish to minimise the value
of Dr. Robb's main conclusions about personality and prejudice,
but such a topic is, in a sense, more obvious than the delineation of
sub-cultures. And yet the latter field of enquiry is of paramount
importance, not only for the purpose to which Dr. Robb has put
it but also for the unravelling of other social problems.

Only one other writer, Dr. Spinley, has given us assistance in
this matter of comparing sub-cultures in this country. In her *The
Deprived and the Privileged* she compares the child-rearing methods of
certain middle-class families with those prevailing in a London slum
area. Clearly the resultant personalities and their standards will be
quite different. And now, for a different purpose, Dr. Robb has
described yet another set of standards and the family relations with
which they are associated. He concludes his book with a generous
list of topics for research. Let me conclude this introduction by
expressing the hope that besides those who will doubtless select from
his list, there will be others who will follow his example by making
further contributions to our understanding of the complex system
of cultures in which we live. Let me also add my thanks to Dr. Robb
for the pleasure and instruction he has given me and for the com-
pliment he has paid be by inviting be to introduce his book.

W. J. H. SPROTT

Department of Philosophy,
The University,
Nottingham.

CONTENTS

LIST OF TABLES

PREFACE

THE study of race prejudice and especially of anti-Semitism has a long history, but it is only in comparatively recent times that any attempt has been made to apply scientific methods to this purpose. Particularly during and since the war, psychologists and sociologists have shown an increasing interest in the problem of anti-Semitism. Their concern has been not so much with the nature of the doctrines propounded by anti-Semites, but rather with the anti-Semites themselves, and with the social conditions under which their opinions gained support.

For the most part these studies have been carried out in the United States, and the work described in this book represents one of the very few attempts to carry out an empirical study of the problem in this country. While it is concerned primarily with the personality characteristics of anti-Semites, all the individuals studied have been members of the same community in East London, and an attempt has been made to relate their personal characteristics to the social situation in which they live.

This study has been made possible only by the active assistance of a number of people. I am very conscious of my indebtedness, which I gladly take this opportunity of acknowledging. My greatest single debt is to Professor Edward A. Shils, who was Reader in Sociology at the London School of Economics, at the time I was carrying out the fieldwork. But for his help and encouragement the work would have been much poorer and might never have been carried out. Mr. J. L. Petersen, of University House, Bethnal Green, was extremely helpful in providing me with introductions when I first visited Bethnal Green, and made a number of useful suggestions.

Mr. John Morris helped to carry out the long and arduous process of using the rating scales described in Chapter IV. Dr. John Spencer, Mr. Hallam Tennyson, Mr. Michael Banton, and Mr. Lionel Rose helped in many ways. Dr. Peter McKellar assisted in experiments with the interviewing methods and Dr. Charles Wrigley gave much valuable assistance with statistics. Many people who lived or worked in Bethnal Green, some of whom I came to know well, and others whom I met only once, allowed me to interview them, to visit their homes, to join them in work and social activities. Without their co-operation the research would certainly not have been possible. The staff of the Bethnal Green Public Library were unfailingly helpful.

In its various drafts the manuscript has been read and criticised in whole or in part by most of the people already mentioned, and also by Miss Elizabeth Bott, Mr. Eric Trist, the Rev. Dr. James Parkes, Dr. Cyril Sofer, and Dr. David Schneider. Miss Theodora Alcock very kindly read the appendix on the Rorschach test results. I am very grateful to Professor Sprott for marking his interest in this study by contributing a foreword. I wish also to acknowledge the advice I received on many points from Mr. John Harvard-Watts, and to thank Miss June Hawthorne who typed the manuscript.

Special thanks are due to my wife who in addition to coping with highly erratic working hours, helped with the rating scales and with the typing of drafts, drew the first draft of the map which appears on page 51, and provided constant encouragement.

The thesis on which this book is based was accepted by the University of London for the degree of Doctor of Philosophy.

CHAPTER I

Introductory

ANTI-SEMITISM as a topic for discussion or a subject of study is neither novel nor unusual. It is upheld or denounced from public platforms, from the soap boxes of street corner orators, and in private discussion. Similarly, the volume of writing on the subject is so vast that it is impossible for any but the most avid student to read more than a fraction of the works available. These include not only the books of scholars, but also novels, plays, pamphlets, popular magazine articles, newspaper reports, and letters to editors, which recount its history, endeavour to explain its existence, support or attack it, or report its latest manifestations. The subject of this concern is not, of course, a figment of the imagination—no social phenomenon is more tragically real.

Amongst this great bulk of discussion, however, there is a comparatively small amount dealing with the people who are actually anti-Semitic. Their doctrines have received considerable attention, but they themselves, except for a small number of the most prominent, have been largely ignored. In recent years, however, attention has been slowly turning from the doctrines to the people who support and promulgate them, and a number of attempts have been made to study them at first hand.

This book is primarily a report on a piece of field research concerned with certain aspects of anti-Semitism, which was carried out during the years 1947-9 in the borough of Bethnal Green in East London. It has the form of a case study; that is to say, it is an account of a single community viewed over a relatively short period of time, and it makes no pretence of being a complete or exhaustive study of the problem of anti-Semitism. In the last two chapters an attempt is made to combine the conclusions drawn from this study with those resulting from the work of others, in order to

I

produce a more general and theoretical statement on the subject of anti-Semitism, but for the most part attention is concentrated on the results of a single piece of research. The main purpose of the research work was to test certain hypotheses, which are set out in detail in the next chapter. The field work was therefore oriented towards the collection of data relevant to this purpose, and the account that follows, being based on these data, will have a similar orientation. It is not therefore a full account of all that pertains to anti-Semitism, even within the community under study: there is much that might be said about anti-Semitism in Bethnal Green that will not appear in these pages. This does not mean that everything omitted was considered to be unimportant or uninteresting, but simply that it was not directly relevant to the task in hand. Therefore, to say that some fact has been omitted or that some aspect of anti-Semitism has not been discussed would be relevant only if the omission affected the task of testing the hypotheses with which we are here concerned. It is, of course, possible to criticise the choice of the particular problem studied, but this choice is a consequence of the interests and training of the research worker concerned, and individual preferences are bound to vary widely.

The amount that can be accomplished by one research worker over a period of two years is severely limited, and it was considered better to concentrate attention on a relatively narrow aspect of the problem and to study it in some detail, than to spread the available resources over the whole field in a more superficial manner. Most emphatically then this is not the whole story of anti-Semitism in Bethnal Green. Rather it is a study of selected features of the general problem of anti-Semitism and it so happens that the data were collected in Bethnal Green. They might equally have been collected in many other places, but so long as attention was focused on these particular aspects of the problem it would have been necessary to procure comparable data. Furthermore, because these data were collected in only one area, any general conclusions drawn from them must be regarded as tentative until such time as they are supported by further evidence obtained elsewhere, though, as will be shown later, a considerable degree of such support is by now available in reports published by other workers, chiefly in the United States.

In view of the statement that the study might have been carried out in almost any locality, an explanation should perhaps be given as to why Bethnal Green was chosen for this purpose. There were actually two steps in this choice, first the decision to carry out the study in a working class community, and second, the choice of Bethnal Green. General considerations concerning the limited resources available made the choice of a single, relatively small area inevitable.

This piece of research was begun after the completion of a study of the methodology of research into national character (Robb, 1946). One of the conclusions reached in that study was that in the past insufficient attention had been paid to variations between sub-groups within nations, particularly to social classes. Supposed descriptions of national character frequently are, in fact, descriptions of the upper or middle classes, or a combination of these. On some occasions the authors of the national character studies are aware of this fact, but very often they appear to assume that their descriptions really do apply to the whole nation. There are many reasons for this state of affairs, but the one which concerns us at the moment is that these authors would have had virtually no information to draw upon had they wished to include the working classes in their descriptions. This applies with particular force to data of a psychological nature, having reference to "normal" working class conditions. Though there are some studies, both sociological and psychological, of certain very limited aspects of working class life, these usually refer to individuals, single families, or very small groups, and are predominantly concerned with crime, delinquency, mental deficiency, and other abnormal conditions, or with special problems relating to children and adolescents. Alternatively they have been of a demographic or ecological nature, giving quantitative information of a highly impersonal kind, and providing only the faintest sketch of the ways in which real individuals live in actual communities.

Psychological research, whether individual or social, has been most usually carried out with middle and upper class subjects. In its most general terms the reason for this is simple: it is easier to do research in this way, since the research worker, either by birth or achievement, always belongs to one of these classes. He naturally finds it easier to deal with his peers, because he thus avoids what is virtually a cross-cultural contact, comparable in important respects with that made by anthropologists studying a primitive tribe. There may even be considerable language difficulties to be overcome. Almost certainly the research worker who moves into a different class in order to conduct his research will have to adjust himself to different value systems.

2   3

As the result of their educational experiences the members of the middle and upper classes usually have some appreciation of the value and necessity of scientific research and an interest in the results achieved, and this means that it is often easier to enlist their co-operation in research of this sort than is the case with those whose education has not normally provided them with such an outlook. Furthermore, the middle class research worker usually has his middle class subjects near at hand. All these factors are especially obvious in the case of university students, and we find, not surprisingly, that in the large majority of psychological research studies, the subjects for experiment and observation are students. Probably the next most frequently used group consists of school children. These are generally taken from middle class homes, or studied without much reference to their social background.

The defects of this situation extend far beyond the boundaries of national character studies. It is now realised, for example, that some of the generalisations put forward by the early psycho-analysts as universal truths, were actually applicable to the Austrian upper and middle classes of the late nineteenth and early twentieth centuries. The spread of psycho-analytic techniques to other countries, and the changes produced by the passage of time have removed many of these misconceptions. It still remains true, however, that the sample of humanity on which psycho-analytic and other psychological generalisations are based is an extremely small and very biased one. One of the major aims in undertaking this research was to make a beginning on the task of filling in these unfortunate gaps in our knowledge, and it was for this reason that a working class community was chosen as the scene of this research.

The choice of Bethnal Green as the locality in which the research was to be carried out was governed by several considerations. First, before the war of 1939–45 Bethnal Green was regarded as one of the most strongly anti-Semitic areas in London. For example, in the 1937 municipal elections the British Union of Fascists candidates polled a much higher proportion of votes in Bethnal Green than in any other part of the British Isles. Secondly, Bethnal Green has a smaller Jewish population than the neighbouring boroughs of Stepney, Hackney, and Shoreditch, which were also considered very strongly anti-Semitic. This reduced the difficulties of making a sample of the Gentile population. Thirdly, Bethnal Green is one of the smallest and most compact boroughs, and has one of the most homogeneous populations in London. The task of studying group influences was therefore of more manageable proportions than would have been the case in most parts of the city. Finally, at the time when this research was being planned, Fascist speakers were again active in Bethnal Green, and regular meetings of considerable size were being held in the borough.

Up to this point stress has been placed on the difficulties involved in studies outside the research worker's usual social milieu, but when these difficulties are overcome several advantages, referred to by Trist (1936) as "stranger value", appear. The observer who is conscious of some novelty in his surroundings and of some detachment from them is likely to observe in greater detail and with more accuracy than the man whose perceptions are blunted by familiarity, or by an emotionally based need to stress or ignore certain aspects of the situation. The present author was doubly fortunate in this respect, for, having been brought up in another country, all aspects of English life had some degree of unfamiliarity and he was not faced with the problem of observing fellow countrymen whose behaviour could only be regarded as odd by comparison with his own—a situation that can become embarrassing for both parties. Indeed, the advantages appear as great for the observed as for the observer. Faced with a middle class research worker from his own country it is not difficult for a member of the working class to feel that he is being patronised or spied on, or is in some other way being put at a disadvantage. A complete outsider can usually be more easily accepted. He does not fit so well into preconceived patterns; even if he is middle class he is not obviously the same as the middle classes to which the working class is accustomed, and in any case, he is only temporarily in the situation and is unlikely to be in a position of power and authority over the man being interviewed. He runs less risk, therefore, of being associated with those powerful and mysterious figures usually referred to as "they". Furthermore, the outsider can ask questions that no Englishman could ask without appearing ridiculous. Questions about the workings of the local government and educational systems can be asked with ease by a stranger—after all, being a stranger, he is naturally ignorant, and why should he not wish to learn?—while the native, unless he is a schoolmaster setting an examination, can have no obvious reasons for asking such things.

There is a further matter which needs to be raised here, namely the connection, if any, between objectivity and membership in a group which is concerned in the research. In the course of this work the author has frequently been presented with opinions on this point, the two extremes being (a) that as a Gentile he should be able to bring some much needed objectivity into a field which, it was alleged, has hitherto been worked almost entirely by Jews, and (b) that because he was not a Jew it was impossible for him to understand what anti-Semitism meant, and that he was therefore wasting his time in attempting such an investigation. While both of these extreme positions can be regarded as untrue, the point is not unimportant; it is often raised in discussion, and deserves consideration, for the subject of anti-Semitism is undoubtedly one which is particularly prone to be discussed with more emotion than rationality by both Jew and Gentile, by both supporters and opponents of anti-Semitism.

There is a strong tradition which depicts the scientist as a detached, unemotional individual, concerned only with facts, and caring nothing for the consequences of his work. If this picture was ever true of the physical scientist—and it has clearly ceased to apply in this atomic age—it was certainly never true of the social scientist, who is perforce one of the subjects of his own experiments and observations, and likely to be closely affected by the results of his own work. Unless he chooses to work on problems remote from all practical human affairs, the social scientist's data are bound to concern matters on which men hold strong opinions, and he can hold himself aloof only at the price of renouncing his humanity. Moreover, no scientist can hope to free himself from the typical value-judgments of his society. He may make himself more clearly aware of them, and try to guard against their effect on his reasoning, but he cannot achieve more than this, and to claim that the social scientist can operate "objectively" only in situations where he has no personal interest at stake is to ask for the impossible. The temptation to stray from the path of scientific rectitude is not confined to those who are studying a problem which affects them directly. Biases and other "subjective" influences (including the wish to find evidence to support a favoured theory) can act far more subtly and just as dangerously even on those approaching a study from a rigorously objective viewpoint. There can be little doubt that students of the natural sciences can be just as prone to such influences. However, the very nature of the observed phenomena, allowing a relatively easy use of strict controls, enables

6

the natural scientist to appear more "objective". Judgment of a social scientist's "objectivity" should, therefore, derive not from his relationship with the problem, but from his use of the controls available and appropriate to a particular research situation, and from the degree to which he limits his findings to the interpretation of his data, and refrains, for instance, from using unacknowledged value-judgments as if they were factual statements.

The claim that only a Jew can understand anti-Semitism is equally exaggerated, though it is undoubtedly true that an essential qualification for competent psychological research is an ability to sympathise in some measure with the individuals who are the subjects of the research. This does not imply sympathy in the sense of agreement with the *content* of the subject's attitudes and opinions, but in the sense of accepting those attitudes as being real, and as having importance and meaning to the individual in question. That is to say, of accepting him as a real individual, no matter how warped and deviant he may be. This sympathy must be extended to all who are subjects of research, to anti-Semite equally with Jew. It is true that only Jews have experienced the precise situation of being the victims of anti-Semitism, but it is equally true that practically every individual has at some time experienced the consequences of some form of prejudice, and it is not impossible to convert such an experience into an understanding of the meaning of anti-Semitism to a Jew. It is also true that only an anti-Semite knows from experience what it is to be a Jew-hater, and an understanding of this is equally relevant to a study of anti-Semitism.

The implication of this position is that the "objective" social scientist is one who is prepared to take *all* the relevant data into account and allow his results to be dictated by those data; one whose task is not merely to name and denounce the villains of the social drama but, more important, to understand these characters (the heroes as well as the indifferent) and try to discover why they behave as they do.

The problem of value-judgments has long been a matter of dispute among social scientists. Though early efforts were aimed at eliminating or denying such "unscientific" matters, there has more recently been a tendency to admit and allow for their inevitability. As Lynd (1946, pp. 183–4) has pointed out, value-judgments always enter into research at some point, for example, in the decision that a particular problem is significant and therefore worth studying. Myrdal (1944) has argued that insofar as these judgments can be recognised and made explicit they need not reduce the "scientific objectivity" of the work.

Anti-Semitism, like the colour prejudice which Myrdal studied, is a topic much discussed in terms of value-judgments, and though not previously closely involved in this discussion, the present writer brought to this work a number of preconceptions. These included the view that the beliefs of anti-Semites with respect to Jews are not factually correct, that anti-Semitism is a disruptive and undesirable force in our society, that its manifestations are sufficiently frequent and important to constitute a serious problem, that it is desirable that anti-Semitism should be reduced and its active manifestations curtailed, and that a much more detailed knowledge of its nature and causes is necessary before effective steps can be taken to this end. It must be left to others to decide on the extent to which these preconceptions have influenced the conclusions drawn from the results of the research work reported here. The execution of this work has not resulted in any change of opinion as far as these views are concerned.

There is a tendency for the problem of measurement in social science to become the centre of heated controversy between those who regard its use as the main indication of a scientific approach and those who maintain that it destroys the subtleties and complexities which are part of the very nature of personality and society. The attitude adopted in this work is that where the data allow of measurement or counting, then statistical methods should be utilised as far as possible, for it is not desirable to use data less accurate than the best that are available. On the other hand, the study of a problem is not to be avoided merely because it cannot be dealt with statistically. The nature of the data available must dictate the use to be made of them, but no useful data should be discarded merely because of unsuitability for some particular form of treatment (cf. Dollard, 1937, pp. 17-18). The tendency towards increased attempts to quantify is undoubtedly a desirable development. At the same time Mannheim's warning that "the mere reduction of a complex of social facts to mensurable elements, gives proof of little scientific insight" (1940, p. 85) should be carefully noted.

An attempt has been made in this book to apply quantitative methods to some of the data. As is usually the case, it was not found possible to define categories which would cover all aspects of the problem under review, and it has therefore been necessary to cover a good deal of the ground in descriptive rather than in numerical terms. The quantitative material and the statistical procedures nevertheless provide a framework for the remainder, and constitute a check on tendencies to wild generalizations and unjustifiable assertions. A detailed account of the techniques employed is given in Chapter IV.

Another problem frequently presented to the social scientist as a dilemma is the distinction between the group and its component individuals. There is a real problem here, but it is doubtful if the usual dichotomous formulation does it justice. Stated crudely the extreme alternatives are, on the one hand, that as groups are composed of individuals the study of group phenomena can be realistically approached only by a study of individuals (Glover, 1946), and on the other hand, that groups are so much more than an aggregation of individuals that they must themselves be the objects of study, and data relating to individuals are comparatively irrelevant in this context.

The view adopted here is that for certain purposes it is legitimate to treat a group simply as the sum total of a number of similar units. Demographers and ecologists rarely need to employ any other approach. For the vast majority of the problems which social scientists attempt to solve such an approach can only represent a first approximation. It is, *par excellence*, the type of problem to which statistical methods can be applied. It is, however, invariably found that explanations based on data of this type are not complete, e.g. that coefficients of correlation are less than unity, which means that there are deviants from the group norm. In many cases this will be a matter of little consequence, but if the explanation of these deviations becomes a matter of interest and importance to the social scientist he will sooner or later be compelled to deal with the individual (Robb, 1952). It is important to note, however, that he never arrives at a "pure individual", for every one of the members of the groups under study will be interacting with, and influenced by, other members, and such relationships, being relevant parts of the situation, must be taken into account (Money, 1949). These relationships can for most practical purposes be divided into three types: those based on the personal qualities of the interacting individuals; those based on the formal or structural connections between the persons concerned, e.g. whether or not one is in a position of authority over the other; and finally, those based on accepted views as to what constitutes appropriate behaviour in the particular situation (Parsons, 1951). Clearly these types of relationship are not independent, and to ignore any of them involves the production of an incomplete account of the behaviour under review, but it is perfectly legitimate to emphasise one type of relationship if this is required by the problem in hand. Until recently, research on the problem of anti-Semitism has tended to ignore the personal relationships concerned, or to deal only with the second and third types. The research described in this book was planned on the assumption that a stage had been reached at which the emphasis needed to be placed to a greater extent on the personalities involved, and hence that more attention should be paid to the approach based on the study of individuals.

This approach does not mean an abandonment of the group for the individual. Those patterned forms of interpersonal relations which we call social and cultural forces have to be taken into account, and because of their patterned and repetitive nature it is possible and convenient to consider them in terms of the group as a whole, rather than to trace the exact process of interaction between each of its members. It is necessary, nevertheless, to be alert for variations from the norm which suggest variations in the interpersonal experiences. The extent to which these variations will be followed up by the research worker will depend on the object of the research and the facilities available. An anthropologist making a first contact with a primitive tribe or a sociologist conducting a community survey will not follow the variations very far, while a psycho-analyst will devote his analytic sessions very largely to this single task.

In accordance with these views this study has been based on a number of individuals who have at the same time been conceived as members of a group in which patterned relationships are operative. The account of the approach to the individual members of the community is therefore preceded by an account of some aspects of the society in which they live. It must be emphasised that these two accounts are interdependent and each would lose most of its value if not supported by the other. At the same time it is true that the main emphasis throughout is on the individual, and that the approach to the problem of anti-Semitism is made through individuals displaying this characteristic, rather than through group manifestations. In general, group situations and patterns of behaviour are taken as relatively constant, but their effect on the individuals who come into contact with them is analysed, while the causes and history of the group situation are given less attention.

The following are definitions of some of the key terms employed in this book. These definitions are obviously insufficiently exact for general use. It has been assumed that it was unnecessary to refine the definitions beyond the point that would enable them to be used here without causing ambiguity.

1. *Anti-Semitism.* An attitude of hostility towards Jews as such, i.e. not towards a particular Jew, and not towards a number of people whom, apart from having an attribute that arouses hostility, also happen to be Jewish. The hostility, to be called anti-Semitism, must be associated definitely with the quality of being a Jew.

Attitudes are, of course, invisible. They may be expressed in a number of ways, only two of which are referred to here. (*a*) Verbal expression, by making anti-Semitic statements. Such a statement is defined as one which is intended to convey the information that all or most Jews are characterised by some trait, or some type of behaviour, which the speaker regards as undesirable. (*b*) Public behavioural expression, by hostile gestures or acts, including applause for anti-Semitic statements.

2. *Jew.* An individual who describes himself as a Jew or who practises some specifically Jewish rite, e.g. attends synagogue, lights Sabbath eve candles, puts a mezuzah on his door post, celebrates Passover or some other specifically Jewish feast, or who has at least one parent who observes some of these practices. The concept of Jew has become so imprecise during the last century that some arbitrary definition that can be applied with a fair degree of precision is absolutely necessary. So far as the writer is aware there is no definition that is not open to objection on some ground.

3. *Working Class.* Here again the need is for some definition that can be applied with a reasonable amount of precision. For purposes of this book it was possible to adopt a definition in largely negative terms. An inhabitant of Bethnal Green is assumed to be a member of the working class if he has not remained at school beyond the age set down as the legal minimum, if he is not an employer of labour, and if, being a clerk or shop assistant, he is not in charge of any shop or office in which other individuals are employed in a position subordinate to himself. This definition does not exclude operators of one-man businesses, or factory foremen and shop stewards, but it does exclude managers of local branches of chain stores and people in similar employment.

CHAPTER II

Theoretical Background and Research Design

THE aim of this chapter is to review some of the earlier literature on anti-Semitism and to set out the hypotheses on which the research described in the book is based. The review of the literature will serve a double purpose. In the first place, by indicating some of the theories concerning anti-Semitism which have been put forward in the past, and by describing previous research, it should make clear the starting point of this project, and the facts, theories, and unsolved problems that appeared to be important when it was planned. Secondly, it will provide a basis for the later discussion (Chapter IX) on a general theory of anti-Semitism.

Writers attempting to explain anti-Semitism usually draw on data from one or more of the following sources: (a) historical evidence based largely on documentary material, (b) casual or clinical observation, (c) deductions from some basic principles which are assumed to be either proven or axiomatic, and (d) the results of systematic experimental and field research. Any of these data may, of course, be obtained at second hand and any given study may use data of more than one of these types.

No claim is made that the following account of suggested theories on the nature and causes of anti-Semitism is exhaustive. The writings referred to have been arbitrarily selected from the great number available for a variety of reasons, usually because either the theory or its author has exerted considerable influence, or because some element in it seems to illustrate a fairly widespread belief about the nature of anti-Semitism. Little attempt is made to classify these theories. So many of them combine a variety of approaches that to place any given theory under a single heading would involve an arbitrary choice as to which of its many elements is to be regarded as the most important. However, some degree of grouping has been employed.

The opinion that anti-Semitism is the logical result of a reality situation, i.e. that the Jews actually have the characteristics alleged by anti-Semites, and the view that anti-Semitic beliefs are the result of ignorance and misinformation, are nowadays so rarely put forward that it has not been found necessary to consider them here.[1] Only general, largely methodological criticisms of the theories described are attempted in this chapter, although obvious inadequacies are pointed out. Factual evidence bearing on the truth or falsehood of the views advanced is brought forward at various points later in the book.

When an author attempts to explain the causes of anti-Semitism by reference to historical material (and not merely to write a purely descriptive history of anti-Semitism) he commonly traces the social, political, and economic happenings which appear to him to have had a connection with the appearance or increase of anti-Semitism. He then endeavours to demonstrate a correlation between the appearance of anti-Semitism and the existence of certain other conditions, though this correlation may not be made very explicit, as, for example, in the *Encyclopedia Britannica* article on anti-Semitism (Pinson, 1947). This and similar works appear to show very convincingly that anti-Semitism is particularly apparent during and following periods of upheaval and unrest; following fundamental political changes; after wars, particularly in defeated countries; during economic depressions; at times of major influx of foreign migrants, especially if some or most of these are Jewish; when there is serious dissatisfaction over corruption in governing circles; and when power-seeking groups use anti-Semitism as a means of increasing influence (Rose and Rose, 1948, p. 303).

Such studies can never provide more than an elementary explanation. They are adequate so long as the only question that is being asked is "At what periods is anti-Semitism most pronounced?" It appears to be well established on the basis of this historical evidence that anti-Semitism does reach its greatest pitch at the times of unrest and dislocation described above, but to say this gives little indication

---

[1] It should be noted, however, that while such a view is rarely, if ever, given as an explanation of anti-Semitism, it seems often to be tacitly assumed as such, particularly in writings and programmes of activities designed to improve inter-racial relationships. These often consist largely of attempts to disprove the accuracy of the usual Jewish stereotype. This point, and its implications, are considered in more detail in a later chapter (cf. Williams, 1947, pp. 7-20).

of the actual mechanisms through which anti-Semitism functions, or of the reason why it exists in times of peace and prosperity, or why some people affected by the dislocation and instability do not become anti-Semitic. Most of the authors quoted above go on to elaborate and refine their general propositions by adducing, for example, historical events which have resulted in the Jews becoming important competitors in certain branches of trade or certain professions (Weinryb, 1946). It soon becomes clear, however, that to achieve a full analysis it is necessary to have recourse to some form of psychological theory; this in fact is what the majority of authors implicitly or explicitly attempt to do.

The simplest of these theories is that Gentiles become jealous, envious or resentful of the success of the Jews, or afraid of being ousted from their positions by them, and that this jealousy and insecurity produces a hatred of the people who are seen as the cause of these unpleasant feelings. In its more sophisticated forms (e.g. Parsons, 1942) this approach includes a more detailed analysis of the psychological mechanisms by which the transformation is made from the original feeling to the hatred of Jews, but the explanations for generalising this hatred from the actual competitors to Jews in general is not usually clear. Nor is evidence produced to show that the persons who experience Jewish competition are those who become anti-Semitic. It is somewhat surprising that so many writers, including Jews, should in this context adopt the typical anti-Semitic phraseology and talk about "the Jews" as if all Jews were virtually identical and interchangeable units. If there was some justification for this in the days when ghetto conditions forced all Jews to conform to a rigid cultural pattern, there is surely none today.

A rather more detailed psychological analysis is made in the use of the concept of a "scapegoat". This seems to be applied most frequently in studies of the rise of anti-Semitism at such times as following defeat in war, and on the appearance of corruption in government. According to this explanation, anti-Semitism is a method of avoiding responsibility either for a single person or the groups with whom he identifies, by placing elsewhere the blame for whatever disaster has occurred, and then punishing the people on to whom the blame is thus shifted. The accusation that the Jews were responsible for the defeat of Germany in the first World War is a frequently quoted example, and evidence suggests that there is an

14

important element of truth in this view. Here again the most obvious criticism is that the theory does not answer all the questions arising from the problem, and, especially, that it overlooks such factors as the large number of patriotic and deeply concerned citizens, who in a time of national disaster do not show anti-Semitic reactions; it fails to show why certain people become anti-Semitic while others in apparently the same position do not. It is a sound theory as far as it goes but the gaps are too numerous for its acceptance as the final answer.

Anti-Semitism can also be viewed as a form of deliberate propaganda—a technique for gaining or maintaining political power. For supporting evidence such theories draw largely on the history of Germany under Bismarck and Hitler (Rose and Rose, 1948, pp. 293-4; Parkes, 1946, p. 195). While there can be no doubt that anti-Semitism has been used in this way, this knowledge includes no explanation of why its use has been so successful. Parkes' attempt to explain this in terms of "a background of dislike, suspicion and hostility arising out of actual Jewish problems" suffers from the same defect as the various economic and historical theories already examined.

A variant on the "intentional propaganda" theme is commonly held by modern Communists (Rennap, 1942; Trory, 1946; Darke, 1952). According to this theory, anti-Semitism is the normal device used by a ruling class to distract the attention of the oppressed classes from the evil doings of their oppressors. In modern capitalist societies this occurs when the capitalists wish to turn away from themselves the wrath of the proletariat. Anti-Semites will appear among the working classes in direct proportion to the weakness of their trade union organization and their lack of class-consciousness. Where these conditions obtain the workers are likely to be deceived by the propaganda and blame their misfortunes not on the capitalists, who are really responsible, but on the Jews. Rennap, for example, claims that support for the Fascists was based upon "disgruntled shopkeeper elements as well as the most backward sections of the workers" and that the strength of this support varied in inverse proportion to the strength and militancy of the Trade Unions and labour movements.

Even if these descriptions and correlations are accepted as facts this theory leaves much unexplained. Like all the theories considered so far it is concerned with the conditions under which anti-Semitism arises. Apart from any other defects, it takes no account of the forms which anti-Semitism takes, the reasons for various stereotypes being used, and for their popularity. As will be seen later, however, there are good reasons for rejecting some of the statements on which the argument is based.

Religious beliefs have frequently been suggested as causal factors in anti-Semitism (Valentin, 1936; Marcus, 1946). It is extremely difficult to disentangle the religious element as a cause from the religious element as a rationalisation. Rose has pointed out (1948, p. 278) that though during the Inquisition the Catholic Church in Spain ceased to torture and kill Jews who became converts to Catholicism, the Spanish people continued to discriminate against these "new Christians". The fact that anti-Semitism has remained so powerful a force in an age in which religion does not stir great passions suggests that this theory is not the real explanation. Equally, the phenomenon of Jewish anti-Semitism cannot be explained in this way (cf. Loewenstein, 1951, p. 42–3).

Probably the most far-reaching modern attempt to find a religious basis for anti-Semitism is that of Maurice Samuel (1940) who claims that anti-Semitism is a disguised attack on Christianity. The anti-Semite is the man who is fundamentally evil, the lover of brute force, the true reactionary. Such a man hates the Christian doctrine of love and goodness. Fearing to make a direct attack on Christianity he turns his hatred on to the Jews, who become unconsciously for him the symbol of Christ the Jew, the frustrator of his own evil desires. On the basis of this analysis Samuel claims that anti-Semitism is qualitatively different from other forms of group prejudice.[1] It might be difficult to deny that Samuel's theory deserves consideration in the case of some individuals and some periods. It might, for example, have been applicable to some extent in the Middle Ages, and to individual anti-Semitic propagandists of recent years, but even if this could be proved it would not explain the widespread acceptance of anti-Semitic views by people whose knowledge of, and interest in, religious beliefs and their origins is slight indeed. Moreover, it merely pushes the problem back a stage so that we are faced with the question of the nature and origins of the lovers of brute force, the true reactionaries.

[1] This theory is not to be confused with the assertion that anti-Semitism is incompatible with Christian teachings of universal brotherly love, i.e. that it is impossible for the same person to be both anti-Semitic and truly Christian (cf. Cook, 1945, for an exposition of this viewpoint). Such a view is vigorously attacked by Samuel as inadequate.

A theory that has many points in common with that of Samuel is the view put forward by Freud (1939). Like Samuel, Freud believes that anti-Semitism is actually an attack on Christianity; but his reasoning is based largely on theories which he has expounded in his earlier books, and he arrives at his conclusion by a completely different route from that followed by Samuel. Very briefly, Freud maintains that the early Jews re-enacted "the great misdeed of primaeval times, the murder of the Father", by killing Moses and denying the deed; the early Christians, under Paul, got rid of their guilt by admitting the killing of Christ and believing that his resurrection absolved them, but they despised the Jews as people who would not admit their guilt; the more recent converts to the Christian religion have only a thin veneer of Christianity over their "barbarically polytheistic" nature and they unconsciously hate their religion for its restraints; this hatred they project on to the Jews, the source of Christianity.

In addition to the difficulties of Samuel's theory, this theory of Freud's entails the acceptance of the "scientific myth" of the murder of the primaeval father and the inheritance of unconscious racial memories, two theories which have not found general acceptance even among psycho-analysts. It is one of the most striking things about this theory that it seems to have found so little support even among Freud's closest followers. Fenichel (1945) referring to this work and the theory of racial memories speaks of Freud's "speculations" and says, "The question must remain open." In his own paper on anti-Semitism Fenichel (1946) makes only a brief and cautious reference to Freud's theory (cf. also Brown, 1942). Even Freud himself in another context gives a rather different explanation of anti-Semitism.

According to this alternative thesis, humanity has achieved a state of civilisation only by surrendering many of its instinctual desires. The principle of psychic economy, however, demands that the energy behind these instincts should be released in some form, and this release is provided by inter-group hostilities. Men can love most of their fellows well enough to co-operate with them if only they can get rid of their feelings of hatred on to the remainder. The Jews, an almost universal minority group, have usually served this purpose. It is their existence that has made possible the existence of culture in the countries where they have lived (Freud, 1934, p. 90). This approach would appear to have more in common with the "frustration-aggression hypothesis" (discussed below) than with Freud's alternative theory.

Fenichel's (1946) account of anti-Semitism, based on orthodox psycho-analytic theory, is more detailed than that of Freud. Unlike Freud he stresses the importance of contemporary social and political conditions. The underlying instinctual drives and character formations which are the basis for anti-Semitism are always present and available in any nation. The problem is why they should be activated at any particular place and time, and for the answer to this question we must look to the contemporary situation. The function of psycho-analysis is to describe the relatively constant human structure which reacts to these conditions.

Accepting the "scapegoat theory" as a generally true but insufficiently specific explanation, he goes on to inquire why the Jews are chosen so regularly as the scapegoats. There are, he thinks, two reasons. The first is the defencelessness of the Jewish people which has enabled them to be attacked with impunity. The second reason is based on "the equation of primitive thinking: Foreign-Hostile". It is an instinctual reaction to be suspicious of foreigners, because one does not know what to expect of them. Because of this it is possible to project on to them the "foreign" instinctual desires of one's own unconscious, and the Jews thereby become accused of rape, murder, incest, the "uncanny crimes", which could only be expected of a strange people, so that they are portrayed as the incarnation of evil. "The Jewish God, and thus the Jew, is the devil, the anti-Christ, the wicked principle directed against God, which crucified God." Added to the uncanny nature of the Jew is his practice of circumcision and his belief that the Jews are a "chosen people".

The well known "frustration-aggression" hypothesis has been used as the basis for an explanation of anti-Semitism, usually in connection with the scapegoat theory. According to this hypothesis, frustration (that condition which exists when a goal-response suffers interference) results in the production of aggression (an act whose goal response is injury to an organism or organism-surrogate) (Dollard, et al., 1946; Miller, et al., 1941). This theory has been used as an explanation of anti-Semitism in more than one way. The simplest version is that the aggression generated by social frustration cannot be released against one's own group and so is displaced onto an "out-group," e.g. the Jews. Varying reasons for the inability to attack the in-group are given: the aggressor must attack a group he knows to be weak (Slawson, 1944); such an act would be likely to disrupt the in-group and would therefore be contrary to the permissible behaviour of the society (Dollard, *et al.*, 1946, p. 87); or it would be productive of more guilt than in the case of an out-group (Brown, 1942, p. 141).

These theories, like that of Fenichel, are based on psycho-analytic theory. Though very plausible, they lack detailed supporting evidence. Even if the existence of the mechanisms referred to has been proved (and the mechanisms of displacement, projection, and rationalisation are very well attested), there is no guarantee that they are in fact operative in this particular case, however likely the assumption may sound. It has been the basic defect of almost all the writings described so far in this chapter that they have been inade-quately grounded in factual research. It is to an attempt to provide empirical evidence on these questions that we now turn.

Experimental and field studies in anti-Semitism and its causes are a recent development, particularly where psychological factors are taken into account. Bogardus' work on social distance (1928), and Lasker's (1929) study of prejudice among children seem to have been the only attempts to carry out any research of this kind before 1930, and even after that date very little work was done until the outbreak of the recent war. Most of the research since that time has been done on a very small scale, consisting usually of the presentation of a questionnaire or attitude test to a small group of students, no attempt being made to tie these results to any other information about the subjects, such as social background or personal history. The majority of these rather trivial studies will be ignored in the summary of research work that follows.[1]

Because the number of cases is so small the material will not be grouped into types of project but each piece of research will be considered in turn. The review will be chiefly critical of the methods of research, though it will be indicated where conclusions are suspect because of faulty methods. A detailed consideration of the conclusions will be reserved for a later part of this book, where they will be reviewed in combination with the results of the present study, in an effort to build up some general propositions about the subject.

The earliest piece of work to be described here was carried out in

[1] For an account of these minor studies see Rose and Rose (1948), pp. 300 ff.

1942 (Campbell, 1947). It consisted of interviewing 316 subjects who were selected as a representative sample of white non-Jewish Americans. The subjects were classified into five groups according to their attitudes towards Jews. Several items of personal data and some information as to other attitudes were obtained from each respondent. The relationships between attitude to Jews and the various other factors were expressed in the form of percentages; no correlations were given. The results can be summarised as follows.

The majority of the sample were not anti-Semitic—11 per cent were pro-Jewish and 50 per cent expressed no anti-Jewish sentiments; 21 per cent showed mild dislike of Jews; 13 per cent tried to avoid personal contact; 5 per cent favoured actively hostile measures. Of the criticisms expressed, the majority referred either to economic activities or to the alleged personal characteristics of Jews, the most common of the latter being that Jews are "clannish". Of the factors found to be associated with anti-Semitism, the most marked were those touching the degree of satisfaction with the personal economic position and the national political situation. The greater the degree of dissatisfaction, the greater, in general, was the degree of anti-Semitism. There was a slight tendency for anti-Semitism to be associated with little contact with Jews and for pro-Jewish attitudes to go with a high degree of contact. The most marked tendency was for people with no first-hand knowledge to be neutral in outlook. Age, religion, and income showed no connection with attitude to Jews but there was a consistent tendency for anti-Semitism to increase with education, this being particularly marked at college level. Men tended to be slightly more anti-Semitic than women.

As a study of distributions this is quite a sound and interesting piece of work on a relatively small scale, and is especially to be recommended as it was something of a pioneering effort, but it is obvious that it touches only the fringes of the problem. No attempt was made to obtain any data relating to the development of prejudice. It is simply a cross-sectional study of the situation as it existed in the United States in September, 1942. It is unfortunate that the statistical material has been treated purely as a series of percentages without correlations or tests of significance.

During the same year an ingenious and somewhat more elaborate study was carried out in New York, using as its subjects 617 students of both sexes from eight universities and teacher training colleges

(Hartley, 1946). The major part of the investigation was the completion by these students of a modification of the Bogardus Social Distance Test. Persons completing this test are asked to indicate, for a number of different groups, how much contact they would be willing to have with the members of these groups. The possible choices vary from a desire to exclude them from the country to a willingness for them to marry into the family. Bogardus' eight-point scale was retained but was applied to a larger number of groups, including religious and political, as well as ethnic, groups. The ethnic groups included three "Nonsuch" peoples, the Danireans, the Pireneans, and the Wallonians. The subjects were also asked to indicate if they, or their parents, belonged to any of these groups.

In his analysis of the results of the social distance test Hartley makes the following points. Although the "general level of tolerance" varies from group to group, the pattern is essentially the same throughout. That is, the rank order of the groups in terms of the tolerance expressed for them is practically the same in each case. (Correlations between the various colleges varied from 0·86 to 0·92.) More detailed study of the results indicates that with few exceptions individuals show the same general tendency throughout all their opinions, in other words, an individual who is more tolerant than the average of one group is most likely to be more tolerant of all others as well, regardless of their nature. This view is strikingly supported by an analysis of the responses to the three "Nonsuch" groups. The mean scores of these were correlated with the mean scores for all other groups. The resulting coefficients ranged from 0·78 to 0·85 and a number of other correlations between groups demonstrated clearly the same pattern. These results leave no doubt that prejudice is a generalised attitude having more reference to the person expressing it than to the group towards which it is shown. That there are also important social factors at work is shown by the fact that the levels of tolerance tended to vary between the different colleges.

A subsidiary part of the investigation consisted of a word-pair test. The results of this test were not entirely satisfactory; although they gave rise to some hypotheses, these cannot be regarded as proven. These hypotheses suggest that people who emphasise similarity between religious and ethnic groups are more tolerant than those who are most aware of differences; that lack of good parent-child relationships is productive of intolerance; that people for whom sex differences are not important tend to be relatively tolerant; that those who view college as a non-aggressive, non-competitive place tend to be tolerant. Personality data obtained from some of the subjects showed interesting trends. From these it appeared that the tolerant individuals were friendly and showed little need to dominate others, shunned violence, were serious and ambitious, sensitive to others, and aware of conflicts over duties and loyalties. The intolerant individuals were described as unwilling to accept responsibility, very conventional, concentrating on pleasurable rather than serious and useful activities, very egocentric, concerned with their bodies and health, relatively uncreative and tending to deal with anxieties by running away from them.

By far the most important points in this investigation are those relating to the generalisation and patterning of prejudice. The data provided by the study, particularly that relating to the "Nonsuch" groups, indicates conclusively that in the case of the subjects studied by Hartley, prejudice (or tolerance) is a generalised attitude having its basis in the individual who expresses it rather than in the groups to whom the prejudice is directed. So striking is the evidence for generalisation that, in the absence of strong evidence to the contrary, it can be assumed to apply to the majority of cases and not merely to the members of this group. This does not mean that cases of isolated prejudices cannot occur, but merely that they are likely to be relatively rare.

Of the origins of this generalised attitude the study gives no information beyond a hint that it may be in some way associated with relationships with parents. By relating to the individuals with high and low prejudice scores various other facts known about them, Hartley is able to suggest that the existence of this generalised attitude is associated with certain personality characteristics, but his results fall short of final proof and give no indication as to the nature of this relationship between prejudice and personality. The operation of social forces is also apparent, though their nature is not clear.

A later piece of research, published at about the same time as Hartley's, began with the clear assumption that prejudice is a function of the personality and experiences of the prejudiced person, and sought to discover something about the factors associated with prejudice (Allport and Kramer, 1946).

This study was based on a questionnaire which was answered by 437 undergraduates of both sexes who were doing courses in elementary psychology. The questionnaire began with the usual personal data including age, sex, occupation, and was thereafter divided into six sections. Of these the first consisted of questions dealing with the amount of contact the subject had had with minority groups; the second was so constructed as to provide a prejudice score for those answering the questionnaire; the third dealt with the sources of his attitudes; the fourth with his attitudes towards his own feelings and beliefs; the fifth with his personal experiences of discrimination; the sixth was designed to elicit self-ratings for prejudices and minority group membership.

A high correlation was found between reports of memories of unfavourable early experiences with Jews and Negroes, and prejudices against these groups. It must be pointed out that this result is open to two interpretations (a) unfavourable early experiences are the cause of prejudice, and (b) prejudiced persons who have not had such experiences invent them as rationalisations for their prejudices. The authors support the latter hypothesis. Prejudiced persons, in the main, claimed either to have taken over their parents' attitudes unaltered, or not to have been influenced by their parents. Individuals who claimed to have reacted against them were usually unprejudiced.

On the whole, the claims of individuals as to what they learnt at school correlated highly with their existing degree of anti-Semitism. The authors conclude that this indicates that American schools do not sufficiently emphasise teaching designed to decrease prejudice. While this may be so, the result also seems to be open to the interpretation that people remember those elements of their school learning which support their present views. For example, a claim that the individual was not influenced by his school was found to be an indication of prejudice. Taken together with the statements regarding parents this suggests that prejudice is associated with lack of insight, as it is inconceivable that an individual is not influenced by his parents and his school.

The results suggest that contacts between persons of equal status (both socio-economic and educational) tend to reduce prejudice, while those between persons of widely different status increase it. There is a slight tendency for any kind of contact to result in less intolerance.

The results are not at all clear on the influence of religion. (a) Persons reporting religion as an important factor in their upbringing tended to be prejudiced; (*b*) persons reporting religious education which included material favourable to minority groups tended to be unprejudiced; and (*c*) many of the unprejudiced subjects gave religious belief as a reason for their lack of prejudice. The authors suggest that "mere exposure" to religion is likely to produce intolerance but that certain types of religious training will work the other way. A favourable reaction to religious influences in upbringing seems to be associated with tolerance, an unfavourable or indifferent attitude with intolerance.

An individual's awareness of being discriminated against seems frequently to be associated with his own prejudices against ethnic or religious groups. This gives some support to the frustration-aggression hypothesis, but there are many exceptions and the correlation is not high. Jews, on the whole, show less prejudice than other groups. The authors suggest that awareness of discriminatory experiences can produce either displaced aggression against other minority groups or identification with them. (There is the further possibility that the experiences of victimization may be remembered or constructed more frequently by the prejudiced than by the unprejudiced.)

There are some miscellaneous findings concerning sociological variable. Women are less prejudiced than men; persons with highly educated parents are less prejudiced than those who have relatively uneducated parents; students of the natural sciences are much less prejudiced than students of the social sciences and they in turn are more tolerant than students of art and literature. People who regard the world as basically hostile, and those who desire more discipline in national life, are usually prejudiced. Those who express sympathy with the underdog are generally tolerant, as are those who are aware of shame and conflict over their own attitudes towards social groups. People who express greater fear of swindlers than of gangsters and those who reject attempts to legislate against prejudices are usually intolerant.

This study goes a good deal further than Hartley's in exploring the nature of correlates of prejudice. It suffers from the usual limitations of the questionnaire, particularly in that there is no check on rationalisations as opposed to genuine memories. The results tend to be a rather disconnected group of observations and no impression as to causality can be drawn from the material.

The next report to be considered is based on field work of a rather different kind (Bettelheim, 1947). Bettelheim's article consists of an account of the observations he made, while a prisoner in a Nazi concentration camp, of the interactions between the Jewish prisoners and the German guards. He relates how a number of prisoners tried to get treatment for frostbite, which was forbidden. The prisoners tried a variety of approaches to the guard, pleading, appealing to his humanity, and pretending they were worse than in fact they were. The only one who was successful was Bettelheim, who approached the guard in a matter-of-fact manner, showed his hands, related a straightforward and truthful story of the origin of the frostbite, and politely but firmly asked for treatment, saying that it would make him more efficient at his work. On the basis of this and other observations Bettelheim draws some interesting conclusions about the nature of Jew-Gentile relationships. He emphasises that anti-Semitism is an inter-personal relationship and that the effect of an anti-Semitic Gentile on a Jew and the effect of the Jewish reaction on the anti-Semite are both important aspects of the problem. At this juncture, only his conclusions concerning the anti-Semites will be summarised.

According to Bettelheim, an anti-Semite externalises his own undesirable tendencies and projects them onto his stereotyped picture of the Jew, in an attempt to rid himself of his inner conflicts. Thus the Jew appears to the anti-Semite to be far more dangerous than he really is because the anti-Semite is afraid, not of the real Jew, but of the stereotype he has created from the evil within himself.

This creation of the dangerous stereotype has two functions. It has to be dangerous because the anti-Semite is afraid of his own inner drives and sees them as threatening, and it is also necessary for the object of his attack to appear in the same light, in order to justify his own pre-occupation with it. To admit that the people to whom he devotes so much aggressive energy are, in fact, not dangerous, would be too damaging to his self-esteem. Because there are no obvious signs of this danger the anti-Semite is driven to postulate secret organisations and conspiracies, which in turn stimulate his anxiety and drive him to even more violent reactions. Bettelheim contends that he was successful in his request for treatment because he managed to place himself well outside the guard's stereotype. He used neither pleadings nor threats and so gave no suggestion of either strength or weakness, the crucial elements in the stereotype of Jewish-Gentile relationships. By behaving in a matter-of-fact manner he enabled the guard to treat him as an ordinary human being.

Bettelheim also suggest that the anti-Semites see in the Jews, who live within the structure of the same society but not fully integrated with it, a working model of their own repressed desires, and so find the Jews a particularly fitting target for their projections.

This study of Bettelheim's has to be evaluated on a rather different basis from those previously described. It does not provide any conclusive evidence, but it is an acute piece of observation made in a situation where an extreme degree of anti-Semitism, and the reactions to it, are very important factors. The conclusions which Bettelheim draws from his observations are hypotheses which are sufficiently well backed by observed behaviour to make them well worth further consideration and testing.

Only one study of anti-Semitism of any consequence has been made in Britain (Eysenck, 1947 and 1948; Eysenck and Crown, 1949). It was based primarily on the use of questionnaires, though other approaches were also used.

The results can be summarised as follows: Individuals' attitudes to social situations are not a series of disconnected events but fall into patterns, so that if one attitude is known, then others can be inferred with some degree of probability. The factorial analysis of the results of questionnaires designed to test attitudes on various subjects suggests rather strongly that one can speak meaningfully of "primary social attitudes". Eysenck claims to have isolated three of these: Tendermindedness, Radicalism, and Emphasis. An individual's particular or specific attitudes, according to this theory, will depend to a considerable extent on his primary attitudes. Eysenck suggests that "almost one-half of the anti-Semitic attitudes in our sample could be accounted for in terms of generalised 'primary attitudes' " (1947, p. 71).

Eysenck lists a number of other attitudes which he finds associated with anti-Semitism (i.e. other manifestations of the particular combination of primary attitudes giving rise to prejudice). As he points out, a difficulty arises here. These other attitudes (warmindedness, vindictiveness, nationalism, white supremacy, aggressive cruelty) can be analysed into practically the same combination of primary attitudes as anti-Semitism, and a scale constructed to measure these will not indicate which, or how many, of these attitudes are shown by the person being tested. Three possible solutions to the difficulty are suggested. (1) There may be other primary social attitudes which determine the particular direction of the specific attitudes. (2) The direction may be determined by chance factors in the experience of the person concerned. (3) The various attitudes are so closely connected that they are rarely found apart but "are all really only different masks for the same fascist face" (Eysenck and Crown, 1949, p. 59).

Eysenck also finds other factors that are associated with anti-Semitism. Men are more anti-Semitic than women, the old rather more prejudiced than the young, the religious more than the irreligious, the Conservative more than the Liberal, the Liberal more than the Socialist, and the less well-educated more than the highly educated. The findings of this study reinforce and extend somewhat the results of Hartley's work. Not only does anti-Semitism appear to be only one aspect of prejudice, but prejudice seems to be only one manifestation of a group of attitudes commonly found in combination. Presumably all these attitudes are expressions of the same basic personality processes, but this type of approach tells us nothing of these.

The study represents a welcome attempt to introduce some degree of exact measurement and statistical analysis into the task of discovering the nature of the correlates of anti-Semitism, but it does not go beyond this. The chief effect of an explanation of anti-Semitism in terms of primary social attitudes is to raise more basic problems. While any increase in our knowledge of the conditions associated with anti-Semitism is helpful, this particular study does little to provide anything in the nature of a causal explanation, for once the existence of primary attitudes has been established the problem becomes one of seeking the origins of these generalised attitudes. A study such as this is a descriptive account of a highly static kind. It is of little assistance in explaining the correlations that are shown to exist, or in describing the processes that lie behind the figures.

A recently published American study employs a technique quite different from any described so far (Ackerman and Jahoda, 1950). The authors of this study collected the detailed case histories of forty anti-Semites of whom twenty-seven had been psycho-analysed, and thirteen had been studied intensively by case work agencies. The data obtained in this way were analysed in some detail and the authors endeavoured, on the basis of this, to build up a theory of the nature and causes of anti-Semitism.

Stated briefly, the conclusion of these authors is that anti-Semitism derives from an interaction of intra-psychic and social factors. The intra-psychic influences produce a personality that is "predisposed" to prejudice, while the external forces determine the form and direction of the prejudice and provide the individual with the stereotypes, the rationalisations and the socially approved situations for the expression of the prejudice. The authors lay great stress on the necessity for taking both these groups of influences into account, but naturally they find it simpler and more convenient to describe them separately at first.

They report that the clinical diagnoses and the presenting symptoms were so varied that no conclusions could be drawn except that there was a complete absence of depression. They conclude that depression, which they describe as a condition in which the "focus of punitive tendencies is directed toward the self", is incompatible with anti-Semitism, as the typical anti-Semitic reaction "presupposes a tendency to blame the outside world rather than one's own self".

These anti-Semites displayed a "diffuse, pervasive, relatively unorganised" anxiety, "not adequately channelised through specific symptom formation"; they have a confused self-image (frequently displayed as a tendency to homosexuality); they have a poor capacity for interpersonal relations; they are strict conformists and fear anything that is different; they have a poor adaptation to reality; they display "little evidence of a consistent value-system protected by a well-developed conscience"; their processes of repression are inadequate. All these factors together constitute the "emotional predisposition to anti-Semitism" and the authors ask, "How does this predisposition arise?"

In attempting to answer this question they point to several factors they consider relevant. These anti-Semites came from homes where there was a poor relationship between the parents; it was usual for the child to have experienced rejection by one or both parents, or to have been used by a parent as a means of compensating for some feeling of insufficiency; discipline in the home was either inconsistent or over-severe; the process of identification with the parents was distorted and uneven with a consequent failure to resolve the oedipal situation, and, in particular, a failure to incorporate the parental relation into an internalised conscience, this being possible only on the basis of a genuine love-identification which cannot exist when the child has been seriously rejected.

In the opinion of the authors, at the level of the individual psyche, anti-Semitism can be viewed as an attempt to "restore a crippled self", something used as defence mechanisms in an effort to ward off the anxieties arising from the situation already described. The anti-Semitic individual refuses to admit the presence in himself of undesirable qualities, or doubts about his own nature and powers. All these are projected on to an outgroup (the Jews) who then become fit subjects for aggression and open rejection. An attempt is made to build up the damaged self by reaction formations and compensatory drives which usually take the form of overt expression of the opposite of that which has been denied or renounced. Finally, an attempt is made to gain strength by associating actually or in phantasy with groups that are seen as powerful and dominant. This is the basis of the strict conformity which is said to be one of the characteristics of anti-Semites.

According to the authors, the two most important roles played by the social forces are the determination of the Jewish stereotype and the determination of the form of the anti-Semitic manifestations. The stereotype always reflects the main emphases of the society to which the anti-Semite belongs. Jews are typically represented as being particularly good at achieving the main cultural values; it is implied that this distinguishes them as an outgroup and they are rejected as such. Thus, in America, the Jewish stereotypes almost always relate to socio-economic matters: ambition, social-climbing, success, wealth, initiative, and so on. Religious items in stereotypes are rare.

This is an important and valuable study based on a great deal of detailed information. There are gaps in the evidence, as the authors do not hesitate to point out, but it is far more detailed than that available in the studies previously described. Nevertheless, the study contains important weaknesses which make it impossible to accept all the conclusions without further evidence.

The most important point is the absence of any kind of experimental control. This study is an interesting example of the desirability of either a random sample or some substitute for it. For example, it is pointed out that poor parental relationships were common among these anti-Semites, but there is no means of knowing whether this is a characteristic of anti-Semites or of analysts' patients. The same objection applied to the statement about the absence of depressive cases. Both these questions could have been settled by the use of some kind of random sampling, or matched control groups. In a study such as this the latter would probably be the more easily managed.[1]

Two other points that call for special mention are the lack of data on the development history of the anti-Semitic attitude, and the relation between the individual attitude and the social background of the specific individuals concerned. The authors point out that the first of these problems is an extraordinarily difficult one, and even with detailed psychoanalytic case histories to draw on it is not possible to say very much about it. They attempt to relate the cases to a pattern of American culture as seen through the eyes of the patients, and they also supply a good deal of information about the family background and personal history of each case; but with a group of this sort, drawn from a variety of situations, it is virtually impossible to do more than provide a very sketchy, generalised social background for the individual studies.

A different technique was adopted in a study undertaken at the University of Chicago (Bettelheim and Janowitz, 1950). The investigation was based on a random sample of 150 veterans of enlisted rank. Each subject was intensively interviewed by a psychiatrically trained interviewer. Direct and projective questions were used and a content analysis made of all the interview records. The subjects were rated on a four point scale for tolerance towards Negroes and Jews. The results were as follows: there was no correlation between anti-Semitism and socio-economic status, nativity of parents, formal composition of the family, political or organisational affiliation, religious denomination, or the veterans' reading and radio listening habits; social mobility was discovered to be a significant factor, those who were downwardly mobile being more intolerant than the upwardly mobile and stable groups; people who recollected the depression as a time of suffering were more intolerant than those who said they had been able to get through it quite well; fears of unemployment and of failure to achieve ambitions were significantly correlated with intolerance;

[1] It is fair to point out that, as a matter of fact, most of the conclusions put forward by these authors are supported by other workers. It is probable that the authors did make use of a form of control by comparing the characteristics of this group with their own experience of analysts' patients, but nothing of this appears in the account of the work.

religious conviction (regardless of denomination) was positively related to tolerance: vague and changing beliefs were associated with intolerance; prejudice against Negroes tended to vary in direct proportion to prejudice against Jews though (in Chicago, at any rate) it was always much higher in the case of the former.

The main conclusion of these authors is that intolerance is related less to the objectively observable external situation than to the individuals' interpretation of that situation. Veterans with long overseas service, wounds, and other experiences of deprivation, were not the most anti-Semitic members of the sample, but those who complained most about the hard times they experienced in the army were the most intolerant. At the same time the authors do not deny the consequences of social factors in the production of intolerance. They discuss at some length the fact that the differences between prejudice against Negroes and prejudice against Jews can be explained largely in terms of the social situation. Again, in describing intolerance as a failure to control the expression of aggression, they make it clear that this failure, though partially explicable in personality terms, is considerably affected by the strength and nature of the social pressures against such expression.

As an application of scientific method to a complicated problem, combined with the use of very detailed data, this study is a considerable improvement on those previously reported. The use of a random sample of subjects, not drawn from a student or other specialised population, marks a change from the usual practice. Long intensive interviews of a psychiatric type form a considerable advance on the simple questionnaire approach, and enable a distinction to be drawn between subjective and objective assessment of frustrations. The result of this seems to be to push the problem back a stage further. Whereas the frustration-aggression hypothesis could be invoked by Allport and Kramer to explain some of their results, it would be of limited value in this case, as it merely provokes the further question why some individuals perceive some situations as frustrating while others do not. Bettelheim and Janowitz do not take up the problem in detail, as their data provide little evidence on this point, though they imply rather clearly that these variations in perception are largely due to previous experiences, especially those of early childhood. Prejudice in this sense is the persistent application to present experiences of patterns of reaction arising from past experiences, but with little regard for their efficacy under the changed conditions.

The most ambitious study of anti-Semitism yet published was carried out by a group of research workers at the University of California (Adorno, *et al.*, 1950). Preliminary reports of later extensions of this project have also been published (Frenkel-Brunswik, 1948; Rokeach, 1948). The study was based on the use of three main research techniques, a questionnaire, projection tests and interviews. The questionnaire contained a number of statements relating to race relations, political and religious beliefs, and other aspects of personal ideology, including a set of items which were intended to reveal "the potentially anti-democratic personality", and the persons taking part were asked to indicate the extent of their agreement or disagreement with each statement. These expressions of agreement and disagreement were given numerical values and the total scores for each of the various sets of attitudes, such as anti-Semitism, ethnocentrism, political outlook, and general anti-democratic trends were obtained. Correlations between the different scores were calculated and in general found to be high. Various forms of the questionnaire were given to more than 2,000 people. Persons scoring very high or very low were subjected to a series of projective tests and individual interviews.

As with many of the other research projects quoted, these results show a tendency for individuals to display great consistency over a wide range of attitudes. Thus anti-Semitic persons when questioned about their religious and political beliefs or their feelings about relationships with friends, spouses and children indicated that they saw the world in terms of rigid hierarchies. Nearly all human relationships in their view were authoritarian and were to be judged by the social and material gains to oneself rather than by the joint emotional satisfaction for all concerned. The most outstanding characteristic of the prejudiced individuals seems to have been rigidity. Once they had adopted a mode of thinking or a form of behaviour they found it almost impossible to adapt it to changed circumstances. This trait was so pervasive that it even affected performance on tasks such as the solution of mathematical problems (Rokeach, 1948; Frenkel-Brunswik, 1952).

The following are some of the other characteristics that stood out in the case of the prejudiced individuals: a marked tendency towards a rigid form of conservatism in political belief; a high degree of deference to powerful people; a strong drive towards social conformity; a refusal to express aggressive wishes, offset by a preoccupation with aggressive themes in responses to projective material; a strong interest in social mobility, social standing and the problem of making a "good marriage"; a greater interest in the external world than in their own mental life (it is reported that they were difficult to interview on the subject of attitudes and feelings); a tendency to take over parental attitudes and to idealise parents (but they showed very ambivalent reactions to parent-figures in projective tests); a high degree of mental rigidity shown by an inability to alter attitudes and modes of reaction under changed circumstance; a strongly moralistic outlook; a utilitarian attitude to sex and religion—regarding them as means to some end such as upward social mobility; and general hierarchical attitude to human relationships.

The studies of children showed a rather similar pattern but with a greater degree of flexibility in the attitude displayed. The children's attitudes were seen as tendencies rather than a rigidly structured system. In addition a good deal of information was obtained about the parents and the parent-child relationships. The ethnocentric child experiences more harsh discipline and sees its parents simultaneously as "providers of one's physical needs and as capricious arbiters of punishment". Parents are, on the surface, idealised, but little evidence is shown of deep relationships.

Studies made along the same lines, using psychiatric patients and criminals as subjects, revealed similar patterns. These results emphasised the fact that the distinction between tolerance and intolerance is not the same as that between "good" and "bad" or "mentally healthy" and "mentally ill". Both the criminals and the psychiatric patients included a mixture of tolerant and intolerant individuals and it is clear that the differences must be sought along other dimensions. There did seem, however, to be some differences in the form taken by mental illness in the two groups, though this could not be expressed in terms of standard psychiatric classification. The tolerant patients showed more insight into their condition, expressed their anxieties more directly and were less likely to convert them to physical symptoms.

What general statements can be made about these eight studies? An attempt to give an account of the details of the prejudiced personality on which they agree will be left to Chapter X, but a few points may be noted here. These studies make certain things very plain: (*a*) prejudice is a highly generalised factor. People who have more than average prejudice against one out-group are likely to have a more than average prejudice against most others. The difference between anti-Semitism, anti-Negroism and general xenophobia are less fundamental than has been commonly supposed. They can best be regarded as slightly different manifestations of basically similar conditions. (*b*) Prejudice is a function of personality at least in the sense that it is dependent far more on the prejudiced person than on the out-group against which the prejudice is directed. A person with a need to express prejudice will somehow find a suitable group to express it against. The existence of a suitable group will not ensure that contact with it will produce prejudice. (*c*) Prejudice is part of a personality pattern, i.e. it is possible to assess prejudice in a person by measuring other aspects of his personality. Although it is known that this can be done the methods at present available are somewhat rule-of-thumb. (*d*) The extent to which the correlates of prejudice vary from culture to culture and from class to class can only be guessed at, but it seems likely that the basic personality traits associated with prejudice show less variation than their behavioural manifestations.

None of the studies tries to link the particular individuals studied to a clearly defined social background. Ackerman and Jahoda are clearly aware of the desirability of doing so, but their attempt goes no further than setting a rather amorphous group of subjects against a generalised and very briefly described background of contemporary American culture, as seen through the eyes of the subjects. Bettelheim and Janowitz obtained a considerable amount of information from each subject about his social background but in terms of a variety of particular categories rather than as an all-over pattern. Further, the variety of social types in the sample studied made the task of placing them appropriately in the general pattern a difficult one. The Californian study while not entirely neglecting the social background did not make it a major part of the study. There would seem to be grave drawbacks to any attempt to assess the roles of personal and social forces in the production of anti-Semitism when the latter have been so inadequately studied.

It is worth noting that, with the exception of the Californian study, all the investigations described here are on a comparatively small scale. They are, nevertheless, the most extensive pieces of

34

research yet attempted on anti-Semitism. When one compares the smallness of the research efforts with the magnitude and complexity of the problem, the wonder is not that so little agreed result has been produced, but that the results are as significant as in fact they are. It is not to be expected that such small-scale efforts made under such a variety of conditions will produce identical results, and only as more and more sets of results become available, with careful descriptions of the conditions under which they are obtained, will there be any hope of giving definite answers to the many problems which these studies leave unanswered, or on which they appear to provide conflicting evidence.

It is, however, questionable whether the confusion is really as fundamental as appears at first sight, particularly in the results of the empirical studies. It seems possible that it is due, in part at least, to an implied but unrealised disagreement as to what constitutes an explanation. In some cases there appears to be an unstated assumption that the discovery of a correlation is equivalent to explaining one of the correlated variables. Thus the discovery that there is a tendency for anti-Semitism to increase in strength and frequency when economic conditions are bad, has been hailed as an explanation of anti-Semitism. As the correlations are not perfect, and as the data derive from the whole population without reference to individual cases, it is certain that economic conditions are not an explanation in the sense of accounting for all cases of the pheno-menon. The correlation can be explained as an indication of a partial cause which must be combined with others for a full explanation; or as a predisposing situation; or as a cause which operates in some cases but not in others. Thus the fact that some investigators have found a correlation between propaganda and anti-Semitism, while others have found correlations with economic conditions or with personality traits, does not necessarily imply that all, or any of these people have been in error.

Such varying theories, all with evidence to support them, suggest either that there are many different reasons for anti-Semitism and that looking for "the cause" is a vain task, or that the suggested explanations are particular cases of a single cause or a group of related causes, which must be expressed by more generalised concepts than have hitherto been employed. That this is, in fact, the case will be argued later.

A far more serious discrepancy exists between the theories

4

summarised earlier in this chapter, and the results of the research work which followed. The theories have been propounded by people who have done little or no research, while the research workers have in most cases been understandably more concerned with presenting their findings than in relating these in detail to more general psychological and sociological theories. This divorce between theory and research is obviously not in the best interests of scientific progress.

All the various approaches certainly agree on two points. The first is that prejudice is not basically a consequence of the behaviour or characteristics of the minority group itself, but is an expression of the characteristics or the social situation (or both of these) of the majority group. This is not to suggest that the views put forward state that Jews and other minority groups have nothing whatever to do with the prejudice situation apart from suffering the consequences. A group cannot be a target for prejudice unless it exists, at least in imagination. (This qualification is necessary in view of Hartley's findings about the "Nonsuch" groups.) Its members must also have characteristics which are identifiable in the majority of cases, e.g. skin colour, language, social customs. Further, it is presumably the case that the reactions of the minority to the discrimination will produce further reactions in the majority group (Bettelheim, 1947), and a complete study of a prejudice situation would involve all of these reactions. Nevertheless, it remains true in an important sense that prejudice arises because of the nature of the majority rather than of the minority group. The existence and characteristics (real or imagined) of the smaller section of people is seized upon by the majority as an opportunity for the expression of certain attitudes which owe their origin to causes other than the existence of the minority group. Any satisfactory explanation of anti-Semitism must account for the development of these attitudes in the majority.

Secondly, none of the studies supports a commonly held popular belief that prejudice is biologically inherited. All the evidence points to the fact that anti-Semitism and other forms of intolerance arise in the course of the individual's social development. In some sense or another he learns to be prejudiced (Rose and Rose, 1948, p. 304).

Both these views are so well established and so extensively documented that no effort will be made here to discuss them further or to adduce further evidence in their support. For similar reasons the proposition that the group of characteristics commonly attributed to Jews—the Jewish stereotype—does not correspond with reality will also be taken for granted. There is a vast literature demonstrating in a completely convincing fashion, over and over again, that these accusations are false when applied to Jews in general, however well some of them may fit certain individual Jews. (Condensed accounts of this evidence can be found in Parkes, 1945, and Golding, 1938).

This brings us to the point at which we can ask the question which has become the central point of research into anti-Semitism. There are certain broad social forces which encourage anti-Semitism: propaganda, economic difficulties, the influence of anti-Semitic parents, teachers, and other adults, on the young. There is no denying the importance of all these and other factors. Yet, as we have seen, none of these influences provides an adequate explanation—some who are exposed to them become anti-Semitic, others do not. We need to know why it is that, in the absence of overwhelming social pressures some individuals choose anti-Semitism and others, faced with the same external situation, do not.

The studies described earlier in this chapter have indicated clearly the general trend of the answer to this question. Phrased very crudely it would seem to be, "Those choosing anti-Semitism have personality characteristics which pre-dispose them to react positively to the social forces that encourage anti-Semitism."

Although the studies referred to are agreed on the point that certain personality traits constitute a pre-disposition to anti-Semitism, there is no obviously close agreement among them as to the precise relation of these traits to anti-Semitism. Furthermore, there is little definite information on the subject of the causes of this particular type of personality structure. As in most other examples of social science research there is a tendency for the subjects to be drawn from only certain sections of the community—the same sections in each case—students and the well-to-do. Finally there is comparatively little attempt to show the dynamics of the relationship between the personality factors and the social forces.

The research which will be described in the succeeding parts of this book was designed to contribute to the solutions to some of these difficulties, and to fill in some of the gaps in the data available.[1]

[1] At the time when this research was planned (November, 1947) not all of these earlier studies had been reported, and of those which had, not all the reports were available in this country. The picture was, therefore, much less clear than appears from the preceding account, although its general lines were beginning to emerge.

There were three main objectives in view. (1) To provide quantitative data on some of the aspects of personality which appeared to be connected with anti-Semitism. (2) To make a tentative approach to the problem of demonstrating the dynamics of the connection between the social and psychological forces in the production of anti-Semitic attitudes. (3) To make a contribution to the task of extending psychological knowledge to groups other than those customarily studied, chiefly with reference to anti-Semitism, but, incidentally, in other aspects of life also.

The theoretical assumptions on which the research was based were as follows:

A. Any comprehensive study of anti-Semitism must take into account the personality structures of the individuals concerned as well as the social forces which affect them.

B. In a community there is likely to be a fairly definite pattern of treatment of most of the individual members throughout life, right from the time of birth, so that, by and large, it will be true to say that individuals of the same age, sex and class will receive (and will have received in the past) similar treatment by parents, spouses, siblings, friends, and other persons having relations with them. As a consequence of this general similarity of experience there is likely to be a general similarity of personality type among these individuals. Personality deviants will appear to the extent that individual experience varies from this norm.[1] In some communities the variations may be so great as to make this view untenable, but it will hold true in stable, long-standing communities.

C. Of all the relations which an individual has with other persons, the most important from the point of view of personality development are those which he has with the persons with whom he comes most in contact during the early years of his life—usually, but not necessarily, his parents—for it is during that time that he does his most important learning. Not only does he learn to walk and talk, to read and write and to dress himself, but he also learns attitudes to things, to people, and to the world in general, ways of reacting to situations, and methods of classifying his experiences. This is

[1] This formulation omits any reference to the influence of innate or biological determinants of personality. The omission is deliberate and was made on the grounds that (a) we know very little about the constitutional determinants of personality, and (b) such knowledge as we do possess suggests that these factors are likely to be considerably modified by later experiences—they probably are limiting rather than controlling factors. For a detailed account of various types of personality determinants, including the constitutional ones, see Kluckhohn and Mowrer (1944), and Kluckhohn and Murray (1948).

tantamount to saying that the main lines of personality development have been laid down by the end of childhood, and that the character of reactions to later experiences will be determined to a considerable degree by the nature of that early personality development.

These assumptions were not hypotheses designed for testing in the course of this research. In any psychological research some basic propositions have to be assumed because as yet there are no established general laws that can be utilised. The alternative is for all research workers to devote themselves entirely to investigations relating to such fundamental topics as personality development and ignore entirely more immediate and more restricted problems such as that studied in the present investigation. These assumptions have been stated here in order to indicate an area in which it was expected to find some of the chief interactions between social forces and individual personalities in the production of anti-Semites. Reference back to the development of the personality types concerned was believed to be necessary if the study was to extend beyond the demonstration of correlations, i.e. if anything approaching a complete explanation was to be produced. The attitude taken here is roughly that expressed by Dollard in setting up his criteria for studying the life history of an individual, particularly his references to viewing the subject as "a specimen in a cultural series", his stress on the role of the family in cultural transmission, the emphasis on the continuous and related character of an individual's experiences, and finally his statement that "the 'social situation' must be carefully and continuously specified as a factor" (Dollard, 1935, p. 8).

The concept of a typical pattern of personality for the majority of members of a given community has become familiar during recent years. It has been developed along similar, though not identical, lines by a considerable number of writers including Beaglehole (1944), Gorer (1943), Kluckhohn and Leighton (1946).

It should be emphasised that the view put forward here does not include the further extension made by some authors, notably Kardiner and his associates (1939 and 1945), postulating that the cultural institutions are largely projections of, and hence in some sense caused by, the personality type that results from the usual pattern of upbringing. So far as this study of Bethnal Green is concerned the environmental situation (which includes cultural patterns of upbringing) is taken as given, and the question that is considered is the effect of this given situation on any individual who comes within its orbit.

It can never be taken for granted that most members of a community will have important personality characteristics in common. This is a matter for empirical demonstration in each particular case. Even if the existence of a characteristic type of personality can be shown, this does not mean that its existence is necessarily of direct relevance to every aspect of life in the community. The present writer believes that the set of experiences which normally constitute the process of growing up in Bethnal Green are such that the development of a personality with some tendencies towards intolerance is on the whole rather likely, though for various reasons only some of these individuals will approach the more extreme degrees of prejudice. It may be that in other communities the prejudiced personalities are more atypical or that they are produced in a greater variety of ways. This is something which can be determined only by investigation. The detailed reasons for the opinion referred to above are set out in Chapters III and IX. At the moment it is only necessary to make the point that while a version of what is usually called basic personality theory appears to have been of value in this particular study of prejudice it will not necessarily be so in every case. It can, furthermore, be only a first approximation. It is useful in showing how people are alike. Insofar as prejudiced individuals are deviants, a study of their characteristics must be focused on exceptions and differences and not on similarities.

The hypotheses which this research was designed to test relate to the characteristics of individual members of the Bethnal Green community.

A. (1) Anti-Semitism is positively correlated with:

(a) Paranoid tendencies.

(b) Fears about ability to control environment.

(c) (i) Pessimism with respect to the self.

(ii) Pessimism with respect to the collectivity.

(Pessimism is defined as the expectation of deprivation.)

(2) Anti-Semitism is positively correlated with a high level of:

(a) Anti-authoritarianism in central persons (leaders).

(b) Submissiveness in follower persons.

(3) Anti-Semitism is positively correlated with a high level of free-floating anxiety.

B. (1) Anti-Semitism is postively correlated with a high level of anxiety-creating situations in any major sphere of life, including important personal relationships.

(2) Anti-Semitism is positively correlated with tendencies towards isolation. (Isolation is defined as an absence of close primary group relationships.)[1]

Given these hypotheses the next problem is that of choosing techniques of research which will make it possible to obtain the data necessary for testing the hypotheses. In this particular case three different types of data were required.

(1) A description, as detailed and accurate as circumstances would permit, of the typical personality of the people of Bethnal Green and of the type of circumstances and experiences that combine to produce it. If there is a typical personality type, produced in a typical manner, the account of the circumstances which produce an anti-Semite should be more meaningful if seen against this background.

(2) A description of the normal life of Bethnal Green and the material, ecological, economic, and historical conditions which affect it. This should include some account of the structure of social relationships, of the commonly accepted value systems, and the situations which are usually regarded as anxiety-producing, or anxiety-dispelling, with special reference to any having particular importance to persons showing the typical character structure.

(3) Information, so obtained as to be susceptible of statistical treatment, relating to the variables listed in the hypotheses. This condition meant that information had to be obtained which would refer to a number of specific individuals, so that the presence or absence of anti-Semitic attitudes in any person could be checked against the presence or absence of the other variables in the same person.

Because of the variety of information required it was necessary to use several techniques for gathering it.

(1) *Indirect participant observation.* Normally, participant observation involves the investigator placing "himself in a position where,

---

[1] These hypotheses derive from some suggested by Professor E. A. Shils on the basis of the Chicago study referred to in the last chapter. Some of the original suggestions were eliminated and others modified after the research had been in progress for a time (after the completion of the pilot phase of the interviewing programme), as it was found that conditions did not permit the gathering of adequate data to test them as they were originally stated. For example, one hypothesis referred to feelings of guilt at the infringement of social and moral rules. When it was discovered that many subjects would have to be interviewed in the presence of other members of their families it was decided that it would not be possible to get the necessary information on this topic.

unknown to the subject, he has an opportunity to observe the subject as he functions in his 'every day' activities" (Wallin, 1941, p. 191). This means that the investigator must be able to assume a role which will enable him to be accepted without suspicion by the subjects he is studying. In the present instance it was necessary to admit that the fieldworker was observing, but only in a general kind of way. The specific topic of his investigations was not revealed and as far as possible he aimed at creating a situation in which his subjects were not normally consciously aware of his observations. (For a more detailed account of this technique cf. Beaglehole, E. and P., 1946, pp. 13–16).

In carrying this out he was able to obtain a temporary position as a part-time barman in a Bethnal Green public house. This enabled him to become acquainted with a number of the local inhabitants, to converse with them informally, and to overhear their conversations. He was introduced to the landlord, and was in turn introduced by him to the customers as a New Zealand student who wanted to learn something about conditions in the East End. He made friends with members of the darts club which met on the premises, and accompanied them when they played matches in other public houses. All this enabled him to gain some insight into the life of the district, the convivial aspect by direct observation, the other aspects by questioning and by inference from statements made to him or in his presence. Another point of no small importance was that he learnt the language of the district. This was invaluable when he later attempted individual interviews as it enabled him to allow the interviewee to run on in his own idiom without continually having to interrupt with questions about meaning. It also enabled him to pick up immediately the significance of many statements made in later interviews, and to avoid making mistakes due to assuming that common English words were necessarily used in the same sense as that to which he was accustomed. To give one example, in Bethnal Green the word "decent" nearly always means "considerable" or "large". Thus "a decent crowd of chaps" means not, as one might suppose, "a friendly group of men", but "a large group of men". To undertake interviewing without first making sure that one understood the finer points of the local dialect can lead to a remarkably large number of mistakes. An East Londoner, who is accustomed to expressing himself in abbreviated forms of rhyming slang, will not lapse into the Queen's English just because he is being interviewed (Franklyn, 1953, pp. 291–4). At a later date in the research work the use of this method of observation was extended by joining the social club attached to one of the settlement houses in the district.

(2) *Interviews with non-working-class informants.* The field worker also undertook a series of interviews with people familiar with the district and whose occupations provided them with the role of participant observers; schoolteachers, clergy, social workers, police, and residents at the various settlement houses. Altogether more than forty people were interviewed in this way. The clergymen took him to visit some of their oldest parishoners who talked about the changes they had seen in the pattern of life in the district during their lifetimes.

(3) *Interviews with local informants.* In the course of the study the fieldworker became particularly friendly with a few members of the community and described to them exactly what he was trying to do. He was able to use them as informants who, in response to direct questioning, could supply him with a good deal of information about the district. They were all men, under forty years of age, and all above average in intelligence and in knowledge of the district.

These three methods of acquiring information were not kept in isolation. For example, when some of the interviewees described certain types of child disciplining as typical of Bethnal Green, an attempt was made to check this information, both by asking other interviewees the same question and by trying to find out from friends in the darts club and at the social club how they disciplined their children and how they themselves had been disciplined by their parents. On the other hand information obtained from these friends was checked by asking the various interviewees how general they thought such practices might be. No statement has been included in the description of Bethnal Green life that was not backed by information from at least two independent sources, unless it is indicated as being based on a single statement or observation.

On the basis of this it can be argued that the reliability of the descriptive material on Bethnal Green life is fairly high. It seems that there are two possible sources of error. In the first place the fieldworker's observations were made on a comparatively small number of people, probably not more than two hundred. There is no guarantee that they constitute a typical sample of the people of the district. This situation was, however, considerably improved

43

by the number and variety of the interviewees. While each of them had possibly observed a biased sample, these biases were probably of several different types, and the high degree of agreement among them suggests that the bias, if it existed, was not of any great consequence.

The second possible source of error arises from the fact that it was, of course, necessary to use selectively the available information. Selection took place in two ways. In the first place, some of the statements made by the informants were deliberately put on one side as being of insufficient importance, and secondly, the fieldworker had to exercise a process of selection on the questions that he asked and the things that he noted in the course of his observations. Such selection is quite inevitable. The problem that arises is whether or not the selection made is the best one, or whether some of the things that have been omitted are not of greater importance than those that have been included. To such a problem there is no simple answer. The selection which was made seems to the author to have been largely inevitable in view of the hypotheses on which this study was based, and its adequacy must be judged from the extent to which the material so selected tests these hypotheses.

(4) *Interviews with a random sample of subjects.* After completing the general survey of the district described above, the fieldworker set about obtaining the data necessary for testing the hypotheses. This was done chiefly through the medium of a further set of interviews. It had by this time been decided, on grounds of methodological simplicity and practical convenience, to restrict the investigation to the adult male members of the community, and an attempt was made to interview a representative sample of this group. The sample was obtained as follows: Beginning with a number chosen at random the address of every two hundredth person on the electoral roll was noted. A call was then made at each address and any adult male available was interviewed. (The details of the interview method are given in Chapter IV.)

These interviews were necessarily brief, and in order to get some of the necessary data it was essential to have longer interviews with at least some of the anti-Semitic subjects. Apart from the difficulties of arranging for longer interviews, time did not permit all these subjects to be interviewed a second time. An attempt was therefore made to arrange longer interviews with the most extreme anti-Semites and, as a control group, with those who showed themselves to be tolerant. (The method by which these two groups were selected is also described in Chapter IV.) The interviews with these subjects, particularly those who were seen more than once and who invited the author into their homes (and in some cases visited his home), also provided useful material on the Bethnal Green social pattern. Some of these men had married women from other parts of England, and these wives' comments on what they considered to be the strange ways of Bethnal Green families were often illuminating.

(5) *The Rorschach Test.* The author also aimed (and was largely successful) at persuading the individuals who were given a longer interview to do the Rorschach test. This was intended particularly to provide data on the presence of paranoid tendencies and anxiety.

We turn now to the results of the general study of the community and a consideration of the importance of the available historical and sociological data available for the problem in hand.

CHAPTER III

Some Aspects of Life in Bethnal Green

THE necessity for studying group patterns as a basis for the study of individual behaviour has been discussed earlier. It is therefore proposed at this stage to describe those elements in the social environment of Bethnal Green which seem to be relevant to the problems in hand, and to suggest some of the ways in which this environment may effect the development of individual personalities. How this material was obtained, and its limitations, have already been described.

The following account refers to conditions in Bethnal Green during the years 1947–9. A more detailed description of Bethnal Green's history may be found in an appendix. It is sufficient to point out here that the district's main period of development was from 1750–1850 and that, with the exception of blocks of flats, most dwellings date from this period. There has been a series of immigrations of foreign refugees since Elizabethan times, and it is probable that some Jews have been living in the borough since the late seventeenth century. Evidence of active anti-Semitism goes back to the closing years of the nineteenth century with peak periods around 1902–1905 and 1935–9. During the second period there was considerable open support for the Fascist party, whose candidates polled well at elections though none was successful.

Bethnal Green has rather frequently been the scene of social surveys of various kinds (Gavin, 1848; Booth, 1902; Smith, 1931; Self, 1945; Glass and Frenkel, 1946; Harding and Hooper, 1948). In spite of this an attempt to write an account of present day life in Bethnal Green is beset by two major difficulties. The first of these is the fact that these surveys have been very largely concerned with such matters as population distributions, trade and employment statistics, the availability of social services, housing conditions, and similar matters. On the whole it is true to say that they have described the people of Bethnal Green in the mass rather than as individuals, and largely in terms of such factors as geographical location, occupation, and economic status. On the basis of these studies and of the Census Reports it is possible to show, in relation to the family, facts such as the following: that families of various sizes occur with certain degrees of frequency; that a family of a given size in Bethnal Green is likely to occupy a certain number of rooms; that on some given date a certain number of families in the district were dependent on a particular trade; that a certain number of heads of families were born in Bethnal Green. There is little indication, however, of the way in which these facts affect the personal relationships between the people concerned. We are told almost nothing of the roles typically played in the home by the various members of the family, or how these roles tend to change in response to the alterations in the external environment which are so fully described by these investigators.

The second difficulty is that there has been no detailed survey of conditions in the borough for over twenty years, that is since the publication of the *New Survey of Life and Labour in London* in 1930 and the Census of 1931. L.C.C. official statistics bring information somewhat more up-to-date in certain limited respects, and in 1945 a small scale social survey of the district was carried out (Glass and Frenkel, 1946). Apart from this rather fragmentary material, it has been necessary to rely on information which the author has been able to gather from interviews with various people in the district, and upon inferences based upon the characteristics of the random sample of people drawn from the electoral roll. Although it is obvious that on this basis one cannot produce an account which is both reliable and detailed, it is possible to provide a general picture which, although somewhat blurred and lacking in detail, should not include any marked distortions. It is assumed that it is preferable to leave blanks rather than include inaccurate data.

Occupationally the picture has not changed in many important respects since the nineteen-thirties. The various trades associated with the manufacture of furniture still provide work for the largest group of Bethnal Green men, with the transport services following as a rather poor second. The firms concerned in the furniture-making are almost all on a small scale, using premises which were originally dwelling houses and where, very often, people still live "over the shop". In some streets practically all the houses have been partly or entirely converted to factory use, so that the few remaining inhabitants are plagued during the day by the noise of machinery, and at all times by the dust and squalor associated with somewhat primitive industrial conditions. There is still an overwhelming tendency for the local industries to be run as family businesses, and to be carried on in small workshops. Out of 470 industrial and wholesale firms only about a dozen employ more than fifty people. Nearly half of this industry is concerned with "woodwork, furniture and allied trades" (Glass and Frenkel, 1946, p. 4). According to the same authorities, eight per cent of all factories and workshops manufacture "clothes, or parts of clothes".

A study of the occupations of a random sample of Bethnal Green Gentile men gives a similar picture. It will be noted that many who are not employed in factories are still concerned in construction with wood as carpenters. Other branches of the building trade are also important.

TABLE 1

OCCUPATIONS OF A SAMPLE OF BETHNAL GREEN MALE GENTILES

	per cent
Furniture making and allied trades	20·5
Transport services	12
Retail trades, personal services and clerical	12
Dockers and market porters	11
Building trades (including carpenters)	9
Engineering, metal, and electrical trades	9
Unskilled labourers	5
Post Office	4·5
Unemployed and retired	4·5
Leather and boot trades	3
Printing trades	3
Clothing trades	3
Miscellaneous	3·5

Woodworking is not only the main occupation in the district, it is also one of the chief areas of interaction between the Gentile and Jewish members of the population. It is possible that this trade employs an even greater percentage of the Jewish than of the Gentile population, and fairly certain that the majority of employers are Jewish. Of the 22 men in the above group who were engaged in the furniture and allied trades, 14 had Jewish employers at the time of interview and only 2 claimed that they had never been employed by a Jew. Of the remaining 87 men, 7 were employed by Jews at the time of interview. Almost without exception the furniture makers had some Jewish workmates, but only 5 of the other workers were in this position. The same situation applies to the men in the clothing trades. All those interviewed, three in number, had Jewish employers and workmates.

The woodworking establishments tend to concentrate in one area of Bethnal Green, corresponding roughly to the western quarter of the borough, with the addition of the area lying to the north of Old Bethnal Green Road. There are some workshops of various kinds in the remainder of the borough but they decrease rapidly towards the east.

This division into "predominantly residential" and "partly industrial" areas is only one in which the borough can be subdivided for purposes of description. Glass and Frenkel, for example, give a division into six areas based on a combination of several criteria. The inhabitants of the borough normally divide the area on the basis of "social standing". Bethnal Green is remarkably homogeneous as far as social class divisions are concerned, and it is improbable that a sociologist, working with a combination of broad "objective" criteria such as standards of housing, income level, occupation, and educational level, would be prepared to subdivide the area with any degree of certainty. There are, however, certain areas which are normally regarded as better or worse than the greater part of the borough. The two "better" areas are commonly referred to as (1) "round Victoria Park" and including Approach Road, Sewardstone Road, and the greater part of Old Ford Road and (2) "over the canal", the extreme eastern area of the borough. The inhabitants of both these areas are conscious of their superiority, refer to their neighbourhoods as "more middle-class, like", speak of the doctors, civil servants, and retired tradespeople who used to live there before the war, and bemoan the fact that recent upheavals have brought in less desirable people "from the slums", who lower the tone of the neighbourhood. Occupationally these people are not easily distinguishable from the rest of Bethnal Green, but they are conscious of their greater respectability. People living in other parts of the borough will boast about the fact that they were born in one of these "better" areas. The people "over the canal" tend to deny their association with Bethnal Green and speak of their neighbourhood as "Bow". On the whole the houses in this area are rather larger and more substantial than those in the rest of Bethnal Green but at the present time they are no less overcrowded.

The undesirable areas are less clear-cut. They include two definite areas, one in the western and one in the south-western parts of the borough, and a number of widely scattered individual streets. The western area is objected to as "foreign" and "Jewish"; the other streets are more usually described as "poor", "spivvy", "not nice", and are believed (probably not without justification in some cases) to have unusually high rates of crime and juvenile delinquency. The remainder of the borough is regarded as being "much of a muchness". These statements are based partly on information gathered during interviews and in casual conversation, and partly on the replies of secondary school children to the questions "In what part of Bethnal Green would you most (and least) like to live, and why?"

It is also possible to subdivide Bethnal Green roughly into Jewish and non-Jewish areas. The evidence for this division is of various kinds. It is derived from information gathered in the course of another investigation,[1] from observation of Jewish names on shops, from the distribution of Jews in the sample of addresses drawn from the electoral roll, and from information supplied by the headteachers of Bethnal Green schools regarding the number of children in their schools who observe Jewish holidays. The statements of some of the interviewees from the random sample have also been useful. Not all of them could be relied upon, however, and so this information does not cover the whole area. A man who made vague or sweeping statements was regarded as unreliable (e.g. "Oh yes, there are any amount of Jews round about" or "There are thousands of them everywhere, the place is full of them") but when a man was able to give the precise number of Jewish families in the street, together with the numbers of the houses they lived in, and the country of origin of the family in each case, it was assumed that his information was fairly correct.

It is because there is no accurate information available about the number of Jewish people in Bethnal Green that it has been necessary to make use of estimates in this way. It had been hoped to make a calculation on the basis of the proportion of Jewish children in the elementary schools, but this proved impossible as none of the Bethnal Green schools serves kosher meals, and therefore an

[1] The author is indebted to Mr. Hallam Tennyson for permitting him to make use of these data.

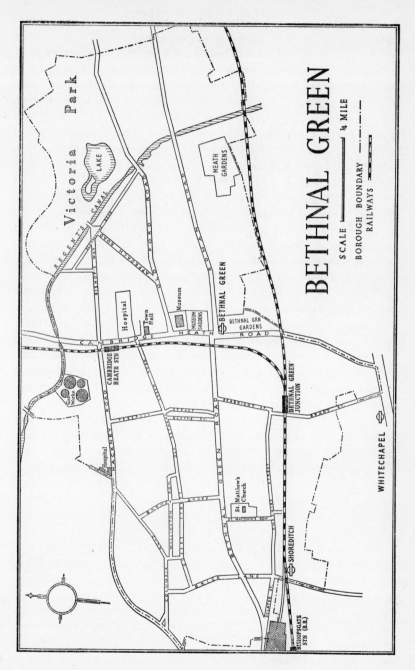

BETHNAL GREEN

SCALE ⸻ ¼ MILE

BOROUGH BOUNDARY ⸺·⸺·⸺

RAILWAYS ▬▬▬▬

Victoria Park

LAKE

REGENT'S CANAL

MEATH GARDENS

BISHOP'S WAY

OLD FORD ROAD

CANAL

BETHNAL GREEN

Hospital

Town Hall

Museum

MUSEUM GARDENS

BETHNAL GRN GARDENS

BETHNAL GREEN ROAD

CAMBRIDGE HEATH ROAD

CAMBRIDGE HEATH STN

Gas Works

TEESDALE STREET

HACKNEY ROAD

BLYTHE ST

FARRANT ST

GREEN STREET

BETHNAL GREEN JUNCTION

BRADY

WHITECHAPEL

BARNET GROVE

WELLINGTON

COLUMBIA ROAD

BRICK LANE

Hospital

St. Matthew's Church

MATTHEW'S ROW

BETHNAL GREEN ROAD

SHOREDITCH

BISHOPSGATE STN (B.R.)

unknown number of Jewish children attend schools in Stepney where kosher meals are obtainable. An attempt to discover how many children cross the border to go to school failed. On the basis of the information available it is estimated that in 1948 not more than ten per cent of the population of Bethnal Green was Jewish, i.e. up to about 6,000 persons. The vast majority of these Jewish people live in two areas, (1) the western end of the borough, an area west of a line formed by Columbia Road, Barnet Grove, and St. Matthew's Row (it will be noted that this falls within the main "woodwork trades area" referred to above) and (2) the district south of the main east-west railway line from Liverpool Street. So far as can be estimated the population of these areas is about sixty per cent Jewish, though it seems certain that the number of Jews is steadily decreasing. Thirty years ago the school population in the western area was about ninety per cent Jewish. As the population of Bethnal Green as a whole has declined fairly rapidly, the decrease in the number of Jews must be proportionately very much greater than that of the Gentiles. There is a third area in Bethnal Green with a marked Jewish population, the so-called "Jews' Island" of Teesdale and Blythe Streets. This is the centre of Bethnal Green's clothing industry, and, while before the war the population seems to have been largely Jewish, now only a few remain. A number of the buildings in these streets are clothing factories which appear to be owned chiefly by Jews.

The main shopping area of the borough, Bethnal Green Road and Roman Road, includes a number of Jewish businesses. The proportion is greatest in the west and decreases towards the east. The precise number of these Jewish businesses cannot be given in either absolute or relative terms. It is, however, quite certain that, in spite of the complaints of some Bethnal Green people, there is no necessity for a person who does not want to do so to trade at a Jewish shop.

Although the author spoke to a number of people who had been in business where they would have had Jewish competitors and whose businesses had failed, not one of them gave Jewish competition as a reason for failure, although two of them were extreme anti-Semites. (The others showed varying degrees of anti-Semitism and tolerance.) The complaints that Jews drive English shopkeepers out of business came chiefly from men in occupations having no connection with these businesses, e.g. lorry-drivers and carpenters.

The Fascists have contested only one election since the end of the war, that for the Borough Council in May, 1949, when they put forward three candidates in the South Ward of Bethnal Green. These three candidates secured 259, 196, and 189 votes and came at the bottom of the poll. The highest vote in the ward was 1,814, the lowest non-Fascist vote was 1,184. (There were eighteen non-Fascist candidates.) If these figures are compared with those for 1937 it is obvious that the Fascists have suffered a severe set-back and that only a small proportion of even the more extreme anti-Semites can have voted Fascist.

There has been a considerable revival of Fascist activities in the borough since early in 1947, chiefly in the shape of open air meetings. There were disturbances at many of these, and for a time they drew crowds of many hundreds. They were greatly overshadowed, however, by the larger and noisier meetings being held during the same period at Ridley Road in Hackney, and were rarely reported in the local press. As at Ridley Road, these meetings dwindled to negligible size and importance when the publicity associated with attempts to disrupt them and to start rival meetings came to an end.

For present purposes this generalised picture needs to be filled out by some details relating to the typical behaviour and experiences of the people of Bethnal Green in the course of their lives. Because the main theme of this book is the relationship between personality characteristics and anti-Semitism, the demographic and ecological facts become important mainly insofar as they affect the attitudes and behaviour of the people concerned, and especially their attitudes and behaviour in relation to other people. An account of these is not available, and it is therefore necessary to attempt to formulate it on the basis of the observations made in the course of the fieldwork for this study. Various aspects of life in other working class districts have been described elsewhere (Collis and Poole, 1950; Franklyn, 1953; Jephcott, 1945, and 1948; Paneth, 1947; Spinley, 1953; Zweig, 1948 and 1952) and though not strictly comparable, as the information on which they are based had been collected by different means and for different purposes, they can serve as a useful check on the account given here. There seem to be no serious descrepancies among these various descriptions.[1]

---

[1] The author is indebted to Mr. Michael Young for permission to read field notes compiled during a study carried out in Bethnal Green and which related in part to some of the topics raised in this chapter.

The account which follows is not intended to present a complete description of life in Bethnal Green. It is a selection of those aspects which are important for this study. Although, for reasons already stated, the author considers that its accuracy should be fairly high, it is presented in an impressionistic manner. The exact verification of the statements made in this chapter would have been a major research project in itself, and it has therefore been necessary to leave them as impressions, albeit impressions which are for the most part based on a considerable number of observations and supported by the opinions of a variety of persons. Doubtless more details of the social structure of Bethnal Green would have added to the value of this account, but the author was trained as a psychologist and was not equipped to carry out such a study on his own, even if time had been available. The co-operation of an anthropological colleague in any case would have been invaluable. This account represents, therefore, an attempt by a psychologist to do justice to a complex topic somewhat outside his own field.

As far as the general external environment is concerned, there seem to be three factors of central importance in determining the way of life and outlook of the typical Bethnal Green male.[1] These factors are (1) the housing conditions and population distribution within the borough; (2) the employment situation and other major economic forces; (3) the low geographical and social mobility which have been characteristic of Bethnal Green until at least very recent times. It will be obvious that in terms both of historical development and present operation, these forces are interdependent, but for purposes of this analysis it is convenient to consider them separately. It is also necessary to note that all these conditions have undergone marked changes during the past few years, and probably at an increasing rate. Since we are interested primarily in men who were adults by the time these changes had become very marked, and since people take time to adjust—especially in their more basic attitudes—to changed external conditions, it is more realistic to consider the influence of these forces as they existed in the pre-war years.

For at least a century the greater part of Bethnal Green has been a densely populated borough. In 1931 the population densities for the four wards varied from 109 to 178 persons per acre, while the

[1] Because the individuals studied in detail in the main part of the investigation were all males this account will emphasise the roles and experiences of the male. It is not, of course, possible to exclude women from the description even where their situation differs markedly from that of the men, but no effort will be made to describe them in the same detail as the men.

average number of persons per room in the whole borough was 1·35. In 1934 over one thousand families of three or more persons were living in a single room, one hundred and five of these being families of six or more persons (*Hackney Gazette*, 4th July, 1934). The buildings in which the people of Bethnal Green are housed can be divided roughly into three types: blocks of flats or tenements of varying age and quality, from squalid slum dwellings to modern well appointed buildings, and owned by a variety of commercial, charitable, and municipal organisations; former middle-class houses occupied usually by two or more families; and, most commonly, terraces of tightly packed houses of three to six rooms, containing, as a general rule, one or two families. The larger houses often have small gardens at the rear, the smaller ones usually a tiny yard, while most blocks of flats stand in paved courtyards. There are three public open spaces, only one (Victoria Park) of any size, all these being in the eastern half of the borough.

As a consequence of these conditions, it is practically impossible to live in Bethnal Green without being in close physical proximity to a great many other people. Even an unsociable individual cannot avoid a large measure of interaction with his neighbours. It is no unusual thing to be able to hear these neighbours, above, below and on both sides. Even some of the post-war blocks are far from sound-proof, and the older ones are usually much worse. The commonest complaint made of flats is that the floors are too thin. The constant and close interaction inevitably causes difficulties, the most common being those arising from noises which disturb other inhabitants of the same building, particularly, as one would expect, the noises made by children. A Bethnal Green parent who wishes to remain on good terms with the neighbours must keep the children quiet, especially in the evenings and during the night. This same pattern has been described as existing in East London towards the end of the nine-teenth century (cf. Besant, 1899, pp. 115-151).

At least until after the outbreak of the last war the employment situation in Bethnal Green was characterised chiefly by low wages and a high level of unemployment. The risk of being "on the dole" was considerable, and even if a man remained in work his family might not be far from the poverty line and would be in constant danger of sinking below it in the event of illness or other misfortune. Furthermore, the incomes of employed men tended to fluctuate because of piece work or of variations in opportunities for overtime.

Many Bethnal Green trades, especially those associated with furniture and building, tended to be seasonal in nature, and many men were regularly unemployed for a period each year; some avoided this by having a second occupation to cover the slack period. The use of spare time work by both men and women as a means of supplementing the family income or the unemployment benefit was a common feature. In these conditions saving was virtually impossible, and such saving as did take place would be effected through local savings "clubs" and would be devoted to such "luxuries" as Christmas, or irregular expenditure on clothes and other essentials. This meant that in the event of difficulties there would be nothing to fall back on, while little could be gained by attempting to plan for the future.

For a man to remain in regular employment was, therefore, not only of basic importance for his family, it was also likely to be a difficult problem for him. The necessity and urgency of keeping a job was constantly before the Bethnal Green man in a way that can hardly be understood by those accustomed to more secure posts. Because of its central importance and because of the rather high risk of failure, maintaining a steady income for the family seems to have become almost a test of manhood, of proper masculinity. In a middle class environment, where security of employment tends usually to be taken for granted, such a test has little meaning, as only the worst failures would not pass. In Bethnal Green the danger of failure is there for all, and every day's work is another hurdle in an unending steeple-chase where there can be no winner and where all the energies are devoted merely to not falling out of the race.[1] As long as a man brings home the housekeeping money each week, he has gone most of the distance toward proving himself a good husband and father. A man who, for whatever reason, is unable to carry out his breadwinning role, unless the failure is only of short duration, falls a great distance in the estimation of himself, his wife and children, and his fellows. If his place as the breadwinner is taken by his son, then the younger man is likely to be treated with far more respect by the family, and given far more comfort and consideration than his father. There are cases to be found where a chronic invalid or cripple is treated by his wife and family as if he were some inferior kind of servant.

[1] Some of the feelings of men caught in such a struggle are vividly described in the novel, *The Ragged-Trousered Philanthropists* by Robert Tressall (1940).

The degree of mobility in Bethnal Green, both social and geographical, is very low. In 1944 it was estimated that seventy-seven per cent of heads of families had been born within the borough (Glass and Frenkel, 1946, p. 6). In some areas mobility is even slighter. One informant who lived in a house that had been occupied by his parents and grandparents stated that he could not remember a new family coming into the street of seventy houses during the previous forty years. Another reported a movement of six families in twenty-five years in a longer street. The absence of social mobility is easy to understand, even if difficult to demonstrate. Where economic resources are slender, where educational opportunity is blocked by the necessity for immediate earning, and where advancement almost inevitably means entering on an unknown way of life which cannot be assessed in advance, the social climber is faced by an all but impossible task.

One consequence of this immobility is that every one is surrounded by people very like himself, most of whom he has always known. Bethnal Green has many points of similarity with a village, or rather with a whole series of overlapping and interlocking villages. The opportunities for close, long-term relationships are greater than is usually the case in a large metropolitan residential area. The likelihood of an inhabitant having neighbours who are strangers, or whose way of life is very different from his own, has until recently been very slight. This immobility also makes it essential for him to be on good terms with his neighbours, as they are likely to be there, for better or worse, for most of his life.

The combination of these three types of influence seems to produce a number of important effects in the lives of the people of Bethnal Green, and many features of their personal relationships can be understood only against this background. The consequences of these conditions begin to show themselves very early in life. It is no doubt normal for a young mother, fond of her baby, to wish to handle it a great deal and to be somewhat distressed when it cries. Circumstances force the Bethnal Green mother to do much more than this. It does not matter too much perhaps if her baby cries during the day (unless her husband, or some other man within earshot is on night duty and needs to sleep) but at night it can be a great disturbance and lead to trouble with the neighbours, or even with her husband, especially if his work compels early rising. Consequently, she is very likely to operate a system of "demand feeding", to pick the baby up frequently, and to carry it about to prevent crying. In the past it has been common, for reasons of poverty and lack of space, for babies to sleep in the parents' bed, and almost unknown for them to sleep outside the parents' room. Nowadays the material factors may be less pressing, but customs are strong, and even though the child has its own cot it will quickly be taken into bed with the mother if this will stop a bout of crying. The wife of one informant considered herself very unusual in Bethnal Green (she had not been brought up there) because she had never allowed any of her children to sleep in the parents' bed, even though the youngest always slept, as a matter of course, in the same room. For all these reasons, and perhaps others as well, the young child in Bethnal Green seems to experience a rather close, warm relationship with its mother, having its wants rapidly gratified, and in general, learning that the world is a good, secure, and comforting place. During the toddler stage especially, the father is also likely to pay a good deal of attention to the child, while there may be grandparents and other relatives who will do the same.

The length of time for which this situation continues is likely to depend on a number of conditions, including the size of the family and the interval before the birth of the next child. The absence of younger children is likely to extend the period, the presence of older ones to shorten it. Looking after a small child in this way is a time-consuming affair and, faced by the difficulties of a growing family, and of housekeeping in circumstances that make efficiency impossible, a mother is sooner or later forced to modify her methods. If she lives in really overcrowded conditions, keeping more than one child with her all the time becomes almost a physical impossibility. The inevitable consequence is that as the child gets beyond the toddler stage he is forced more and more out of his mother's company, and loses much of his close relationship with her. Since this change does not take place overnight, he is not pushed out entirely and without compensations. He may find himself turned over to the care of others for a good deal of the time, perhaps a young unmarried sister of his mother, or his own older siblings (the existence of these is likely to make his own change in status both necessary and possible at an earlier age than otherwise) or older children of neighbours. There will almost certainly be other children of his own age in the same position, and it is from this mixed group of children that he must seek some of the comfort and security that formerly came from his mother. Thus the neighbourhood, whose demands have done much to force him into this position, is the means whereby the blow is softened, and the demands made tolerable.

In spite of these aids, however, the child experiences a considerable change in his way of life, and this must on the whole be felt as a change for the worse. He is less often the centre of attention, he has much less contact with his mother. Playing outside, and with other children, no doubt has its pleasures and excitements, but it would appear that the change is rather too great and too sudden, and takes place at too early an age for easy adjustment. Other changes in treatment also take place. As the child approaches school age, and becomes more obviously amenable to reason and punishment, the overworked mother, under pressure to respect the needs of the neighbours, is less and less likely to use her former pleasant but time-consuming methods of keeping the peace, and so scoldings, slaps, and requests to go and play with other children are likely to become increasingly frequent, not because the mother loves her child the less but because such methods are an obvious and simple method of achieving a result she feels she must obtain at all costs. By the time the child sets off for school he has had to revise considerably his early notions of the world in which he lives. His beliefs have been rudely though not unbearably shaken, and some of his expectations of constancy and dependability have gone. Life is harsher, and much more uncertain, while adults, and especially parents, appear to be less reliable than earlier experiences had indicated.

The child's most usual reaction to this feeling of partial loss would seem to be to cling all the more strongly to all that he still possesses, that is, to the parents who have proved something of a disappointment, and to the group of children with whom he plays. They may be somewhat imperfect but they are his world. He minimises their imperfections and, particularly in the case of his mother, endeavours by means of idealisation to convince himself that everything is as good as before. Of course, not all children have exactly these experiences. Some are fortunate enough to live in less crowded conditions in a house with a garden, or have a mother with exceptional qualities, and so avoid this change, or experience it later or in a slighter degree. Others experience a sharper break, perhaps after a less satisfactory beginning, but by and large the picture approximates to that given here, because in the circumstances it would be difficult for people to behave otherwise.

The father's position in the family is difficult to describe. The absolutely crucial nature of his role as breadwinner has already been indicated, but in some other respects his position is very different. Schoolteachers, social workers and others who have contact with Bethnal Green families nearly always agree that the real head of the family is the mother, but a few stress the importance of the man as the final authority. The disagreement seems to be based on a sharp division of labour between men and women and a difference of opinion as to which role is to be regarded as the more important. One consequence of the man's economic importance is that so long as he remains in work he can claim, if he wishes, almost complete exemption from all other tasks connected with the family. Again, it is essential for the well-being of the family that he should be kept as fit for work as possible. Therefore he tends to get first consideration in the comforts and amenities of the home; his rest must not be disturbed, he must be well fed at all costs, and no unnecessary demands must be made on him. From this point of view his role appears rather like that of a despotic monarch. On the other hand his abdication from responsibility for activities within the home leaves his wife in a central position as far as closer relationships within the household are concerned. The importance of the economic as against the purely parental role of the man can be seen in the extent to which a boy on starting work comes to be regarded as a family breadwinner with all the privileges and absence of restriction which go with this position. Such privileges are not granted to the boy who continues his schooling beyond the minimum age of leaving, and this situation is no doubt a powerful deterrent to any boy who could extend his period of education if he so wished.

The men appear to take a great deal of interest in the smaller children, especially at the toddler stage, and may spend a great deal of money on gifts and treats for them. Fathers frequently boast of the things they have bought their children: in fact, the buying of rather expensive and elaborate, though often unsuitable and unappreciated, presents for his children seems to be a man's regular method of demonstrating his goodness as a father. In spite of this, a father is unlikely to have much close contact, especially with the older children. Often he seems to appear as a rather remote figure, by contrast with the mother, and even more than she, is he likely to be seen by the child as inconsistent and unpredictable. The tendency for the children to play outside the home, and the man's long working hours combine to ensure a rather small degree of contact between father and children, even if he does not follow the common practice of spending at least two evenings a week and part of the week-end away from the home with his friends. Again the pattern varies from one family to another. While a few fathers show such a degree of indulgence that almost every whim of the child's is gratified if at all possible, a few will be consistently harsh and punishing; but the majority oscillate rather suddenly and erratically between the two, without ever reaching the extremes, a situation which tends to confirm the child's impression that the world is a somewhat disturbing and unpredictable place.

As the boy grows older the chief change in his way of life is his gradual transfer after he begins school from the group of children of mixed ages and sexes to a uni-sexual gang of boys of his own age. This gang becomes one of the most important influences in his life. Outside school hours he spends most of his time with these friends and, to the extent that his home is unsatisfactory, the gang is likely to provide some degree of compensation for lack of support and security. It is, of course, true that even in districts where it is customary for boys to spend much more time within the home, the local group of age-mates plays an important part, especially in providing support in conflicts, whether open or suppressed, with parents. In Bethnal Green, where, as we have seen, circumstances tend to push the child out from the centre of his family rather early, and where he is under great pressure to grow up and become a wage earner, its importance is very great indeed. It is easy to see how this kind of experience will reinforce and emphasise the development, already noted, of neighbourhood loyalties and group solidarity, especially in circumstances where the boys, when grown up, tend to stay in the neighbourhood.

The degree to which groups of this kind, with some modification of membership, persist into adult years is very striking. Such a group often becomes associated with one of the local public houses and may form the nucleus of its darts team and supporters. Men who have once become integrated into such a group will often go to considerable lengths to avoid its break-up. In the public house where the author worked, about half the members of the main group of "regulars" had at some time, usually following marriage, moved to another part of the borough, but they continued to use the same public house as their social centre. Some of them walked more than a mile at least twice a week to drink and play darts with their friends, not because they had been unable to make new contacts—most of them had built up a connection with the nearest public house to home and were getting known in the new district—but because of the strength of the ties in the old group. Where ties are so strong, a rejection by the group is clearly a major disaster, as also is a failure to become properly integrated within a chosen group.

There is one characteristic type of behaviour which seems to be closely related to this theme of group solidarity. This is the very marked aggressiveness which is displayed in almost any circumstances, and is nearly always masked by a display of joviality. The aggressiveness is most marked between adolescents of opposite sexes. Here it often becomes a kind of mock fight, and one frequently observes struggles between groups of teen-agers standing about on street corners or outside youth clubs in the evenings. Among the young adults and older adolescents it is chiefly displayed as a kind of competition in the use of insulting names, telling the other person that he, or she, is ugly, stupid, untidy, lazy, and so on, all with an air of mock anger and joviality, and sometimes developing into the same type of physical conflict as among the younger people. This latter feature is not seen so much among the adults, though one man will sometimes make a threatening gesture towards another, and occasionally towards a woman. The pattern of aggression among the adults is usually one of insults, accusations and threats, often made laughingly, but sometimes with a serious face, and on some occasions it is impossible for the newcomer to the district to distinguish jest from reality except by watching the faces of the other bystanders. Even courting couples will behave in this way.

In the case of real quarrels it is customary for comparatively slight restraint to be shown, while little attempt is made to disguise emotions. People tend to quarrel openly but fairly briefly, and once feelings have been relieved in this way, memories of the dispute appear to be quite short. The commonest cause of trouble seems to be the children. Two adults (especially women) will quarrel over something that the child of one has done in relation to the other, or because one adult has punished another's child (this is very definitely against local customs: the proper course is to ask the parent to punish), or simply because the children have quarrelled and each supports her own child. However, considering the opportunities that arise in such a crowded area, serious quarrels seem to be remarkably infrequent.

The mock quarrelling described seems to be a means of expressing anger without disturbing the unity of the group. This system enables people to get rid of a considerable amount of aggression without causing any real trouble and so leaving the group solidarity unimpaired. It might almost be true to say that it is the quarrelling that is real and the joviality that is a pretence. The struggling among adolescents has presumably the additional function of providing some indirect sexual satisfaction through physical contact.

A further indication of group solidarity in the face of a difficult environment can be seen in the amount of mutual aid, in the form of loans of goods and services, that goes on all the time among households in any neighbourhood. The extent of communal help and the speed with which it is forthcoming in cases of sickness, death, or other misfortunes is quite remarkable. The collection (usually called "a whip round") taken up along a street or among the members of some group is a common feature of such efforts at support in time of trouble.

In view of the importance of the local group to its members it is not surprising that the pull of local loyalties tends to be much stronger than rules and authorities imposed from without. This situation could be seen more dramatically at the beginning of the century and earlier when group action against external authority was carried to an extent which made it unsafe for a solitary policeman to enter some parts of the borough, and the "School Board man" endeavouring to enforce school attendance was treated as a hated foe. Although Bethnal Green is now as peaceful and lawabiding as any London suburb and a stranger can wander safely and at will, the distinction between the things that must be done because they are "right" for Bethnal Green and those which are done because "they" enforce the performance remains in many subtle ways. Thus, a man who steals even a small sum from a neighbour or a workmate is subject to a degree of condemnation that is unlikely to be visited on a man guilty of a much larger theft elsewhere. The unpardonable crimes are those against the group, or those which bring the group into disrepute, while those against outsiders, although deprecated, are usually placed in quite a different category. Open display of authority, even within a local group, is viewed with some suspicion. People who are in informal leadership positions, e.g. chairmen of local committees, or captains of darts teams, will ostentatiously ridicule their position, and their "followers" will do likewise. There appears to be remarkably little competition for leadership, as the really important thing is to be a freely accepted member. The problem of hierarchical position is of little importance, and such concern as is shown in this respect seems to be directed mainly at preventing the leaders from rising too far above the others.

This outline of some of the important influences on the behaviour and outlook of the average Bethnal Green man can now be briefly summed up with the emphasis on the consequences of these influences, and particularly on the situations which the man is likely, as a result, to find particularly gratifying or frustrating. The picture which seems to emerge is that of a man whose needs and whose expectations of satisfaction are rather delicately balanced, though with the likelihood that in most circumstances the level of satisfaction will be adequate. The really critical tests will come in two areas, namely those of economic security and personal relationships, especially within a small local group.

The importance of economic factors is in many ways straightforward and obvious, as it is in all sections of the community. No matter where a man lives, or what his standard of living, economic failure and unemployment are serious matters. However, for the Bethnal Green man, whose share in the family tasks is largely confined to this one field, and whose risks of failure are so high, these assume added importance. Naturally men will vary considerably in their view of how much unemployment constitutes failure, in how soon they give up hope of finding work, and in the extent to which they make do with odd jobs, but there are only a fortunate few who can realistically consider themselves as safe against the forces of economic depression.

Personal relationships are equally crucial but their importance has a less obvious basis. The comparatively high degree of separation from the mother, which follows a very happy and secure early experience, and which must appear to the child as involving a degree of desertion and cruelty on the mother's part, seems to leave a basic anxiety which is alleviated, but not entirely removed, by the support obtained from close group membership, and which is to some extent reinforced by the later rather inconsistent behaviour of both parents. If all goes well, this basic anxiety will do no more than result in the dependence on the group and the idealisation of the parents, described earlier, but its existence leaves the individual more vulnerable to threats of further "desertions", while another actual experience may reactivate the old anxieties. It is likely that the threat of economic failure gains some added strength from this situation, for the man's position in his home, and the degree to which he is esteemed by his family, will depend, in part, on the extent to which he fulfils his economic obligations.

It is against this background that the facts set out in succeeding chapters must be evaluated, for it is clear that, because of his different background and experience, the Bethnal Green man will interpret many facts in a way that will not be immediately obvious to the outsider. It will be argued later that it is only by interpreting data in this way that apparent contradictions between the results of research carried out in different areas can be resolved.

CHAPTER IV

Interviews and Rating Scales

URING the past few years much has been written about the
topic of interviewing and a great deal of research on the
subject has been reported. Various types of interview,
from the rigid questionnaire form to the free interview, in which
questions are avoided as far as possible and the interviewee is allowed
to speak as and when he wishes, have been advocated (Hertzof,
1948; Merton and Kendall 1946; Young, 1935). Many of the freer
techniques have been developed by therapists and, although these
have been used chiefly by them and by social case workers, social
science research workers have also shown considerable interest,
particularly since the publication of reports on the Hawthorne
project (cf. Roethlisberger, 1939). It would certainly be too much
to claim that all social research workers have abandoned the older
type of formal questionnaire-interview, but is undoubtedly true
that within recent years it has become widely recognised that a more
flexible form (variously called "guided", "focused", "qualitative",
"open-ended", etc.) has a valuable part to play in social research.

It is not proposed here to enter into a detailed consideration of the
arguments in favour of abandoning the questionnaire interview,
but merely to indicate very briefly why a more flexible form was
used in this particular study. The actual method used will then be
described in some detail and its values and weaknesses discussed.
This latter task will be attempted chiefly by comparing the form
and situation of this interview with that found in other circumstances,
notably in social case work.

The form of the interview was largely determined by the circumstances in which it had to be carried out. The interviewees could not
be told the subject of the inquiry. Had the actual topic been
announced it is highly probable that many would have refused to

participate, and certain that most would have returned highly stereotyped answers to most of the questions. The most fundamental circumstance that had to be taken into account was that the interviewees were not, in the ordinary sense of the term, volunteers. True, they had a choice in the matter; they could either submit to the interview or not, just as they pleased. But it was not obvious to them when the interview began, what it was all about, nor that they were likely to gain anything from it. In short, there was no necessary motivation for the interview on the part of the interviewee. A later part of this chapter can be anticipated by pointing out that this situation differs greatly from that obtaining in the usual non-random group of interviewees. Such a group consists usually of individuals who have either consented to, or asked for, an interview because they believe it will help them in some way (e.g. an analyst's patients or a social case worker's clients) or they have volunteered to be interviewed in response to a definite and open appeal for subjects for a piece of research. The motivation in this latter case may be of various kinds—interest in the results of the research, a desire to earn the gratitude of the research worker, hope of monetary reward, hope of an opportunity to obtain psychological assistance in some personal difficulty—but in each case it is strong enough to induce the individual to volunteer to be interviewed and to be prepared to respond to a number of questions with detailed personal information.

One of the major defects of groups of both these kinds is that they are not randomly selected, and may, indeed, show a very high degree of bias in some direction, and it becomes important to know whether or not the results obtained from such groups can properly be generalised to the whole population. In this study an attempt has been made to interview all the members of a sample which, while not strictly random, approaches this condition closely enough to avoid the most obvious forms of bias in selection. The selection of a group of people in this way, while overcoming some difficulties, introduces others, as there can be no guarantee that they will have any strong motive for taking part in an interview. The subjects were not volunteers but conscripts, and the fact that they submitted very willingly, in most cases, to this conscription, does not eliminate the difference that this made to the interview situation.

Under these circumstances a fixed set of questions would have been useless. It was necessary for the interviewer to lead the conversation away from the ostensible subject of the interview (housing),

6

to the actual subject (Jews). It was not possible to do this in the same way in every case, and there had to be a sufficient degree of flexibility in the interview to enable this transition to be made smoothly and without arousing the interviewee's suspicions. In addition it was necessary to obtain information concerning the subject, his present attitudes and past experiences, which had no obvious connection with the topic of housing, and here again a flexible approach was necessary. What, in fact, had to be done was to supply the subject with some motive for continuing the interview, or at any rate, remove any motives for breaking it off. In cases where a follow-up interview was desired the creation of a positive motive was necessary. As the method which would operate with one person would have been useless with another it was essential for the interviewer to be able to vary his approach.

At the same time it had to be recognised that the material obtained from the various interviews had to be comparable in order to be of any use for purposes of statistical treatment, and therefore all interviews had to rest on a similar basis, aim at obtaining similar types of information, and include always a certain number of basic questions. Most variation was allowed in the way in which these were introduced and the manner in which the transition from one to another was made. It was, however, desirable that the interviewee should always express his own feelings and not merely those provided for him by the interviewer, and the flexibility of the interview gave an opportunity for allowing him to emphasise those things which were of greatest importance to him, without having his attention dragged away to some other topic merely because it was next on the list of subjects to be dealt with.

For reasons already stated the interviewees were not informed of the real object of the interview. The ostensible topic was the housing situation with special reference to new housing areas and satellite towns. This subject was chosen chiefly because it was thought to be one which most people, because they had some definite opinions to express, would be willing to discuss with the interviewer. It also provided a convenient jumping-off ground for various topics, and, because of the frequency with which housing difficulties are referred to in anti-Semitic propaganda, gave the interviewees an early opportunity of making anti-Semitic remarks should they wish to do so. An anti-Semitic statement, for purposes of this study, is one which is intended to convey the information that all, or most,

Jews are characterised by some trait, or some type of behaviour that the speaker regards as undesirable. Statements were judged very strictly and any remark that appeared even slightly unfavourable was judged anti-Semitic if it was generalised in any way. The degree of anti-Semitism of any individual is therefore likely to have been overestimated rather than underestimated.

The interview opened with the following statement: "I am carrying out a kind of social survey, trying to find out what the general opinion is about the plans to build new towns outside London to reduce the overcrowding in the city. The kind of thing I am trying to get at is this; suppose you or some of the other people about here were given the opportunity of going to one of these new places, would it make any problems or difficulties for you?"

The answer to this question almost invariably related to the man's work, and gave an opportunity for discovering his occupation, and whether or not he wanted to, or would be prepared to, leave his present firm or trade, and what he thought his chances were of getting other employment. This part of the interview varied according to the interests and attitudes of the interviewee, and always included a question relating to his attitude to leaving his present neighbours and living among new ones. The opportunity was also taken of informing the subject (sometimes in answer to a direct question) that the interviewer was a New Zealand student studying in this country, who was interested in housing problems and had discovered that publications on the subject of new towns did not seem to refer to the ideas of the people who were likely to live in them. He thought that these opinions were important and had decided that the only way to discover them was to go round and ask the people concerned.

The next section of the interview began with the following question: "One of the things I am trying to find out is how hopeful people are of having these plans carried out. You know, of course, that if we find ourselves in the middle of another war or a bad slump these plans are likely to be held up, or perhaps scrapped altogether. What do you think our chances are of remaining at peace for, say, another twenty years? . . . What do you think of our chances of remaining prosperous for the next twenty years or so?" From here the conversation usually went on to the man's employment history, his experiences during former depressions, his war service, and (if he was interested in the subjects), his views on international affairs, economic and political policy, and so on. Any interviewee who had by this time made an anti-Semitic statement was rated 1.

Following this discussion came two more questions. "What people do you think should be given priority in getting houses in these new towns?" and "Are there any types of people you would keep out of these new towns altogether?" An answer to either of these questions which indicated that the subject thought Jews ought to be excluded gave him a rating of 2. The interviewer then went on (if no anti-Semitic answer had been given) to explain this second question. "The reason I asked you is that other people I have spoken to have suggested keeping out various types, and I wondered what the general opinion was. Some of the people who have been suggested were Communists, Negroes, Fascists, Foreigners and Jews." If this brought forth an anti-Semitic statement in response the man was rated 3. If not, the interviewer added "I think the Jews have been mentioned most frequently." An anti-Jewish response at this point earned a rating of 4. If such a response was still not forthcoming a rating of 5 was given. An interviewee who was rated 5 at this point but who later made an anti-Semitic statement had his rating changed to 4.

From this point onwards the interview took one of two forms. If the rating that had been given was 1 or 5 attention was concentrated on finding some way of maintaining contact in order to get a second, longer, and more intensive, interview. The usual method of doing this was to get the subject interested in discussing something, i.e. the way in which Bethnal Green had changed during his lifetime, the kind of work he did, the affairs of his trade union, or any other topic on which he talked willingly, and then to ask if the interviewer could come back some other time to hear it in detail instead of having to cut it short. Sometimes it was not necessary to make the request, as a spontaneous invitation would come first. If the man's rating was 2, 3, or 4, the interview was prolonged for as long as possible, and covered chiefly the man's work, his union, his relations with foreman and employer, his contacts with Jews, and any other topics which appeared to interest him. The usual duration of an interview was twenty-five to thirty-five minutes, but many extended to as long as an hour. The second (and any subsequent) interviews were similar to the final section of the first interview, that is, they were relatively unstructured and the course of the conversation was determined primarily by the interests of the interviewee. At the end of the second interview, or on some sub-sequent occasion, the subject was asked to do the Rorschach test. This was introduced as a kind of afterthought having no apparent relation to the original reason for contact. It was referred to as an "experiment" and as being concerned with the way in which the imagination worked. It was explained that a number of people were interested in collecting as many sets of answers as possible from varying types of people, and the subject was asked if he would help out by doing it. This completed the collection of data.

Almost invariably the interview took place at the door of the house. On only twenty-one occasions was the author invited inside during the interview. On four occasions he had to conduct the second, longer interview, also on the doorstep. These doorstep interviews included several occasions when he had to stand in the rain throughout the interview. Occasionally some excuse would be given for not inviting him in, such as lack of room, or the house being untidy, and in a few cases the man remarked at the end of the interview that he would have suggested coming in if he had realised how long the discussion would continue. In the vast majority of cases, however, the question of entry into the house was never mentioned.

The form of the interview was developed in a short pilot survey of twenty interviews undertaken in Hackney and Bow, districts bordering on the northern and eastern boundaries of Bethnal Green. Lack of time prevented the carrying out of a detailed scheme to validate the form of the interview. Changes were made in the original draft on the basis of impressions formed during the pilot concerning the effectiveness of various statements and questions in eliciting the information required. The pilot was carried out by two interviewers, one doing the questioning while the other observed reactions and later compared notes with the questioner.[1]

The most fundamental question that can be raised in connection with the interview is whether or not the five groups into which the subjects are divided during the interview do, in fact, correspond with the strength of these peoples' anti-Semitic attitudes. The interview was based on the assumption that the strength of an attitude could be measured by the degree of specificity of the stimulus required to produce a statement of opinion reflecting the attitude.

[1] The author is indebted to Dr. Peter McKellar for assistance in carrying out this pilot survey.

Thus a person rated 1 was an individual who reacted with an anti-Semitic opinion to statements which, on any rational basis, had no close or direct connection with Jews and no suggestion of the rejection of anyone. A rating of 2 resulted from a stimulus suggesting that some individuals or groups should be rejected. Rating 3 was awarded following a more specific suggestion of rejection, while persons rated 4 and 5 were those who responded to, or resisted, a highly specific stimulus for the rejection of Jews.

As this basic assumption was made strictly *a priori* it would have been desirable to test it empirically. For reasons already stated this did not prove feasible, but some evidence on the matter can be brought forward. Of the seven individuals who were rated 1 and who were interviewed on one or more subsequent occasions, none showed any tendency to depart from an extreme anti-Semitic position during the additional interviewing time. At the other end of the scale, of the ten persons who were rated 5 at the end of the first interview and who were seen on further occasions, only one made any anti-Semitic statement during the later interviews, and this was a single remark of a comparatively mild nature. A further important indication is the extent to which the progression in anti-Semitic rating is matched by a change in the Jewish stereotypes expressed. It is unlikely that this consistent change in the same direction was purely fortuitous. It would appear, therefore, not unreasonable to assume that the rating scale employed in connection with this form of interview has a degree of reliability sufficient for the purposes of this study, i.e. it enables the extreme cases to be distinguished from the less extreme with a considerable degree of certainty, while the intermediate cases are arranged in an order corresponding roughly to the degree of intensity of the attitude displayed.

As the nature of much of the data presented in this study has been determined very largely by the interview situation it is important that this should be clearly understood. Something has already been said on this point, and stress laid on the importance of the absence of a known and relatively strong motivation in favour of undertaking the interview. There were, of course, exceptions, but these constituted a small minority who were motivated by some personal need to express themselves at length to a stranger. Had no attempt been made to obtain a random sample it is possible that the majority of interviews obtained would have been with individuals of this type. It is well known, for example, that anthropologists' informants are frequently drawn chiefly from among the deviant members of the group being studied, and special care has to be taken by the field-worker to allow for this. There is no reason to suppose (unless precautions are taken to ensure that this is not the case) that a non-random sample of informants used by a sociologist or psychologist would not also be markedly biased in this way.

Absence of motivation means a weakening of rapport between interviewer and subject, with the result that the interviewer feels that he must be constantly on his guard to avoid a sudden breaking off of the interview. He must not, for example, bring too close to the surface any area of the subject's experience which is a source of too much clearly-felt anxiety. This would not only result in breaking off the interview, but is undesirable on ethical grounds. Here again the situation is in marked contrast to that found in a therapeutic situation where the psychiatrist, or case worker, deliberately raises anxieties in order that they may be worked through and disposed of. The position may be summed up by saying that it is necessary for the interviewer in this unmotivated situation to deal only with the relatively superficial aspects of the interviewee's personality and experiences, or at any rate only those which are sufficiently well defended to be handled in this kind of situation without giving rise to conscious anxiety. In general, resistances cannot be attacked and overcome because this always involves the production of anxiety. Questions which would be asked without hesitation in any case-work situation must be avoided altogether or approached with great circumspection and the interviewer must be constantly ready to beat a retreat to safer ground. For example, straightforward questions on attitudes to parents and the family situation, which are a commonplace in any case-work interview, were usually impossible, or very difficult, in the interviews conducted on Bethnal Green doorsteps, even when the wife or other persons closely concerned were not actually present, as was sometimes the case. As a general rule information on such topics had to be obtained by inference from more general statements, or from parenthetical remarks.

The knowledge that this motivation may be lacking and that the rapport is therefore of a somewhat tenuous kind naturally has an effect on the interviewer. He has less confidence in his ability to handle any situations that may arise in the interview; he is more prone to skirt around delicate subjects; he becomes unwilling to probe more deeply when any resistance appears; unless he forces himself to take a certain number of risks he quickly slips into the attitude of always "playing safe" and so picking up much less information than would have been possible in the particular situation. These tendencies to caution can be valuable in that they make the interviewer less likely to forget his obligation to leave his subject no more anxious or unhappy than when he found him, and to conclude his research without having created a situation which would make it difficult for other research workers to interview in the same district, but on the whole they seem to operate much too strongly and the worker has to beware lest reasonable caution becomes undue timidity. Occasionally an interviewee is found who is so eager to talk that it becomes obvious at a very early stage of the interview that almost any question will be accepted, or even welcomed, but for the most part the interviewer must conduct the interview with the thought constantly in his mind that an unwise question will terminate the discussion.

There is one further factor that complicates matters for the interviewer in circumstances such as those described here. Unless he is peculiarly insensitive he is burdened with the feeling that he is not playing an entirely honest part. He is using a subterfuge to obtain information which the interviewee might not be willing to give if he were aware of the purpose for which it is being used. It is not necessary to stress this point too forcibly. Certainly it is true that the persons interviewed had tactily agreed to be questioned about their views on housing, and it might be argued that, as they had accepted the fact that they were taking part in research, the actual topic was of no great importance. It must also be admitted, however, that the most important parts of the interview were those which the subject believed to be friendly conversation, and this was particularly true of second and subsequent interviews. It is not entirely pleasant to return home and record for purposes of research the details of a conversation which the other person believed to be an informal chat. The fact that a person's statements on various subjects are used for drawing conclusions about his character and personality does not of itself constitute an important issue, as all of us carry on this activity constantly in our everyday social and business activities. It is one of the characteristics of human intercourse that continual mutual assessments are taking place. The problem lies in the means which were used to obtain access to these people's statements and opinions in the first place.

To sum up briefly, it can be said that the chief weakness of the interviewing technique adopted was the absence of a known motivation in favour of being interviewed on the part of the subject, and a consequent serious limitation on the part of the research worker in the amount of information which he was able to obtain about the subject, particularly with reference to the deeper layers of the personality. On the other hand, however, it did demonstrate that some approach can be made toward the study of randomly constituted groups, on a different level from the merely factual or conscious attitudinal level attained by the usual opinion polls and social surveys. Information can be obtained by this indirect, fairly flexible, approach, which would not be accessible to the direct, standardised, questionnaire method of interview. In some circumstances it is possible to contact sufficiently unselected groups of individuals through techniques other than sampling, and to follow this by an uninvited, unannounced approach to the persons selected. Use of these alternative techniques usually permits an easier and longer contact, with a consequent improvement in the amount and quality of the data. Adorno and his associates, for example, were able to gain access to groups sufficiently varied for their purposes by contacting institutions with which these people were associated. When, as in the present case, the subject chosen for study is a community, it is necessary to contact representatives of those members of the population (possibly the majority in Bethnal Green) who have no close associations with any formal institutions and are unlikely to be reached in this way. Such a situation necessitates either an approach through informal networks—a slow and laborious method unsuited to conditions where time is strictly limited—or a more direct approach of the type actually used.

Here, however, two special difficulties arise which, although not peculiar to student investigators, are likely to be particularly important for them. The first stems from the situation in which the student is endeavouring to establish a relationship with the interviewee. Unless some institution which is sponsoring the work is prepared to let its name be used as a means of introduction, or unless the student in question is fortunate in being able to obtain the backing of some influential person or organisation, he is left in the position of having to "sell himself", i.e. to create rapport, with nothing to back him up except the impression that he is able to create in the mind of the interviewee in the first few minutes of the interview (perhaps even the first few seconds). In the present study, for example, the interviewer appeared before the subject, unexpectedly, as an anonymous, New Zealand student, asking questions about the subject's opinions, apparently merely in order to gratify his personal curiosity. This is a difficulty not normally faced by the representatives of well known organisations such as the much publicised samplers of public opinion, or a recognised official or quasi-official body like the Social Survey or a University, and it reduces still further the degree of motivation in favour of being interviewed.

The impression gained from this interviewing was that the fate of any given interviewer was largely settled within a very short period—usually by the time the introductory statement was completed. By then the interviewer had been classified in some term having a special meaning to the interviewee, such as the snooper, the authority figure, the spy, or the sympathetic listener, and had been reacted to accordingly. Compared with the relatively clear and consistent picture presented by some other possible callers—a doctor, a health visitor, or an insurance agent for example—he was a vague and shadowy figure, a kind of walking Rorschach blot on which any role could be, and was, imposed. The solitary, unsupported research worker lacks that opportunity for definite self-labelling which ensures that the perception of the "blot" is clearer and more favourable from the beginning. This makes his task particularly difficult if he hopes for a development of the relationship beyond an initial meeting.

The second of these special difficulties is the lack of training and experience on the part of the interviewer. No organisation seriously concerned with field research would employ untrained interviewers on actual research projects, but the student investigator has no alternative but to train himself in the course of carrying out his own piece of research. Given the time and resources this training could form part of the pilot phase of the investigation, but in the study under review this was not possible. It would be unthinkable for a student in any of the natural sciences to pass through even the briefest course of training without being given some knowledge of the tools of research normally used in the particular branch of science. It is, however, a measure of the lack of research orientation, and of the low status of social science in academic circles, that it is not merely possible, but usual, for a student of this subject to reach post-graduate status with no knowledge or experience of inter-viewing techniques. It is especially frustrating for him, when, having realised his deficiences, he is unable to secure this training in any way except by the highly unsatisfactory method of self-teaching by trial and error, helped out to some extent by a study of text-books. As long as student research workers have to commence their work in an entirely untrained state, the standard of that work will fall unnecessarily low.

Only one topic remains to be dealt with in connection with the interviewing methods employed—the recording of the material collected in the interviews. From the earliest days of social science field work the problem of recording has haunted the investigator. Those who have been concerned chiefly with the achievement of maximum rapport have insisted that no notes must be taken during the interview itself, while those whose chief interest has been in accuracy and verifiability have insisted on a full report being made during the interview. Occasionally it is possible to use some method which enables a record to be made with or without the subject's knowledge, either by a dictaphone or a concealed stenographer, but this is most unusual. Attempts have been made to develop a method whereby detailed records of essential points can be made without much disturbance of the interview, by means of a system of coding on a specially designed form (Kinsey, *et al.*, 1948, pp. 35–62).

In this particular case the merits and demerits of the various methods are irrelevant, as no recording during the interview was possible. Most of the important questions in the interview were those which were introduced apparently casually and without forethought. To have recorded the answer would have given the game away immediately. Furthermore, several of the questions were of a somewhat personal type, and others were treated as such by some subjects. (For example, it was not always easy to find out a subject's occupation by a direct question early in the interview, and the topic had to be approached carefully later in the discussion.) Had their answers been recorded, it is probable that the subjects would either have refused to reply or would have given highly stereotyped answers. An already tenuous rapport would have been hopelessly broken.

The only question that concerns us then is the accuracy with which the interview was recorded after it had been completed. In this connection it is necessary only to detail the precautions taken to ensure that, as far as possible, error was reduced to a minimum. In the first place the interviewer had had a considerable amount of experience of this type of work, having, in the course of the preliminary observational work described in Chapter II, recorded detailed reports on well over one hundred hours of conversation. Secondly, he made it an invariable rule to record each interview in the form of brief notes within a few minutes of its conclusion. In no case did he carry out any further interviewing or conversation before doing this preliminary recording. The interviews were then recorded in full, on the basis of these notes, as soon as possible, usually the same evening, occasionally the following morning. Recalling the course of the conversation was less difficult in these cases because of the partly structured nature of the interview. The standard questions and their invariable sequence gave a rough framework on which to build the report, and unexpected cues for a change of subject were fewer and easier to remember. On the whole it would seen reasonable to claim that errors and omissions in these reports are not of a frequent or serious nature.

When all the subjects had been interviewed and rated on the five-point anti-Semitism scale the problem remained of rating these same individuals on the traits which were thought to be associated with anti-Semitism. There is no standardised test material available for measuring these particular variables and in any case it would not have been practicable to have made use of it in interviews of this sort. The only material available, therefore, was that provided by the records of the interviews. While the interviews had been designed to provide information on the variables under consideration, there was no simple automatic way of converting these into a numerical quantity which could be handled statistically. The only method available was to assign to each interview record a score for each variable. For statistical convenience a five-point scale was used in each of these cases also.

The crudest method of carrying out this procedure would be for the investigator to assign the score on the basis of his impression of the interview record. Such a method would be open to serious objections on the grounds of consistency and reliability, and it was therefore necessary to employ various devices to meet these objections. The procedure adopted in this case was as follows.

Arrangements were made for all interviews to be rated by three judges working independently. Ten interviews taken at random were rated first, then discussed in detail by the three raters in order to clear up any uncertainties. After this the remaining interviews were rated. All three judges were social science graduates.[1] Each rater was supplied with the following instructions as a guide in the task of assessing the interviews.

1. Mark all the interviews on the first scale, then all of them on the second scale and so on. Never mark the same interview on two scales simultaneously or in succession.

2. Remember that it is highly improbable that no cases will fall on the extreme points of the scale. Therefore if you discover that you have not marked any individuals 1 or 5 for any scale you should reconsider your markings to see if some of the more extreme cases should not be marked in this way.

3. Some of the interviews will not contain sufficient data for the individual concerned to be marked on every scale, but he should be given a rating for any scale where this is at all possible. Any rating about which you feel dubious as a result of paucity of data should be specially noted and dealt with as indicated below.

4. Keep very strictly to the definitions and scales given, even if you personally disagree with them. It is more important that all judges should rate the individual on the *same* scale than that the scale should be "right" in any absolute sense. If you have doubts about the meaning or applicability of any of the scales you should make a careful note of this when rating the first ten interviews so that you can discuss it with the other judges.

5. Always rate with a whole number, i.e. do not rate any individual as $4\frac{1}{2}$ or as 3–4. If you feel that an individual falls between two points on the scale you should give him the rating to which you think he most nearly approaches. The difficulty should be noted and the reason for the final decision given.

6. Attached to each interview record are several slips of paper, each one being marked with the title of one of the rating scales. On each slip you should note, (a) the appropriate rating, and (b) the location of all the data used in deciding the rating. (The location should be given by means of the line reference numbers in the margin of each interview.)

7. Each rater should keep a log-book, noting in it all difficulties

---

[1] The present writer was one of the judges. He is indebted to his wife and to Mr. John Morris for their work in carrying out the rating as the other two judges.

met with and the reason for the solution eventually arrived at. This is particularly important in the case of the first ten interviews scored, as the value of the discussion with the other judges will depend on these records being available.

8. Difficulties which arise in the marking of the later interviews should be noted and discussed subsequently with the other judges.

Then followed details of the four rating scales, defining the variables and giving examples drawn from the interview material.

I. *Feelings of Competence Scale.* This scale is intended to measure the individual's own estimate of himself, in relation to his ability to control his environment, including persons with whom he has relations. *This scale is to be applied twice.* In the first case it should be used to assess the individual's estimate of his own personal capabilities; the second time to assess his estimate of the power of any groups of which he is a member, and whose failure or success he believes will affect his own well-being, e.g. his trade union, the country as a whole, the working class.

1. Shows feelings of helplessness, of being controlled by other people, by fate, or by the social and economic system, in such a way that he has little or no control over matters which are important to him. Examples: I can't do anything about it—it all depends on people who won't take any notice of me. It's no use our government trying to do anything to avoid a slump—we are so closely tied to America that we just have to go the way they go.

2. Feels that some major decisions which concern him are outside his control. Examples: Any statements similar to those under 1, but used in contexts which suggest that the area of powerlessness is not limited, e.g. I would like to own my own business but it is almost impossible for a wage earner to save enough.

3. Is dubious and hesitant about his powers or shows conflicting evidence about his feelings.

4. Feels that he always has a chance of getting what he wants though he may not be confident about it. Even though things are difficult it is worth making the attempt. Examples: I know it is hard to get repairs done these days but if I keep at them long enough I expect they will do them. The next five years will be difficult ones— if we can get through them we will be all right.

5. He believes that he can usually achieve what he sets his mind to. You can always get people to do what you want, or to treat you properly if you handle them in the right way. Examples: Our

union can usually get what we want because they keep on good terms with the governors and approach them in the right way. In the long run the working class will always get what they want because they are a majority.

II. *Optimism—Pessimism Scale*. This scale is intended to measure the degree of expectation of deprivations and gratifications. The individual or the group is conceived as being affected at some time in the future by the actions of other people or external forces, and as the recipient of the deprivations or gratifications resulting from this situation. This contrasts with the previous scale where he is regarded as being the initiator of actions (or as being unable to initiate actions). The first scale refers mainly to his estimate of the present position, this scale refers exclusively to his expectation of the future. *This scale should also be applied twice*. The first rating is to be with respect to the individual's expectations for himself as a person; the second with respect to his expectations for the collectivities to which he belongs, e.g. nation, firm, union, trade, class, etc.

1. The future is seen as very black and there is really very little to look forward to. Example: There will certainly be another war within five years and with atom bombs you know what that means —one of them will wipe out London.

2. The future seems uncertain but on the whole is more likely to be unpleasant than otherwise. Example: There will be a slump for certain if the Tories get back and it looks as if they are likely to.

3. Uncertain, contradictory statements, or states "no opinion" in reply to questions relating to wars and slumps, but gives no other data on which to be rated.

4. The future is uncertain but on the whole is likely to be satisfactory rather than otherwise. Example: Of course you can never be certain that you will not be sacked but I think I'm pretty safe.

5. The future, on the whole, is rather rosy and in any case is certain to be at least as good as the past. Example: I think the country has got to the stage where we can go right ahead and get at least back to pre-war standards.

III. *Authority Scale*. Before attempting to rate any individual on this scale it is important to decide what individuals or organisations are regarded as authorities. An employer (usually referred to as the "Governor") can safely be assumed to be an authority, but trade unions may or may not be so regarded. In the same way the government may be looked on as anything from a branch of the Labour

Party and therefore as something of which he is almost a part, to a Jewish secret society which issues imperative commands. Other possible authorities are, the police, local bodies, civil servants, landlords, foremen, the upper classes, schoolteachers, and sometimes even the interviewer.

1. Is disposed to accept authority without much question, either because he regards legitimately constituted authority as something that ought to be obeyed, that is, regards obedience as a moral quality, or because he regards it as the only sensible and natural thing to do. Praises life in the army and makes special approving mention of discipline. Example: What else can I do but obey him—he's the governor, isn't he?

2. Regards obedience as better than disobedience but does not believe that one should necessarily obey one's superiors. In general obedience is better, causes less trouble, and is pleasanter than disobedience. If authority is challenged it should be done through the recognised and properly constituted channels. Authority may be criticised on specific points but the criticism is always less than approval. States without qualification that he enjoyed life in the army. Example: I don't like unofficial strikes—if you have elected men to represent you, you should back them up.

3. Uncertain, changing and contradictory attitudes.

4. Authority is at best a necessary evil. It should be regarded with suspicion and promptly opposed if necessary, but this opposition should preferably be through recognised legal channels. May approve authority up to a point or on some specific matters but this is always outweighed by criticism. Prefers jobs where he is not constantly supervised. Mentions dislike of discipline in referring to service life. Example: I don't believe in being silly about going against the governor, but you have to keep your eye on him.

5. Strongly anti-authoritarian and rebellious. Stresses discipline as the main reason for disliking the services. Has virtually nothing favourable to say for authority and is inclined to oppose it on principle without much thought on the precise issues involved on any particular occasion. Example: There's no sense in negotiation and that sort of thing—there's only one way to get what you want and that is to strike for it.

IV. *Isolation Scale.* Isolation is defined as the absence of close affectional ties.

1. Is without any very close affectional ties or fears that he may

be deprived of those he has, e.g. his wife is old and in bad health. Even in this latter case he has few of these ties.

2. Has a number of contacts with relatives and friends but none of them are very close ties. Does not see very much of these people and does not normally exchange visits with them. If married is not on particularly affectionate terms with his wife, or may have separated from her.

3. Is on good terms with his wife and children but has no other close friends and takes part in no social activities. Does not belong to any clubs and if he has interests outside the home they are of a solitary nature, e.g. going to the pictures on his own.

4. Has a happy family life and some social activities outside his home, such as visiting relatives, but largely confines himself to his home.

5. Has a happy family life and a variety of social contacts outside the home. Keeps in close touch with relatives or several close friends. Exchanges visits fairly frequently with these friends and with relatives. If he belongs to some club or other organisation he takes a considerable interest in its activities.

The purpose of the discussion following the marking of the first ten interviews was to ensure that the scales could be applied to the data available and that the judges were doing the rating the same way. Ratings were compared and disagreements discussed. As a result, a few minor amendments were made to the rating scales. After this discussion the remaining ninety-three interviews were rated by each judge. Throughout the entire rating procedure each rater kept a record of the sections of the interview records used for determining the rating given. The purpose of this record was two-fold: (1) to ensure that the same items were not used for more than one rating, i.e. that the various scores assigned to one individual were based on different sets of data, and (2) to ensure that the various judges were using approximately the same data for rating on any given variable.

When the ratings by the three judges had been completed they were collected together and compared. In those cases where all three ratings were identical no further action was taken. If the ratings were spread over more than three points they were all discarded as too unreliable, and no rating was given. For example, if the three ratings were 1, 2, and 4 it was assumed that the data available were not adequate for an accurate rating, and consequently one was not given. If, however, the ratings were 2, 3, and 4, or 2, 2, and 4 they were retained.

The next task was to decide on the method by which these ratings on which opinion varied could be given a single score. There were two possibilities, the first being to use some automatic method such as taking the central score when the ratings were of the 2, 3, 4 order, and taking the majority decision when two of the ratings were identical. It was eventually decided to adopt the other alternative of discussing each rating at a meeting of the three judges in order to compare reasons for the ratings which had been given and to come to an agreed decision wherever possible on the rating that was to be given. In those cases where complete agreement was not achieved the majority decision was taken. It was discovered in the discussion that disagreements on ratings had been due almost entirely to two reasons. The most common was a hesitation on the part of a judge between two adjacent scores, say 2 and 3. Very often all three would have had this doubt, two finally making one choice, and the third the other. The second cause for disagreement lay in one or more of the judges having overlooked some relevant piece of evidence. It was this possibility which made the discussion method of deciding final scores seem better than the automatic taking of the middle point. There were very few cases where there was genuine disagreement among the judges as to the rating that should be given. These few cases are represented by the ratings which were finally given as a majority vote.

The variable on which most difficulty was experienced was social isolation. Here there was considerable discussion on the question of what was to be regarded as satisfactory evidence of a good relationship, and the question was never solved to the entire satisfaction of all the judges. A high proportion of the majority decisions appeared on this one variable. The isolation scale cannot be regarded as particularly satisfactory. The probable explanation is that the concept is so complex that to measure it on a single scale on the basis of brief interviews is almost impossible. A series of scales dealing with such variables as husband-wife relationships, parent-child relations, interaction with neighbours, social contacts at work and outside the neighbourhood would probably be required (Curle and Trist, 1947, p. 262). This would demand longer and more detailed interviews than were possible on this occasion, in order to provide sufficient data. As it stands the isolation scale can be regarded only as a rough-and-ready approximation—somewhat better than a purely subjective estimate by the interviewer, but not having a very great degree of accuracy.

The following tables give details of the extent to which agreement on the ratings was secured among the judges.

TABLE 2

AGREEMENT AMONG JUDGES AT FIRST RATING

Agreement on rating	142
Agreement that rating not possible . .	56
Two judges agreed	324
Three different ratings retained . .	88
Ratings discarded as unreliable . .	8
Total	618

As can be seen from this table there were 466 cases out of the 618 (i.e. 75·4 per cent) where at least two of the judges were agreed on the ratings to be given. (This does not include the 56 cases where there was agreement on the impossibility of giving a rating.) The same fact can also be expressed in the form of correlations between the ratings given by the three judges.

TABLE 3

INTER-CORRELATIONS BETWEEN JUDGES' RATINGS

A and B	. 0·78
B and C	. 0·78
C and A	. 0·76

From these figures it can plainly be seen that there was an extremely high degree of agreement among the judges, and on the basis of this material it is difficult to avoid the conclusion that the judges were, in fact, rating the same variables by very similar standards. The measure of agreement was of course greatly increased during the discussion following the rating, at the end of which there were no cases where at least two of the judges were not agreed on a rating, or alternatively agreed that the inadequacy of the data prevented a satisfactory rating being made. In those cases where one judge dissented from the decision of the other two the majority view was taken as the final rating.

It might be wondered, if the final rating was based on a discussion, why the judges first rated independently and not as a group. There were two main reasons: first, such a procedure would have prevented a check on the degree to which the ratings really were determined by the data available. The high correlations resulting from independent judgment disposes of this doubt. Secondly, the practical difficulties of arranging such a discussion in a satisfactory way, giving each judge equal opportunity of forming and voicing his opinions, would have been very great. The discussions which were held following the independent ratings were greatly facilitated by the fact that by this time each judge was very familiar with the material (having read each interview record at least six times), and had in his possession notes on the material made during the rating process.

By the end of the discussion the amount of agreement among the judges as to the ratings to be given was as follows:

TABLE 4

AGREEMENT OF JUDGES ON FINAL RATINGS

Agreement on rating . . .	446
Agreement that no rating be given .	119
Agreement by two judges . .	53
Total	618

There were two further tests of the extent to which the ratings represented a reliable evaluation of the interview material. Both of these were referred to in the instructions to the judges, and related to the extent to which any one judge used different parts of the data for rating on different variables, and the extent to which different judges used the same material for rating the same variables. Each judge kept a record of every line of print on the interview record to which he referred in making any particular rating. A detailed analysis of the record of one judge discloses that 5,376 lines were referred to in the process of rating, and of these 556 (i.e. 10·3 per cent) were listed twice. Of this total number of lines the other two judges referred to 73 per cent and 76 per cent respectively in reference to the same variables. These figures support the view already expressed that the three judges were indeed rating the same variables on the same basis, and that the ratings did undoubtedly refer to something actually contained in the interview material.

The most serious deterrent to carrying out rating and validating procedures of the kind described is the amount of time consumed. In fact the whole of a field study of this kind is so intimately bound up with questions of time that a special mention of this factor seems desirable. The figures given below refer only to the interview programme with the random sample of cases and the analysis of the results, and do not take into account the time spent in the general study of Bethnal Green.

The time taken by the interviewing, i.e. by actual face-to-face contact with the subjects amounted to about one hundred and fifty hours. In addition to this a great deal of time was spent in locating the addresses obtained from the electoral register, in unsuccessful visits, in repeated attempts to contact people who were out, or in fruitless interviews with people who were discovered to be Jews, not working class, or in other ways outside the sample.[1] In addition brief notes had to be made immediately after each interview. In all nearly four hundred hours were spent in carrying out the whole of this programme. As almost all interviewing had to be done in the evenings in order to find the men at home, this involved spending at least five evenings a week for seven months on the task. So many men in Bethnal Green go out for the evening at the weekends that unannounced calls were more likely to be unsuccessful than otherwise. Whenever possible second and subsequent calls were arranged at weekends.

The process of recording the interviews took almost as long as making the interviews themselves, while the clerical work involved in preparing the interviews, rating scales, instructions and record sheets for the work of rating took about a further one hundred hours.

The actual process of rating was one of the most time-consuming parts of the work; as it involved three people it needs to be expressed in man-hours. The initial independent ratings took about three hundred man-hours, while the discussions following this consumed some thirty-five to forty man-hours, i.e. a full twelve hour day of each judge's time. The bulk of the interview records (approximately 100,000 words) means that any study of the whole group is a long task. Merely to look through and count the number of instances of any type of statement, for example, involves about two hours' work, even when one is very familiar with the material. When all these activities have been carried out, the statistical calculations even when made mechanically require many more hours of work.

---

[1] An interview once begun could not be broken off suddenly without leaving hostility and suspicion behind, so that even when the interviewee was known to be unsuitable, something approximating to the full interview procedure had to be gone through.

In addition to the rating scales requiring consensus of opinion on the part of the judges, rating was carried out on two variables where it was considered that the data were sufficiently objective to make the use of judges unnecessary. These scales applied to age and to experience of unemployment. In the case of the age variable the actual age in years was converted to a five-point scale for convenience in correlation calculation. The ratings were given as follows:

21–30 years .	. 5
31–40 years .	. 4
41–50 years .	. 3
51–60 years .	. 2
Over 60 years	. 1

Experience of unemployment was rated on the basis of the following scale:

1. At least one period of more than a year of unemployment.
2. At least one period of more than a month but less than a year in duration.
3. More than one period of unemployment but with no periods of more than a month.
4. One period of less than a month.
5. No unemployment.

It is possible to quarrel with the actual time intervals chosen for this last scale, but as any choice, in the absence of detailed research into the question of the precise significance to the worker of varying periods of unemployment, is bound to be arbitrary, the choice of these particular intervals can be justified on the ground that they are graded in order of length and to that extent should succeed in arranging the subjects into an order roughly corresponding to the amount of deprivation suffered as a result of unemployment. It is true that many factors such as the existence of other resources, such as savings, employed children, opportunities for part-time jobs, and "fiddling", will affect the amount of deprivation suffered over a period. In a study of this kind, where experience of unemployment is only one factor among many, the use of such refinements would provide far too many complications, as they would demand practically a separate study to themselves. All that can be hoped for in these circumstances is to attempt a broad, general measurement of the influence of this particular factor. If it is of the importance claimed by some writers its significance should appear in spite of the crudity of the measure.

CHAPTER V

The Results of the Interview Programme

THE list of addresses to be visited in order to carry out interviews with a sample of adult males was obtained by drawing on every two hundredth name in the electoral register. In this way a list of 216 households was compiled. Of these, twenty-eight proved to be Jewish;[1] two were aliens (identified by speech); three were newly arrived from other parts of the British Isles; twenty-four fell outside the definition of working class; nine of the dwellings visited had no adult male inmate; three houses had been demolished. All these considerations reduced the sample to 147 individuals. Of these 103 were actually interviewed, that is 71 per cent.

The forty-four individuals who fell within the sample but who were not interviewed can be accounted for as follows: in eight cases the man refused to be interviewed, without giving any reason; in five cases a woman answered the door when the interviewer knocked, and refused to let him see any of the male occupants—in all cases this was an extremely abrupt refusal with no reason given;[2] in six cases the man of the household was ill and his wife or mother thought he ought not to be disturbed; in eight cases the man was home at irregular and infrequent hours, the wife was unable to say definitely when he would be in, and three calls at varying hours failed to find him—most of these men were long-distance drivers; in eight cases there was no reply in three visits at different hours, followed by a fourth call several weeks later; in six cases the

[1] A few Jews were identified by name and dropped from the sample immediately. This was done only in the most obvious cases. The remainder were identified while being interviewed.
[2] In six cases the door was answered by a woman who was unwilling to call the man but when she had been persuaded to do so he agreed to be interviewed without difficulty. There was no correlation between the wife's unwillingness to call the man and his anti-Semitic rating.

interview was begun, but the interest of the interviewee could not be maintained and the interview was broken off before a rating for anti-Semitism could be given. The length of these six interviews varied from two to twenty minutes. This last was exceptional and concerned a man who contrived to answer all the questions in such an equivocal manner that it was impossible to rate him on any variable. None of the other five interviews lasted more than ten minutes. In three of these cases, where interest was not maintained, the interviewee was an old man, rather deaf and obviously not enjoying standing at the door—one was so deaf that he was unable to understand any of the questions; the other two were middle-aged men who insisted that they were very comfortable in their present homes and had no views on the new towns. (In the five other cases where the interviewee stated that he was satisfied with his situation and did not have any opinions it was possible to continue the interview. There was no correlation between an expression of housing satisfaction and anti-Semitism on the part of these men). In the case of the remaining three individuals who fell within the sample but were not interviewed the interview began but was interrupted suddenly before any ratings could be made; once the man was called to a meal, once to go out to keep an appointment, and once he had to break off to attend to a rapidly filling bath.

The composition of these various groups can now be summarised in the form of two tables.

TABLE 5

COMPOSITION OF ORIGINAL SAMPLE FROM ELECTORAL REGISTER

Jewish	28
Alien	2
Non-London (recent arrivals)	3
Non-working class	24
No adult male in house	9
House demolished	3
Adult male working-class sample	147
Total	216

TABLE 6

COMPOSITION OF ADULT MALE WORKING-CLASS SAMPLE

Interviewed successfully	103
Man an invalid	6
Irregular hours of work	8
No reply	8
Interview interrupted	3
Women refused interview (no reason given)	5
Man refused interview (no reason given)	8
Not interested	6
Total	147

In cases where the man played a passive part in the unsuccessful result, there is no reason to suppose that the loss of these cases makes any difference to the pattern of the results, as there would seem to be no very likely or obvious connection between such things as hours of work and anti-Semitism, nor is a wife's attitude to her husband's being interviewed likely to be connected with this variable.

The active refusals are likely to be a more serious matter, but further consideration suggests that two different factors are operative here. It would seem from experience with second interviews that the tolerant are more likely to refuse interviews than the anti-Semitic. On the other hand the "not interested" group have a rather high average age (about 45–50) and this is more likely to be associated with anti-Semitism than with tolerance. These two influences may very well cancel each other out, especially as the number involved is not large. On the basis of these considerations it seems reasonable to claim that, while the figures for anti-Semitism based on these interviews cannot be taken as an absolutely accurate description of the distribution of anti-Semitism in Bethnal Green, there is no reason to suppose that they are seriously in error. They are certainly more accurate than the estimate of any unsystematic observer, no matter how well informed he might be about the general climate of opinion in the district.

The problem of non-response is one which is constantly appearing in sociological research, but it cannot be said that the frequent discussions have produced much result beyond the rather obvious conclusion that every effort should be made to ensure that the failures are as infrequent as possible in the circumstances (Bureau of Applied Social Research, 1948, pp. 47–9, and Yates, 1949, pp. 107–108). The figures for the present research can be compared with those available from other surveys. For example, a study of the population of Baltimore by the United States Bureau of Census in 1947 produced a refusal rate of 8 per cent (Bureau of Applied Research, 1948, p. 49). The study by Lazarfeld of the Presidential election campaign in Erie County, Ohio, showed a refusal rate of 14 per cent (Lazarfeld et al., 1948, p. 159). This is described as "remarkably low" for repeated interviews, while the National Opinion Research Centre in the United States reports refusal rates on a series of surveys, varying from 7 per cent to 18 per cent (Sheatsley, 1948). Thus, although the rate for this survey (29 per cent) is rather high, and the results (as far as distributions are concerned) must be accepted with some caution, it is probably not unsatisfactory in that the comparison is with studies conducted by organisations specialising in this kind of survey, and in most cases asking a smaller number of more direct questions.

The actual distribution of anti-Semitic opinion in Bethnal Green is shown in Table 7.

TABLE 7

DISTRIBUTION OF ANTI-SEMITIC OPINION

(1 = Highly prejudiced. 5 = Tolerant)

	Ratings				
	1	2	3	4	5
Number of cases .	9	18	14	44	18
Percentages . .	8·7	17·5	13·6	42·7	17·5

The question at once arises as to how these results compare with those of other investigators. This question is not easy to answer because of the great variety in the methods that have been used for measuring and classifying attitudes towards Jews and other minority groups. There seem to have been no figures published for Great Britain which can be used as a basis for comparison. Some of the American results, however, can be considered as roughly equivalent.

From a survey of public opinion poll results, Bettelheim and Janowitz (1950, pp. 7–8) conclude that 5 to 10 per cent Americans form a hard core of extreme anti-Semites, while between 30 and 60 per cent display anti-Semitic reactions to a lesser degree. This leaves a tolerant group of at least 30 per cent. In their own sample of Chicago men the same authors found a tolerant group of 41 per cent; "stereotyped" anti-Semites constituted 28 per cent (from the description given this group seems to correspond roughly with group 4 in the present study); 27 per cent were "outspoken" anti-Semites (equivalent to group 3); 4 per cent were "intense" anti-Semites (groups 1 and 2) (Ibid. pp. 12–16). Campbell (1947) on the basis of a nation-wide sample reports 61 per cent tolerant and pro-Jewish;

21 per cent expressing "mild dislike" (presumably equivalent to group 4); 13 per cent "dislike Jews, tend to avoid close personal contact; against discrimination except for specified social restrictions" (equivalent to group 3 and perhaps group 2); 5 per cent "show active hostility towards Jews".

The results obtained for Bethnal Green appear to be consistently higher in terms of the level of prejudice than any of these other studies. While it is true that in the present case anti-Semitic statements were judged very strictly (it is clear from their account that Bettelheim and Janowitz would have included in their tolerant group a number of individuals who were classed in group 4) this would not wholly account for the difference. It does not, for example, explain the larger number of extreme anti-Semites in Bethnal Green (groups 1 and 2) especially as it is for these groups that similarity of criteria for classification is closest. This high level of prejudice is, of course, consistent with the known history of Bethnal Green in terms of support for Fascist candidates at elections. It also suggests that since the war behaviour may have changed more than underlying attitudes; that is, while still disliking Jews, people do not express this by voting for Fascists. Apart from any other meaning that can be given to them, these results should dispose of the surprisingly frequent statement that anti-Semitism is a middle class phenomenon and rare among the working class (Sartre, 1949; Zweig, 1948, p. 64).

The figures require little further comment at this point. Only one inhabitant of Bethnal Green in eight is completely tolerant, but more than half of the remainder have to be openly invited to express their anti-Semitism before they will do so. The anti-Semitic statements of this group are highly stereotyped, backed by few signs of emotion, do not include the grosser accusations common in the statements of the men rated 1 and 2. They are, generally speaking, people who will not oppose anti-Semitism, rather than those who will make any effort to propagate it.

A record of the political affiliations of the members of the sample reveals only one point of significance. Liberals, Socialists, and people without party affiliations show almost exactly the same proportions of individuals with the various ratings as does the general population. The small group of Conservatives, however, is definitely placed at the anti-Semitic end of the scale and a comparison of the distribution for Conservatives and Socialists gives $X^2 = 17.09$ (P 0.01)

thus showing the difference as highly significant. The single supporter of the Fascists is rated, not surprisingly, 1. There were no Communists in the sample.

TABLE 8

DISTRIBUTION OF ANTI-SEMITISM IN RELATION TO POLITICAL OPINION

	Rating					Total[1]
	1	2	3	4	5	
Socialist .	3	9	9	26	13	60
Liberal . .	1	4	3	6	4	18
Conservative .	3	1	0	1	0	5
Fascist . .	1	0	0	0	0	1
No party .	0	2	1	6	0	9
Not known .	1	2	1	5	1	10

[1] These figures agree quite closely with the proportions of votes cast in the 1950 General Election, the main difference being that the above table underestimates the Liberal vote. As the sample consisted only of men, one could not expect an exact correspondence.

Each individual was rated, not only for anti-Semitism but also for some of the variables referred to in the hypotheses listed in Chapter II. It was not possible to make every interview sufficiently detailed to collect data which would enable all the individuals to be rated on every variable. Apart from the general difficulties described in the last chapter there were certain more specific ones which reduced the amount of data obtained. By far the most important of these was the one already mentioned in connection with interviews that were broken off before any ratings were made and which therefore had to be counted as complete failures. In a very large proportion of cases the interview was brought to an end by the intrusion of some external factor, most commonly by the man being called to his evening meal. The hour of the evening meal varies enormously in Bethnal Green and it was impossible to choose some time which was unlikely to interfere with it. There were also other interruptions such as the arrival of visitors, and the interviewee having to depart to keep an appointment.

These interruptions became serious because of the general difficulty of absence of motivation to continue the interview on the part of the subject. In those cases where the interviewee was keen to continue the discussion either the interruption was brushed aside, or he suggested completing the interview at a more convenient time. It is also certain that the amount of data increased as the interviewer's skill became greater. There is an obvious difference in the amount of data available in the early and the later interviews. Throughout the whole series of interviews it remained true that the data which could be obtained directly on the interviewee himself were less than those obtainable on the groups to which he belonged and on his attitudes towards these groups.

The variables on which the subjects were rated were: (1) Feelings in relation to ability to control the environment. This rating was made twice; once in relation to his attitude towards groups to which he belonged. This was done in order to see whether there were any individuals who felt that they gained power from group membership in spite of personal weakness, or any who felt themselves strong in spite of the impotence of the groups to which they belonged. The groups most usually referred to were the nation as a whole, the working class as a whole, and the trade union to which the man belonged. The choice of groups was left to the man himself. (2) Feelings of optimism or pessimism. Again the rating was made twice, once for the individual and once for the group. (3) Attitude to authority. (The individuals were classified into two groups, central persons or leaders, and followers, and a correlation with anti-Semitism made separately for each group.) (4) Degree of social isolation. (5) Age, and (6) Experience of unemployment.

Each of these sets of ratings was correlated in turn with anti-Semitism. The correlations, the number of cases for each variable, and the degree of significance in each case are listed in Table 9.

TABLE 9

CORRELATIONS BETWEEN ANTI-SEMITISM AND OTHER RATED VARIABLES

	r.	N	P[1]
Control of individual over environment .	0·33	88	< 0·01
Control of group over environment .	0·47	91	< 0·001
Pessimism or optimism for self . .	0·55	79	< 0·001
Pessimism or optimism for group . .	0·59	101	< 0·001
Attitude to authority for leaders . .	0·57	26	< 0·01
Attitude to authority for followers .	0·25	59	0·05
Isolation	0·50	54	< 0·001
Age	0·28	103	< 0·01
Unemployment	0·15	90	> 0·1

[1] All values of P were obtained from Fisher and Yates (1949), p. 46.

The first striking thing about this table is the high degree of significance for almost all the variables. The two exceptions are experience of unemployment, which is below the level of significance, and the attitude of followers to authority which barely achieves significance at the 0·05 level. The correlation between age and anti-Semitism, though lower than most of the others in the table, should be noted. It is particularly interesting in that it contradicts the assertion made by almost every person interviewed who claimed to know anything about anti-Semitism in the East End, namely that young people tend to be more anti-Semitic than their elders. One man, formerly a prominent member of the British Union of Fascists, and well acquainted with the organisation in Bethnal Green, assured the author that practically all the support for that body and its successors came from young people. The correlation agrees, however, with the writer's observations of audiences at Union Movement meetings in Bethnal Green where the most regular attenders, and the most regular contributors to the collection box that is passed around at these meetings, seem to be old men. Two explanations of this clash of opinion seem feasible. The first is that this sample contains no adolescents and it is not unlikely that this age group would supply the Fascist movement with many recruits. This would involve the assumption that young men in their twenties and thirties are less anti-Semitic than the adolescents.

Such a situation does not provide as many difficulties as might at first be thought. According to the account of the Bethnal Green character structure and cultural patterns given in Chapter III, the period of life between twenty and thirty-five may well be, on the whole, one of the most satisfactory that the average Bethnal Green man experiences. Marriage provides him with much of the companionship and feeling of being wanted that he so much desires. It has not yet brought the more serious economic problems of a large family of older children. The fear of age has still not descended upon him. The adolescent, as is well known, is burdened with his own troubles and anxieties, and is probably at his lowest ebb as far as stability of relationships both within and without the home is concerned. The very high degree of aggression which he displays has already been described. It is noticeable that adolescents tend to be the second largest group at the Union Movement meetings and very often the most vociferous.

The second reason that suggests itself for the belief in the strength of the anti-Semitism of the young is that they are more likely to take active steps such as joining an organisation, cheering at meetings, marching in processions and so on, than would be the case with older men. It is also possible that a less strong attitude would be required in the younger persons to produce a tendency to action. Their greater vocality at meetings has already been noted. In view of this it is not impossible that both the correlation obtained and the opinions of the observers referred to may both be in large measure correct, in spite of their apparent contradictions.

The figures in Table 9 support several of the hypotheses put forward in Chapter II. These hypotheses are that anti-Semitism is positively correlated with fears about one's ability to control the environment, with pessimism with respect to the self and to the collectivity, with a high level of anti-authoritarianism in central persons, and with tendencies towards isolation. The hypothesis that anti-Semitism is positively correlated with submissiveness in follower persons is also supported, but less strongly. The importance of the correlation with isolation is somewhat reduced by the relatively large number of cases that could not be rated on this variable, but the correlation is so high that it is unlikely that an increase in the number of cases would bring it below the level of significance.

When ratings distinguish between the group and the self the clearest result is that the self-rating is consistently higher than the group rating. The mean for ratings on the individual's view of his own power to cope with the environment is 3·33 while that for the group is 3·22. In the case of the optimism—pessimism ratings the means are 3·33 and 3·07. The attitudes to the self and the group are nevertheless very closely connected, as can be seen by the fact that the inter-correlations in these two cases are 0·67 and 0·74. These differences can probably be explained very simply on the assumption that the individual could not usually bear to think of the blackest aspects of the future as applying specifically to himself, but was able to apply some of his worst forebodings to the group.

One factor that does not appear in the tables of data and which refers to a problem that is really outside the cope of this thesis may be mentioned here. It is commonly accepted that men are more anti-Semitic than women (Eysenck, 1948; Allport and Kramer, 1946; Slawson, 1944). While conclusive figures on this point cannot be given for Bethnal Green it can be said that of all the cases (thirteen in number) where it was possible to form an impression of the degree of anti-Semitism shown by the wife of the interviewee, only one was not at least as anti-Semitic as her husband and in practically all these cases her anti-Semitism appeared to be stronger. (The single exception was a young woman from the north of England who had come to London for the first time after marrying a man from Bethnal Green. She seemed to be completely puzzled by her husband's anti-Semitism—he was rated 2). There were five cases where the wife was seen but where it was impossible to form an opinion on her attitude to Jews. The meagreness of these data on the women of Bethnal Green would make any discussion of possible reasons for this difference (if it really does exist) mere speculation, but it does suggest that on such matters cultural variations may be very marked.

This interview programme also permitted a study of the stereo-types of Jews current in Bethnal Green. There are some interesting changes in stereotype as one progresses from the more to the less anti-Semitic. Those who are rated 1 for anti-Semitism are most inclined to accuse Jews of the more heinous crimes, of being firebugs, swindlers, warmongers, and traitors. They also state that Jews have too much political and economic power, occupy the best houses, are lazy, cowardly, selfish, and (surprisingly) great eaters of poultry. Physical appearance and personal habits are practically never mentioned, nor are speech, Communist affiliations, or qualities as employers. Frequently mentioned is the alleged role of the Jewish Board of Guardians in providing large sums of money to any Jew who wants to set up in business in opposition to Gentiles. (Always referred to as "English".) On the whole the description refers to matters well outside the realms of reality and the personal experience of the man concerned.

Individuals rated 2 and 3 are more vague in their descriptions, ascribe fewer characteristics to Jews, avoid accusations of most crimes (though the giving and receiving of bribes is referred to rather frequently)—it is also these groups who referred most often to Sidney Stanley as a Jew. Physical characteristics begin to make an appearance—Jews are described as big, fat, large-nosed, and dark haired. Reference to Jews as small businessmen is made frequently by these individuals, and they are several times described as good employers though often with a qualification. ("Jews can be better governors than Englishmen," said one man, "They don't

expect to be called 'Sir' and they pay well, but they make you work
for your money." Several others said: "They (Jews) are always
fond of the big shilling.") Personal behaviour is referred to, especially
by the 3 group,—Jews are dirty in their habits, arrogant, pushing,
and cocky, and they talk loudly and gesticulate. (Whitechapel is
sometimes referred to as the "Land of the Waving Palms"). Where
"dirty habits" are described in more detail they are related almost
entirely to the cooking and eating of food and the disposal of scraps.
("If Jews lived in this flat they would just toss their scraps over the
balcony into the courtyard." "Jewish buildings always smell of
cooking." "Streets where Jews live are often littered with bones
and fish heads.") It should be unnecessary to add that although the
writer has spent a good deal of time around the scenes of these
alleged unsanitary practices he has never witnessed them.

The stereotypes of group 4 anti-Semites contain more, and more
varied, items than any other. The Jews are practically never accused
of serious crimes though it is often suggested that their business
practices are not the most scrupulous. It is frequently said that they
cut prices and drive Englishmen out of business. This criticism is
often combined with an admiration of their ability as keen and
clever businessmen. They are usually described as well-to-do, with
nice motor cars, and houses, and a liking for the best seats at any
entertainment. It is almost always stated that they are keen to make
money but the way in which they set about this is variously described. Very often they are portrayed as thrifty and hard-working,
sometimes as lazy people who will only take well-paid jobs that
do not involve physical exertion ("There are no Jews in my job—
it's too poorly paid, and too much hard work," was a frequent
comment), sometimes as employers who know how to get their
money's worth out of their employees. They are often described as
good employers, rarely as a cause of unemployment. Physical
appearance, accent, and personal habits are important points in
descriptions, but these are vaguer and less derogatory than with the
other groups. "Dirty" is still a comparatively common term of
abuse, but it is used by only six out of the forty-four in this group.
All the characteristics described by the group 4 anti-Semites are
reasonable in the sense that some people (both Jewish and Gentile)
could easily be found to whom many of these descriptions would
apply. Taken individually they are all well within the range of
experience of the ordinary man and they lack that air of extravagant

phantasy typical of the plottings and high life described by group 1. The only extravagance involved is in applying them indiscriminately to all Jews.

One attribute that is ascribed to Jews by all four groups of anti-Semites is their group solidarity. The terms used to express this, however, vary considerably from the group 1 individual who sees them plotting against the Gentiles, to the group 3 man who regards them as rather exclusive and cliquey ("They don't mind sharing in our affairs but we must keep out of theirs"), to the man in group 4 who says "There is one thing about them—a Jew will always help a Jew, whereas some Englishmen will cut your throat for tuppence." The favourite word used by the great majority of interviewees to describe this quality of solidarity is "clannish", but the connotation, as has been pointed out, varies greatly. "They're a clannish crowd," said a group 2 anti-Semite, "they'll have nothing to do with you unless it's for their own good. An Englishman can buy from their shops but they'll never buy from his." A group 4 man said, "I will say this for them—they're clannish. They never let each other down." An accusation made by every group is that Jews contribute to the housing shortage by managing to get more houses than Gentiles and by using houses as factories.

The tolerant men of group 5 have the least to say about Jews. Most commonly they make some remark emphasising that Jews vary as much as other people ("There's good and bad in all races"). Often they are described as "No different from us", "Very decent people", "Kind and helpful". Again "clannishness" is referred to, always with a favourable connotation. They are often described as good employers, frequently with considerable detail of actual instances of thoughtfulness or generosity on the part of the interviewee's Jewish employer. Several tolerant people emphasised that it is usually possible to distinguish Jews by their physical characteristics.

An attempt was made to see if any of the social, occupational or residential variables referred to in Chapter III had any connection with the amount of anti-Semitism found in the members of the random sample. For this purpose the sample was subdivided in various ways on the basis of occupation, residence, and other criteria, and each subdivision re-divided according to the number of individuals at each position on a five-point scale for anti-Semitism. X^2 was then calculated for each of these groupings. The results of these calculations are set out on p. 101.

TABLE 10

DISTRIBUTION OF ANTI-SEMITISM IN RELATION TO EMPLOYMENT BY JEWS AND NON-JEWS

	Anti-Semitic Rating				
	1	2	3	4	5
Jewish employer . .	3	1	4	9	5
Non-Jewish employer .	5	16	10	34	13

$X^2 = 4\cdot387$. This gives $P = 0\cdot4$ which indicates that there is no statistically reliable connection between degree of anti-Semitism and working for a Jewish employer.

TABLE 11

DISTRIBUTION OF ANTI-SEMITISM IN RELATION TO THE PRESENCE OR ABSENCE OF JEWISH WORKMATES

	Anti-Semitic Rating				
	1	2	3	4	5
Jewish workmates . .	2	1	5	9	6
No Jewish workmates .	6	15	9	34	12

$X^2 = 4\cdot982$. This gives $P > 0\cdot2$ indicating that there is no statistically reliable connection between degree of anti-Semitism and working with Jewish workmates.

TABLE 12

DISTRIBUTION OF ANTI-SEMITISM IN RELATION TO RESIDENCE IN JEWISH OR GENTILE NEIGHBOURHOODS

	Anti-Semitic Rating				
	1	2	3	4	5
Lives in Jewish district .	0	3	3	9	6
Lives in Gentile district .	9	15	11	35	12

$X^2 = 4\cdot342$. This gives $P > 0\cdot3$ indicating that there is no statistically reliable connection between anti-Semitism and residence in a Jewish district.

TABLE 13

DISTRIBUTION OF ANTI-SEMITISM IN RELATION TO
SOCIAL CLASS OF NEIGHBOURHOOD

	Anti-Semitic Rating				
	1	2	3	4	5
Lives in "lower" class area .	1	0	0	1	3
Lives in "middle" class area.	7	16	11	35	14
Lives in "upper" class area .	1	2	3	8	1

$X^2 = 10 \cdot 347$. This gives $P > 0 \cdot 2$ indicating that there is no statistically reliable connection between neighbourhood residence and anti-Semitism.

In view of the theory (referred to in Chapter II) that there is a definite connection between anti-Semitism and amount of trade unionist activity it is worth noting the extent to which this is true for the people studied here. The figures are available only for the most extreme anti-Semites and the tolerant individuals.

TABLE 14

DISTRIBUTION OF ANTI-SEMITISM IN RELATION
TO TRADE UNION MEMBERSHIP

	Active Unionist	Inactive Unionist	Non-Unionist
Anti-Semitic .	2	4	2
Tolerant . .	4	2	3

$X^2 = 1 \cdot 48$. This gives $P = 0 \cdot 5$. There is therefore no statistically significant connection between union membership and degree of anti-Semitism. (All values of P obtained from Fisher, 1943, pp. 112–113.)

The tables show clearly that there is no connection between these variables concerned with residence and occupation, and anti-Semitism. Obviously, therefore, the causal factors for anti-Semitic attitudes and opinions must be sought elsewhere.

It is important to note that these demonstrations of the absence of significant relationships between factors of occupation, inter-racial contact, and residence in the different areas of Bethnal Green, do not dispose entirely of the possibility that the presence of Jews in the district has some connection with the appearance of anti-Semitism. All that has been demonstrated is that such differences in degree of contact as are provided for in Bethnal Green do not have a significant effect upon the amount of anti-Semitism displayed. A really adequate consideration of the effects of contact would require a comparison between areas where there is a far greater range of possibilities, e.g. between Bethnal Green and a provincial town with no Jewish inhabitants. The figures available do indicate, however, that degree of contact cannot be more than a partial cause, or a secondary influence, in the production of anti-Semitism, as it is possible, within the range of degrees of contact provided in Bethnal Green, to find examples of every degree of anti-Semitism. We can, therefore, safely disregard, for the moment, the factors of contact in searching for conditions which show a significant relationship with the existence of anti-Semitism.

CHAPTER VI

The Extreme Anti-Semites

FOLLOWING on the general account of the results of the interviews with the sample of Bethnal Green men, we come now in this and the following chapter to more precise descriptions of the individuals who were studied in greater detail, that is, the men who fell into the two extreme groups of the classification, groups 1 and 5, the extreme anti-Semites and the tolerant people.

Of the nine individuals who fell into the anti-Semitic group, five were interviewed on three or more occasions, two on two occasions, and two were interviewed only once. Of these last two, one was given a normal first interview and agreed to be seen again, but in five further calls at varying times he was not found at home; the other was interviewed for a very short period only and then became so enraged on speaking of the Jews that he began to shout abuse at his wife, mixing this with accusations against Jews, and finally slammed the door in the interviewer's face. The seven men who were interviewed on two or more occasions all completed the Rorschach test. The extreme anti-Semites, on the whole, were far more co-operative in the matter of second interviews and the Rorschach performance than were the tolerant group.

A brief description of each of these individuals follows. For purposes of convenience and anonymity code numbers were used to refer to all interviewees in the records and this usage has been retained rather than the alternative procedure of constructing fictitious names. All personal details have been altered sufficiently to ensure anonymity.

B.6

Personal details. Age 66. Married but with no very close attachment to his wife. Two daughters, aged 21 and 14. Occupation;

fitter, continues to work though past the retiring age. Politics;
Conservative. Stated three times in the first interview (without
being asked) that he was not a Fascist but admitted that he has
attended a number of their meetings, knew the names of their
principal speakers, and described with considerable anger the
behaviour of some Jews at one of these meetings. He referred to
Union Movement as "the so-called Fascists" and "the anti-Yid
Party" and said they had a lot more support in Bethnal Green
before the war. Spare time interests; reading, films (which he goes
to by himself) and solitary walks. No religious beliefs. Health good.
Was unemployed ("walking the stones") for several months in 1930.

Social and institutional contacts. Belongs to no clubs. No close friends.
Used to belong to the British Legion but gave it up, he says, because
it fell into the hands of the Jews. Trade Unionist but not keen.

Ethical views. Stresses that he does not drink, smoke or swear and
is insistent on setting a good example to his womenfolk. Stresses
parents' duties towards their children. Regards other people's ethical
views with some cynicism: e.g. says the Churches wouldn't oppose
a national lottery if they were offered a percentage of the profits.

Competence of self and membership groups. Both explicitly and by
inference he makes it clear that he personally, and the groups which
he recognises as including himself (Gentiles, working class, Englishmen, etc.) are lacking in political power, locally, nationally and
internationally. The best of everything has been in the past, he
thinks, except those things which affect children, so he has had the
worst of it all along. Good people won't take office in organisations,
so you can't get rid of the incompetents who are in power—this
is the trouble with the Trade Unions. He would make political
office inaccessible to all whose family had not been in Britain at
least three generations.

Attitudes to parents and authorities. Says he was strictly brought up.
Speaks almost reverentially about his father and quotes him as an
authority on political and economic matters. His father has been
dead over forty years but he applies his father's views to contemporary problems as though they had been enunciated yesterday.
Describes how his father punished him as a boy and always made
him go to bed earlier than the other boys, but says he deserved it
and it was good for him. He has a great admiration for the aristocracy and a strong belief in the virtues of strict discipline.
Distinguishes between "the real aristocracy, who won their titles in

the field" and "the pseudo-aristocracy who bought their titles and would sell their country". This last remark is accompanied by a peculiar gesture that he makes whenever he speaks of the Jews. Says nothing directly about his employer but implies that he is short-sighted, mean and rather unpatriotic.

Jewish stereotype. His chief complaints refer to their alleged political power, nationally, locally and in the Trade Unions. He also complains that they get priority in housing and are firebugs. He asserts they will burn down buildings to get insurance without worrying if there are people in them. They engineer wars to suit their convenience. The war with Germany was due to them and now they want one against Russia.

Future outlook. He thinks wars and slumps are both inevitable, the former because of Jewish plottings, the latter because nothing can be done to prevent them. He looks forward gloomily to the day when he will have to retire to live on his old age pension.

Reaction to interview. He was not at first keen to be interviewed but gave the impression of not being sufficiently assertive to refuse, though at the same time he seemed to enjoy expressing his opinions. By the end of the contact (three interviews) he was quite friendly but would obviously not form a close relationship.

Rorschach test results. Definite psychotic tendencies of a paranoid type but no signs of deterioration. Very anxious about deprivations (castration anxiety).

C.7

Personal details. Age 69. Married and seems to be very attached to his wife. No children. Occupation; market porter, could have retired but carries on doing light work. Politics; Labour. Spare-time interests; football pools, walking, solitary drinking. No religious beliefs. He reports his doctor as saying he is in good health but gets very anxious over even slight symptoms and visits the doctor quite often. Has never been unemployed.

Social and institutional contacts. No clubs. No close friends. Keeps in touch with his own and his wife's siblings—occasional letters and visits. Trade unionist and attends union meetings regularly. Belonged with his wife to a shelter club during the war.

Ethical views. Emphasises his morality and reliability by comparing himself very favourably with the majority of the people in Bethnal Green of whom he speaks disparagingly. Extremely proud of never having been late for work in his life. Condemns stealing by market porters, chiefly on the grounds that it is silly as you are sure to be caught. Says he is not opposed to gambling but paints a lurid picture of the consequences of becoming addicted to it and even more of the awful fates that may befall people who win large prizes. He has never won anything.

Competence of self and membership groups. Alternates between suggesting that he and his groups are in a reasonable position and implying that they are not; e.g. Trade unions help their members to get increased pay, but they can't stop prices rising, so they are no better off; Britain and Russia could live at peace, but Russia and America cannot, so we will be involved. Sees a continual conflict between strong and intelligent effort on the one hand and blind uncontrollable forces on the other, with no necessary victory for the former.

Attitudes to parents and authorities. Stresses his father's good qualities as a skilled workman, a good provider and a stern but just parent. Says his greatest regret is that he did not follow his father's trade. He is strongly opposed to strikes, believes in regular disciplined behaviour. Very conscious of class distinctions and emphasises that he was born in the best part of Bethnal Green.

Jewish stereotypes. Jews talk about you behind your back, will not work hard, are cowards, wealthy, eat only the best foods and get priority in housing to the exclusion of the "English".

Future outlook. Worried about his age (he is also proud of it in a way, and emphasises it by always saying he is "in his 70th year"), and about the prospect of a lowered standard of living when he retires. Nervous about the possibility of the house burning down and takes elaborate precautions to prevent this. Thinks there is likely to be another war soon.

Reactions to the interview. Friendly and co-operative. Eager to talk and very ready to express his opinions.

Rorschach summary. Very disturbed personality, of a markedly schizoid type with the possibility of paranoid trends. Low intelligence. Unable to express emotion easily.

F.14

Personal details. Age, 47. Married, but separated from his wife. Daughter aged 19 and son aged 13 who live with their mother. He lives with sister and brother-in-law with whom he is on moderately good terms, though the brother-in-law thinks that F.14 is lazy and doesn't help enough in the house. Occupation; french polisher; and ex-regular soldier (corporal). Politics; Fascist. Spare time activities; drawing, but only does this rarely and always copies other pictures, never draws from life. No religious beliefs. Health good. Has never been unemployed. Has a scrap-book full of photographs of Nazi Leaders and scenes from Belsen. Says he kept them "just for interest". Is proud of having met William Joyce whom he says was "a very fine man".

Social and institutional contacts. No clubs and no close friends. Only contact with relatives is with sister and brother-in-law. Not a trade unionist.

Ethical views. Says little about these directly. Indirectly he implies that other people's morals are at a low level; e.g. Londoners are snobbish and unhelpful, politicians are corrupt, the government is dishonest (nationalisation is theft). Said he did not associate much with fellow soldiers in the army as they spent their time in pubs and got drunk. Most of his other statements in regard to ethics have a self reference either in implying that he is exceptionally helpful and generous (e.g. for sending a tube of tooth-paste to a French family who had helped him to escape at Dunkirk or for presenting the interviewer with a picture that had obviously been part of an advertising display), or in expounding grandiloquent and impracticable schemes which he would like to put into operation for improving the lot of poor and invalid children.

Competence of self and membership groups. He is a superpatriot of a very nationalistic kind, but at the same time laments that Jews, Socialists and the forces of evil have brought England so low that it is hardly worth living here any longer. He would emigrate but the difficulties that are put in one's way make it hardly worth while. At one moment he thunders out boasts of the true Englishman's love of liberty, at the next moment he mourns that nowadays one's fellow citizens are so corrupt they can only be despised. ("The country is absolutely rotten.") He himself is always the model of the true Englishman, but even he cannot get anywhere. "Everything I do seems to have a barrier built right across it." He contradicts himself every few minutes but his statements seem to add up to saying that things should be wonderful because the English are the salt of the earth but the situation is so bad that even the English can't cope with it.

Attitudes to parents and authorities. Obviously and deliberately avoided talking about his parents apart from one approving remark about his mother. Very anti-authoritarian. Thinks trade unions are a good thing: "they keep the bosses down." Accuses his boss, on apparently very flimsy evidence, of "fiddling the income tax" in some way that results in the boss making, and F.14 losing, money. "I am going to see this through. If he has been tricking me he will find he has taken on the wrong man", and he goes on to speculate in great detail as to whether the boss will be fined or imprisoned when his crime is exposed. Says he (F.14) practically runs the business and implies that the boss is incompetent. His solution for all problems is "There ought to be a law about it" or "If I were in power I would make a law."

Jewish stereotype. His complaints about Jews are numerous and varied, and frequently contradictory. Says they are cowardly, did not join the army, but hid in the A.R.P. and N.F.S., then later details the perils that he and his sister faced in these same services. In the same sentence he said that Jews were the main capitalists and the leaders of Communism. "Ninety per cent of Communists are Jews." Says they are black marketeers and firebugs. (Calls fire engine bells "Jew's wedding bells"). Almost any topic of conversation will bring him on to the subject of Jews and he tells long detailed stories to illustrate his assertions. Says Jews import cheap foreign labour to increase their profits and put Englishmen out of jobs, then, describing a luxury flat he claims to have seen in the course of his work, he says, "The Jewess never did anything to keep it clean. She floated round all day in varnished fingernails. It was all done by some poor Welsh girl who would be thrown out as soon as she was not wanted. The Government should send people round to inspect places like that."

Future outlook. He expects nothing but disaster. He was the most pessimistic of all the subjects. Even in his most manic moments his statements implied that his hopes would eventually come to nothing. He is sure there will soon be another depression. He expects a war with Russia. When asked what he thought the outcome would be he said, "The outcome won't be of much consequence to us. With the atom bomb and all that, this place will be the first to be wiped out."

Reaction to interview. Friendly and apparently very co-operative except in his refusal to talk about his parents. He was, however, less co-operative than he appeared since he said nothing about his wife and children and implied that he was single. The information about his marriage came from his sister. He changes rapidly from ebullient enthusiasm when he strides up and down, shouting and waving his arms, to a depression when he sits slumped in a chair and complains bitterly. There were six interviews including a visit to the interviewer's home.

Rorschach. Marked schizophrenic tendencies. The possibility of his deteriorating cannot be ruled out. Very excitable, uncontrolled, eager to impress, low average intelligence.

G. 2

Personal details. Age 58. Widower. Three adult children. Lives with widowed daughter. Occupation: clerk. Politics: Conservative. Made one favourable reference to the Fascists and said that Jewish domination of the local councils prevented Mosley hiring public halls and putting his point of view. Spare time interest: Has motor cycle. Has some rather vague religious beliefs. Health: suffers from asthma and rheumatism. Has never been unemployed but went bankrupt when he tried to open a small shop.

Social and institutional contacts. No clubs or close friends. His closest relationship appears to be with his small grand-daughter. Belongs to a trade union but is not keen and does not attend meetings.

Ethical views. Complains of declining moral standards, chiefly in terms of failure to perform certain actions, like going to church. He is especially upset because people no longer send their children to Sunday School, though he adds that when they did it was chiefly in order to get rid of the children for an hour or so.

Competence of self and membership groups. Practically everything he says is in terms of weakness and despair. He does not believe that it is possible to do anything constructive or to have any certain knowledge. (He pointed to the stars and said "These fellows who tell you the stars are a certain distance away, and such and such a size—they don't really know—my guess would be as good as theirs —or at least, your guess would.") He describes himself as "full of discontent". He doesn't vote because his vote would never make any difference. He concluded his views on housing by saying "I can't do anything about it. No one takes any notice of me and I don't suppose they will of you." The past was much better than the present. ("There was a time when you could get drunk for sixpence —now it costs about £2.")

Attitudes to parents and authority. He praises his father for his strictness and describes the thrashings he received as a boy. He speaks bitterly of the ingratitude of the young and the pernicious effects of education. "Some people say the children are getting cleverer. I think they are just getting more artful. Sometimes I think artfulness and education go together." (His son, of whom he had obviously been very proud, won a scholarship to a grammar school, graduated from the University, achieved a high rank in the Civil Service, and then refused to have anything more to do with his father who has not heard of him for some years.) He is a great believer in discipline at work and complains that office boys are treated too easily these days. "I can remember getting many a clump on the head when I was learning my job. Of course you cannot do that now. That's all wrong—an occasional clump is a good thing." He speaks in rather awestruck tones of prophecies which he says were made many years ago by his father, and his colonel during the first world war, and which he thinks have all come true, about the increasing power of Jews and Chinese. Complains about restrictions and regulations, objects to working for other people, hates to take orders.

Jewish stereotype. They have too much political and economic power. ("They control all the Town Halls.") They exclude other people from the use of their possessions by closing their estates to the public and letting flats to Jews only. They should be legally restrained from actions of this sort. Jews are the only people now who have large families—no one else can afford it. Soon they will outnumber us. They own all the shops and factories—only one shop in twenty in the main street of Bethnal Green is owned by a non-Jew. Related how he and his friends, when schoolboys, had made a practice of stoning Jewish boys as they came out of school.

Future outlook. Sees no hope for the future. Expects further wars and slumps and feels that nothing can be done to prevent them. Is worried about his age and the fact that he will get no pension from his firm. People are becoming better dressed and less happy.

Reaction to interview. He was obviously not keen to be interviewed but seemed unable to resist when the interviewer carried on asking questions. At the second interview he again showed disapproval but then suggested going inside. The impression he gave was of someone whose frequently expressed anti-authoritarian attitudes were only a façade—he would never put them into practice.

Rorschach. An obsessional character with some degree of confusion. Average intelligence. Marked signs of repression and possible paranoid trends, certainly makes use of projection.

I.4

Personal details. Aged 76. Married. No children. Occupation: retired bus driver. Politics: Labour. Spare time interest: gardening. No information on religious beliefs. Health good. Has never been unemployed and held the same job for thirty years before retiring.

Social and institutional contacts. No clubs. No close friends. Keeps in touch with his brothers and sisters but does not see them very often. Was a member of a trade union but was not very keen. Sees little of his neighbours—"I keep myself to myself." Would not like a flat to live in, "I like to be able to shut my front door and I know I am on my own—you can't do that in a flat."

Ethical views. Is very insistent on the virtues of hard work and punctuality. "These strikes are all wrong. People get paid too much these days." Thinks strikes should be forbidden by law.

Competence of self and membership groups. Is very conscious of lack of support through having no children, saying mournfully "We are all on our own." Identifies himself chiefly with old age pensioners. They are the only people who aren't paid enough. "No one ever takes any notice of them or worries about their troubles." He objects strongly to child allowances and to the policy of building flats instead of houses for old people.

Attitude to parents and authorities. He did not mention his parents. His attitudes to authorities are contradictory. On the one hand he complains bitterly about having been retired two weeks before he qualified for special benefits after thirty years of service, and tells with great delight of an occasion when he got the better of a policeman who had charged him with a driving offence. On the other hand he is very class conscious, mourns the passing of the horse buses, saying that driving them was "a gentlemanly job", and his happiest memories are of gifts and favours from rich and titled passengers in the horse bus days. He said, "In those days we knew our place and our manners."

Jewish stereotype. Says Jews are warmongers (for financial reasons), wealthy, live in luxurious West End hotels, and are lazy.

Future outlook. Not very hopeful. He must just stay where he is, getting older and lonelier. He says there won't be a war if Russia keeps quiet but the Jews stir things up when they want to as the Jewish diamond merchants did in South Africa. There won't be any more slumps if people work hard enough, but they probably won't.

Reaction to interview. Was very friendly, took the interviewer inside, showed him the garden, some testimonials and some old photographs. Agreed to a further visit but was out whenever calls were made subsequently.

O.2

Personal details. Age 36. Married. Two sons, aged 8 and 4. Occupation: lorry driver. Politics: Liberal. ("I hate the Communists. They are quite mad. They are as mad as the Blackshirts . . . the Blackshirts hold meetings near here . . . they just get up and complain. That isn't very clever—I could do that easily. . . . What does take brains is to find some remedy and they don't do that—they just complain and criticise.") Spare time interest: reading. Has some uncertain religious beliefs—says "I am not a strong churchman but I believe in religion. Sometimes I have had my doubts but at other times I had great relief from prayer." Health good (but his wife is in poor health). Has had two periods of unemployment totalling ten months. Is a charge hand—was a senior N.C.O. in the army.

Social and institutional contacts. No clubs. No close friends. Says he used to "go around with the boys" a lot before he was married, but not since. Was a keen trade unionist for 15 years (says he was dismissed five times from jobs for union activities), but resigned recently when the union refused to support a friend whom he thought had been unjustly dismissed.

Ethical views. He brings up ethical issues frequently, his comments nearly always taking the same form—first a remark that he doesn't consider himself perfect, then a complaint about unethical practices on the part of other people (bribery, theft, black-market, sexual perversions), then gives an example which usually seems to implicate himself in the practice he complains of. He describes this as "beating them at their own game" which he says is the only way of dealing with dishonest people. His objection to bribery is not so much that it is dishonest as that it puts him at a disadvantage. It takes a £15 bribe, he says, to get a council house and he can't afford this. He usually exonerates the other dishonest people also by saying, for example, that their pay is so low that you can't blame them for stealing and taking bribes, and thus shifts all the blame off on to "the authorities". He is very concerned about teaching his children the right ethical and religious beliefs but it is difficult. "You can get clever men arguing on both sides and how is a man in my position to know what is right. I am not clever enough. All I can do is to accept what I was taught when I was young and teach it to my children." Talked a lot about being upset by thoughts of the people he had killed during the war and implied a lot of guilt over associations with a group of homosexuals before his marriage.

Competence of self and membership groups. His attitude to his own capabilities is expressed quite clearly in the remark just quoted about religion. Also he followed his remark on people who complain and do nothing by saying, "I have no idea of what should be done. I am just an ignorant working man and there is nothing I can do about it." He reads a periodical published by one of the banks from which he finds out about the things that are wrong, but can't understand the articles well enough to follow the suggested remedies, so that his efforts to understand only make him more depressed. He doesn't think you can do much about economic forces. "If labour gets plentiful again, wages will come down, in spite of the unions." When complaining about the prevalence of corruption in local government he says he knows it goes on but he can't prove it, and no one would take any notice of him.

Attitudes to parents and authority. His upbringing seems to have been highly erratic. He has memories of "moonlight flittings" when they were behind with the rent. His parents separated early and he was brought up by his mother. He is highly ambivalent towards his father—admires his ability as a craftsman but dislikes his treatment of his mother, though he continually understresses this. Very attached to his mother. Talks a lot about the duties of a good husband and emphasises his own virtues in this direction (helps with the dishes, minds the children while his wife goes to the pictures). Makes a show of disciplining his children strictly but does not succeed. Puts the blame for troubles on to leaders and authorities, but then names all the leading politicians and specifically exempts them from blame. Blames some of the second rank men and then exonerates them and blames "the system". If the stories he tells are true he is well able to stand up for himself against employers: e.g. he talks of threatening violence in order to get back pay.

Jewish stereotype. They are mean, operate the black market, drive hard bargains, are unscrupulous businessmen, full of low cunning, unpatriotic, dirty in their habits, have foreign accents and gesticulate. They are the only people for whose misdeeds he does not find an excuse.

Future outlook. Just as the present is bleaker than the past so the future is likely to be worse still. There will probably be another slump, but he doesn't really know, he isn't qualified to express an opinion. He is sure there will be another war. He went on to complain that people get too despondent these days and always look on the dark side of things. As long as you get people thinking like this there will be wars.

Reaction to interviews. Very friendly and co-operative through three interviews. Invited interviewer inside on each occasion and made tea. Willingly arranged further interviews though carefully making them when his wife would be out, as she was at the time of the first interview.

Rorschach. A very neurotic record. There were only six responses, so a detailed assessment is impossible. The feature that stands out with the greatest clarity is fear of anything connected with sex, especially masculine sexuality, and anxiety over quite strong homosexual tendencies.

Q.4

Married and seems not to be on the best of terms with his wife. Age about 55. He worked himself into a great rage over the way in which Jews and other foreigners get the best of the houses while people like himself who have to pay the rates have to live in hovels. He slammed the door early in the interview.

Q.7

Personal details. Age 56. Married and has a good relationship with his wife. One child (married daughter). Occupation: street sweeper. Politics: Labour. Spare time interest: making furniture. No religious beliefs. Health: he has suffered from rheumatism and asthma in the past but has fairly good health at the moment. (His wife has heart trouble.) He has had long periods of unemployment and frequent shorter periods. Also when he and his wife were running their own polishing business he had long stretches of illness when he couldn't work. Most of his life has been a struggle with ill health and poverty.

Social and institutional contacts. No clubs. No friends. Does not keep in touch with any relatives. His son-in-law has forbidden their daughter and granddaughter to visit them and this upsets him greatly though he adds that he thinks relations are better apart— seeing them always means quarrelling with them. He is a trade unionist but says he doesn't really believe in unions and didn't know the name of the union he belongs to until he found his card. Doesn't mix much with other people—says he doesn't know his next door neighbours. "They are all very inquisitive and I have nothing to do with them. When I come home all I want to do is to shut my door and stay there."

Ethical views. Emphasises the virtues of hard work and independence. He has never been out of work through his own fault. He is not like the men who are content to live on the child allowance and unemployment benefits. Any man who is out of work today should be ashamed of himself.

Competence of self and membership groups. He stresses the efforts he has made in the past and the fact that they have come to nothing. He seems to have little sense of belonging to any groups except such vague and negative groups as non-Jews. Such groups as "nation" and "working class" appear to have no meaning for him. His summing up of his life story was "Life is one long battle and you get no help from anyone." (Of all the people interviewed he was the one whose experiences most warranted such a conclusion being drawn from them.) He has not voted for some years. "I don't see that it does much good. They have never done anything for me."

Attitudes to parents and authority. His father died when he was small. He speaks with affection and admiration, but with no factual details, about his mother, who was killed in an air raid, and describes her death and burial as if it were an important symbol for the whole country. He likes working on his own and without supervision. Implies, but does not explicitly state, accusations of cruelty, meanness and double dealing against the man from whom they got their french polishing work. (He was not Jewish.)

Jewish stereotype. They are cowards (ran away during the blitz), wealthy, unscrupulous, get all their benefits at the expense of

Englishmen: "If you allow one Yid to set up a stall he will soon have pushed two more stalls off the street." They have an organisation that gives them money to set up in business and outdo the English.

Future outlook. Things look as good as ever they have at the moment, because he now has a steady job that he likes, but he expects another war in which London will be wiped out by the first atom bomb. In any case there can be nothing left in life for him. "When you get to a certain age you just have to face up to the fact that there is nothing in front of you." He dwelt at great length on the horrors of war, illustrating them with very detailed accounts, of his work on Civil Defence during the last war, digging bodies out of ruins, and other unpleasant duties.

Reaction to interview. Very co-operative and friendly throughout two interviews. Seemed delighted to have someone to talk to about his troubles.

Rorschach. An obsessional character. Low average intelligence. A high degree of repression. Some suggestion of psychotic trends of paranoid type but these are not conclusive. Latent homosexual tendencies.

S.11

Personal details. Age 42. Married. A son aged 14 and a daughter 13. Occupation: foreman painter and decorator. Politics: Conservative. ("They are the best of a bad lot.") Spare time interests: rambling. No information on religious beliefs. Health is good but he has had a deformed arm from birth. Has never been unemployed.

Social and institutional contacts. He belongs to a rambling club and has some friends among the members. Little contact with his relatives who are scattered all over London. Doesn't belong to a union. Says they are all very well as long as they don't interfere with a man working harder and earning more.

Ethical views. Emphasises moderation and caution in all things, particularly the latter quality where money is concerned. Says he won't gamble even to the extent of doing football pools, and adds that he expects they don't usually pay out the proper prize money as there is no way of checking on how many people got the right answer and if they say there were 300 you couldn't know if this were true or if you were the only one. Stresses that he is a good and dutiful parent, arranging for a good education for his children and at the same time complains how much this costs. He contrasts his own morality with that of his neighbours who he says don't come up to his standards.

Competence of self and membership groups. Says little directly about himself, but implies that he is a dependable and worthy character. Stresses the situations in which he has some power, especially at work, but also implies that he is alone against a hostile world. He is scornful of the "general run" of people in Bethnal Green, calling them "ignorant fools" and "a poor lot". "If you shook them up in a bag you wouldn't pull out many good ones." Gives the impression that he feels isolated and as though he does not belong to many groups (apart from his rambling club), except rather large and vague ones like "Gentiles". (He was one of the few people interviewed who used this word.) Says England is going downhill rapidly and he would like to emigrate. Seems to feel guilty about this implied desertion, and insists that he is not a rat leaving a sinking ship.

Attitudes to parents and authority. Says nothing about his family in general. Is also reticent about his employers, merely describing them as "a large and old-established firm". Was very critical of political leaders, and especially of taxation policy which, he said, took away all incentives to work harder. Gives the impression of being very dictatorial to his subordinates and very obsequious to his superiors when in a face to face relationship, but with a façade of rebelliousness when talking about them. Very class conscious. Would like to move to "a better class neighbourhood" though he has a very comfortable flat. Would especially like to live in Chelsea.

Jewish stereotype. Jews are Communists and it is the spread of Communism that is the main trouble in this country. The country is "infested" with Jews. He knows that according to statistics there are only 450,000 Jews in Britain but he doesn't believe this. There must be at least five million. They should be strictly controlled. They are "mean, greedy, and dishonest", and they make big fortunes by "twisting it out of Gentiles". His whole manner and voice changed when he talked about Jews. He hesitated a moment before producing his first anti-Semitic remark (about Communism) then said, "I can see you are a Christian, a Gentile" and went on to give his opinion.

Future outlook. The past was rather better than the present. He is undecided about the future. He has a sure job and will get a good pension but he is very nervous and depressed about the possibility of another war which he thinks is very likely. The economic outlook is very black. Even Government securities are no longer safe.

Reaction to interview. Very reserved at first. By the end of the fourth interview he had become much less so, but gave the impression that he could never be really friendly and welcoming. He invited the interviewer in only at the fourth visit in order to do the Rorschach test, but just into a spare room and obviously avoided having to introduce his wife or children.

Rorschach. The predominant characteristic of this record is anxiety which is associated with human relationships, with sex and with vague dangers. Marked obsessional traits and a considerable degree of repression. Slightly above average intelligence.

These brief summaries are intended to provide some fairly detailed evidence of the way in which certain patterns tended to run through all the pictures which it has been possible to build up of these people. The patterns most clearly indicated can be described as follows, additional extracts from the interview records being included as illustrations.

(1) There is a continual insistence on the idea of deterioration. The past is best, the present is unattractive, the future is black. Q.7, who comes nearest to providing an exception here, is prevented from conforming exactly to the pattern by overwhelming pressure of reality factors. Only a psychotic could have regarded a past such as he had experienced as better than his present condition. Yet even Q.7 at the height of his happiness expected only disaster in the future. G.2 says, "At one time people used to go out and walk in the streets a lot more in the evenings, but now all the streets are empty. Now that the shops can be lit it might make a difference, but what is the use of going out to look at shops that have got nothing in them, or, if they have got it, are too dear for you to buy, or else the shop is shut anyway."

(2) Associated with this idea of deterioration is the feeling that the difficulties with which they are faced are too great to be overcome. It is also noticeable that the difficulties are almost always impersonal, inexorable forces. Trade cycles, the actions of other nations, the inaccessibility of certain knowledge, are among the factors mentioned. F.14's statement, "Everything I do seems to have a barrier built right across it" is expressive of the typical attitude. The cause of the difficulty is never in the individual himself.

Here again F.14 illustrates the trend very clearly, if in a somewhat gross and exaggerated fashion. He is the embodiment of the true Englishman, a man of courage and resource with an unconquerable determination to bow to no one. But even so he is powerless, for other Englishmen are no longer true; they have become cowardly and corrupt and so F.14 and the few like him are left in an exposed and hopeless position. G.2, complaining about increasing fares, said, "The only thing I can think of is that some people in this country get more than they earn. But I don't know and I wouldn't be able to find out. You can easily drive yourself silly thinking about problems you can't solve. It's best to leave them alone."

(3) Nearly all are concerned with ideas of power. Jews have power. The groups they themselves belong to have none. Things ought to be set right by legislative action, i.e. by the application of power to the situation, and if this power is applied, that should be enough to right the wrongs. The use of manipulation and social pressures, the treatment of human beings as individuals is not suggested. The individuals are to be dealt with *en masse* by legislative action. B.6 says, "The worst thing about Yids is that they get into Parliament. They will do anything for their own race but they soon forget all about you and me who put them there. . . . War was inevitable from the time Hitler threw the first Jew out of Germany. Straight away the Yids in Parliament engineered the treaty with Poland and then war was bound to come. . . . The Bethnal Green Jews were the scum of Poland and Russia. The restriction acts were a good thing, the only trouble was they were not passed soon enough. . . . It should be impossible for any man to get into Parliament unless he has three generations of British blood in his veins."

(4) Nearly all are concerned to maintain some rigid standard of behaviour which will single them out as virtuous examples to others. One gets the feeling that they want some simple set of actions, the performance of which will assure them they are worthy people. B.6 emphasises the example he sets his daughters in not drinking or smoking. C.7 contrasts his sobriety and punctuality with the careless and dissolute habits of his fellow citizens, while G.2 insists on attendance at Church and Sunday School even when it is only a meaningless gesture. In the same way S.11 contrasts his thrift and caution with his neighbours' shiftlessness and habits of gambling, while I.4 and Q.7 extol hard work as the prime virtue.

(5) The followers, B.6, C.7, and I.4 all stress the virtues of discipline, obedience and doing a full day's work. They oppose strikes,
are conscious of class distinctions, and "know their places." I.4 said,
"On the old horse buses we used to have a lot of lady and gentlemen passengers. In those days we knew our places and our manners.
Sometimes some of the gentlemen would sit in the seat right behind
the box and talk to me and ask about driving. In cold weather I
might offer them a rug. Often I would get big tips and often a
cigar." The central persons, those who exercise some kind of
leadership (F.14, G.2, O.2, Q.7, S.11) are less inclined to do this.
They tend to emphasise the need for discipline in those below them,
while at the same time they are very critical of their superiors.
Thus O.2 states, "When I worked for the (Jewish) firm over the
road it was a fight for my wages every Friday night. They would
always try to bluff me out of them just on principle. I have had to
hold my fist under their noses at times to get the wages I was
entitled to. At the same time I did fairly well out of them. It was
easy enough to knock off (sell) a box of fish from the loads fairly
often." There seems to be a fairly marked tendency by the men
in this group to regard their parents and especially their fathers as
objects of veneration and beyond criticism, though examples of
benefits from parents nearly always refer to material gains. For
example, C.7 says, "My father was a strict man when dealing with
us children but always very just. We were exceptionally well
clothed and after we grew up we could often get cheap furniture
from my father. He was a very clever man and was employed on
making special types of furniture." The main decoration in his
sitting room is a large picture of his father.

(6) There is a very strong tendency (S.11 is the only exception)
for these people to have no close relationships outside the home
and very few group interests of any sort. Trade union connections
provide a partial exception. Nearly all belong to unions and C.7 and
O.2 can be classed as active members. The absence of friends, lack
of contact with relatives, the preference for solitary pursuits in
spare time is very marked. Q.7, for example, does not know his
next door neighbours even by sight though he has lived four years
in his present house. His first thought when he comes home, he
says, is to get inside his door and shut the other people out. He has
relatives but prefers not to see them. Meeting relatives means
quarrelling with them.

The following table shows how close is the correspondence in this group between the rating for anti-Semitism and the ratings on the other variables which are listed in Table 9. It is obvious that the correlations are rather higher for this extreme group than for the whole sample of 103 individuals, except in the case of unemployment. Some of these ratings illustrate clearly the patterns described above. The tendency to regards one's personal power as

TABLE 15

RATINGS OF THE EXTREME ANTI-SEMITES

	Variables							
	B.6	C.7	F.14	G.2	I.4	O.2	Q.7	S.11
Control of individual over environment . . .	3	3	1	1	2	3	2	3
Control of group over environment	2	3	1	2	1	1	1	2
Pessimism-optimism for self .	2	2	1	1	2	2	1	2
Pessimism-optimism for group.	1	2	1	1	2	2	1	2
Attitude to authority—leaders .	–	–	5	5	–	4	4	4
Attitude to authority—followers	1	2	–	–	3	–	–	–
Isolation	2	4	2	1	3	3	2	4
Age	1	1	3	1	1	4	2	3
Unemployment . . .	2	5	4	3	4	3	1	5

greater than that of the group can be clearly seen. Even F.14, who receives an equal rating on these two variables, is an example of this tendency, as his opinion of the group power was much lower even than his opinion of his own slight capacity to control his environment.

One other hypothesis, that anti-Semitism is correlated with the existence of anxiety-creating situations, can also be illustrated from data drawn from these cases. A distinction has to be made here between actual reality situations, and those situations to which anxiety is attached by the individual concerned without any apparent objective justification. This latter case constitutes an indication of free-floating anxiety. One difficulty which does arise is that of distinguishing between present and past anxieties. When does an anxiety-creating situation cease to create anxiety? For example, is G.2 justified in showing anxiety over his son's desertion of him, even though this happened some time ago? It has not been possible to lay down any satisfactory rule on this point, and an arbitrary decision has been made in each case. It is possible to give the following list of anxiety-creating situations for each of the eight individuals under discussion. (Expressions of fear of atom warfare have been treated as indications of free-floating anxiety. Obviously this danger is virtually the same for all and undue attention to it cannot be regarded as a normal reaction to an objective situation.)

B.6. His approaching retirement. He has already reached retiring age but continues to work. Sooner or later he will have to give up and his standard of living will fall.

C.7. The same situation exists for this man. In his case it is made worse by the fact that he has no children to supplement the family income.

F.14. His uncertain domestic situation. His only home is with his sister and brother-in-law and he is on only moderately good terms with them.

G.2. His health is not good. He will shortly be retired and because of the break in his service when he went into business on his own he will get no pension from his firm. He has been deserted by the son of whom he was so proud.

I.4. He is entering a very old age with no children to look after him and his wife (who is only a year younger), and no friends or relatives of any kind in close contact with him.

O.2. His wife is in poor health.

Q.7. His wife has a very weak heart and his own health, though better than in the past, is only fair. He has virtually had his only child and his grandchildren taken from him. He lives in a most unpleasant house, which has rotten floor boards, falling ceilings, and is alongside a busy railway line.

S.11. He is deformed.

It is difficult to evaluate these situations or to arrange them in any kind of order corresponding to the degree of anxiety. It is certain that B.6 is in a relatively happy situation while Q.7 has very real reasons for his anxious feelings, but the intermediate positions are not clear. Moreover, as one is not in possession of detailed information about O.2's knowledge of his wife's condition (information which he would not supply), it is impossible to make any approach to an accurate estimate of the quality of the situation. Therefore all that can be done in this case is to assert that all these individuals have some real cause for anxiety, but B.6's case is sufficiently favourable for him to be classed apart from the remainder.

CHAPTER VII

The Tolerant Group

TOLERANT individuals proved more difficult to interview on a second occasion than was the case with the extreme anti-Semites. Of the eighteen men who received ratings of 5, six were interviewed on three or more occasions, three on two occasions (of these three, two refused to do the Rorschach test), and the remaining nine were seen only once. These nine failures arose in various ways. In four cases an interruption broke off the interview before a second call could be arranged; two, although very friendly during the interview, refused to arrange a second meeting; three agreed to a second meeting, arranged a time and date, were out when calls were made at this time, and on subsequent calls (two in each case), the door was always opened by some other person who said that the interviewee was not at home and that it was not known when he would be in. It therefore appears that these three individuals were deliberately avoiding a second interview in spite of having been, in each case, very friendly and co-operative on the first occasion.

In the following brief summaries of data on the tolerant individuals, only those who were interviewed on two or more occasions are dealt with, but all members of the group are listed in the table of ratings which appears later in the chapter.

A.2

Personal details. Age 31. Married and has an affectionate relationship with his wife. Two sons, aged 6 and 2. Occupation; cabinet maker. Politics: Liberal. Spare-time activities: drawing and gardening. Also takes quite a keen interest in politics—reads the parliamentary news and checks on the movements and speeches of the local M.P. "to see if he is doing his job properly". Slight religious beliefs. Health good. Has never been unemployed. As a youth he had successful psychiatric treatment for a skin disorder—he saved up and paid for this himself. He won a scholarship to a technical school at 14 but the death of his father forced him to go to work. His mother died soon after.

Social and institutional contacts. Belongs to an art club and is secretary of a gardening club. Has several friends in the neighbourhood and keeps in touch with his siblings—occasional visits. Keen trade unionist—has been a shop steward.

Ethical views. Stresses tolerance and equality of opportunity. Advocates equal pay for women on both ethical and economic grounds. Emphasises the importance of creativity—wants to provide opportunities for creative self-expression for himself and his children. Only comment on gambling was that he used to do the pools but gave up as the odds were too heavily against winning.

Competence of self and membership groups. Believes that in general he can get what he wants if he tries hard enough and views groups in the same way. His attitude to politics is characteristic—it pays to take an interest and to make sure that the key people are doing their jobs.

Attitudes to parents and authorities. Says his father was too strict. He is trying to avoid making his father's mistakes with his own children. Thinks his father's early death may have helped him in the long run by forcing him to be independent. Believes the most important thing with children is to be consistent. Says little about his employer but implies he is good—doesn't drive his men too hard.

Jewish stereotype. There are many types of Jew—just like the English. They work hard but that is nothing against them. Says they have been used as scapegoats, especially since the Fascists started encouraging this. Most people don't like the Jews, but he doesn't mind. Jewish parents encourage their children to work hard at school which gives them a reputation for cleverness and the others "who are interested mainly in getting into the football team" become jealous.

Future outlook. He thinks slumps and wars are on the whole rather unlikely. He intends to emigrate to Canada where he expects that life will continue to be satisfactory for him and give greater opportunities to his children. Has taken out insurance policies to cover the education and apprenticeships of his children. Is slightly worried in case he loses these on emigrating.

Reactions to interview. Friendly and co-operative. Interested in giving his opinions and in asking the interviewer questions about life overseas, experiences of emigrants, etc. Three interviews including a visit to the interviewer's home.

Rorschach summary. Mainly a very healthy record. Slight signs of immaturity. Fairly well controlled, but certainly no rigidity. Possibility of slight hysterical tendencies and some repressed homosexuality, but no prospect of this becoming overt.

C.2

Personal details. Age 27. Married. One son aged 2. Occupation: upholsterer. Politics: Labour. Sparetime activities: social drinking with relatives, and other social amusements. Also does extra work to make more money. Was very interested in religion as an adolescent but not now. Health good. Has never been unemployed.

Social and institutional contacts. Belongs to local Labour party and to a social club. Has close contact with his own and his wife's families and with several friends. Is opposed to trade unions and does not belong.[1] Says he gets more money by working in a non-union shop. "I think unions are a bad thing. They always seem to cause trouble. There are far more strikes in union shops that in non-union ones. I have never belonged to a union and don't intend to join".

Ethical views. Mildly critical about the amount of drinking in Bethnal Green. Says he likes to go to a pub, but for sociability, not for hard drinking. Expressed guilt over the fact that during a short period in the Service Police during the war he had had to arrest men for types of offences which he had committed himself, such as appearing in public improperly dressed, and other mild "crimes".

Competence of self and membership groups. Believes you can make yourself felt politically by being active in your local political party. Has considerable confidence in his own and other people's capacity to control the environment.

Attitudes to parents and authorities. Has a great admiration for his father who is a chronic invalid. Says father has spent himself in the service of others. Considers he was strictly brought up but was better off than most Bethnal Green children as he was not turned

---

[1] The expression of such views by an active Labour Party member is commoner than might be supposed. People join political parties (and other organisations) for a variety of reasons, but certainly not always because they know and support all their basic tenets.

out to play in the streets. Thinks most Bethnal Green parents neglect their children. Compares his own and his father's disciplinary methods—says he is less strict and gives various reasons including the fact it is easier to be indulgent to one child than to six. Speaks highly of his (Jewish) employer. Regards strikes as wrong. Not bothered by class distinctions. Clearly aware of the existence of a social scale and the possibilities of mobility but doesn't want to change and doesn't care if his son doesn't. As long as the boy trains for a good job he will be happy.

Jewish stereotype. Jews are very varied. The rich ones are high and mighty, like most rich people, but the majority of them are poor and they are like everyone else.

Future outlook. Thinks there may be another war but doesn't really know. He is sure there won't be another depression, thinks prosperity is here to stay.

Reaction to interview. Friendly and co-operative. The first interview was interrupted, at which he seemed upset and asked interviewer to come back again to finish.

Rorschach. A markedly depressive record. Record too sparse for detailed picture. Depression is neurotic and not psychotic in character. Average or low average intelligence.

E.8

Personal details. Age 33. Married and has a good relationship with his wife. Three children (daughters aged 6 and 2 and a son of 4.) Occupation: carpenter. Politics: Labour. Says he is really a Communist but won't join the Party because he dislikes Stalin. Spare time activities: politics, painting and dog-racing. Tries to work out betting systems and is often sure he has succeeded, but never has enough money to try it out. No religious beliefs. Health good. Has not been unemployed. Was a senior N.C.O. during the war. Extremely carefree, easy-going person. Earns good wages (£11 a week; rent is 7s. 6d.) but spends lavishly, especially on food and on the children and is always short before next payday. "We eat big meals at the weekend and go short the rest of the week."

Social and institutional contacts. Is an active member of the local Labour party, and of a small, very left-wing political discussion group. Has several close friends. A keen trade unionist (shop steward). Frequent visits to the houses of friends, usually for political discussions. Very pleased at one interview because he had just succeeded in arranging for his best friend to come and work on the same job as himself.

Ethical views. Appears to be almost completely unconcerned with moral issues of any kind except loyalty to friends and fellow workmen. Stresses this loyalty very strongly. His wife's family are mostly criminals and keep wanting him to "come in on a job". He says he has no objection to breaking the law if he can make some money out of it, but these people are all so stupid and keep getting caught and he doesn't want to spend six months in jail. His in-laws say it is all right because the money is waiting for you when you come out but he says he doesn't think it is worth it. Makes no attempt to exercise any control over any of his children. Is mildly upset because his mother-in-law has taught his daughter to swear, but says he hopes it will have become fashionable for women to swear by the time she grows up and then it won't get her into any trouble.

Competence of self and membership groups. Tremendous self-confidence and even more belief in the power of organised groups. The aim of the discussion group he belongs to is to "ginger up the Labour party" and he obviously means this to be on a national and not just on a local level. They have started their own news sheet which he hopes will eventually develop into a daily newspaper. Thinks that when the unions fail to get what they want this is because of the lethargy of the men at the top and the task for individuals like himself is to organise things on the job and force the hands of the officials. Says, "The average trade union organiser has a nice house a bit out of the city, and he likes to get home with his weekend clear for a bit of gardening, so he is against strikes because they mean his weekend is broken into." This is especially the case with the older men who feel they have earned a rest, and so it is up to the younger ones to push things along.

Attitudes to parents and authority. Doesn't say a great deal about his parents. Speaks quite critically of his father with whom he disagrees politically, but also expresses sympathy with his father's position (a crippled ex-regular soldier). Seems to have had a much closer relationship with his mother. Says he was very strictly brought up but has no stories of beatings or severe punishments. Is very anti-authoritarian on principle. Believes in organising against employers, but says that he insists on having a genuine grievance before calling a strike. His present employer is a very good one—insists on a high standard of work, but pays well and is otherwise

WORKING-CLASS ANTI-SEMITE

friendly and easy going. E.8 has a great admiration for one of his
friends who won't take a job with a good employer, but looks for a
place where the men are being exploited, organises a strike and
gets things in order and then moves on elsewhere. E.8 lives in one
of the oldest and most dilapidated houses in Bethnal Green and
keeps up a running fight with his landlord over repairs. He relates
these quarrels with great glee. The landlord happens to be Jewish
but he doesn't mention this. Says he is very unpopular with the
leaders of the local Labour party because he insists on talking about
housing and other political matters when they are more interested
in arranging the annual ward picnic and matters of that sort. He was
recently thrown out of a Labour party meeting because he insisted
on asking an M.P. a lot of awkward questions.

Jewish stereotype. Says Jews are just like other people and anti-
Semitism is "silly". Criticises his wife's family for their anti-Semitism
(his mother-in-law spits after Jews in the street), and says they use
this as an excuse for not doing anything positive about their troubles.
He tells of Jews who have done him good turns. His wife is at
least moderately anti-Semitic and laughs excitedly as she tells of
some of the pre-war Fascist marches and fights.

Future outlook. Does not expect slumps or wars. Things have
improved a lot for the working man, mainly because of the unions,
and as long as they stick together things will be all right.

Reaction to interview. Invited interviewer in at once. Very friendly
and co-operative. Six interviews.

Rorschach. Mildly psychopathic, but with no signs of deterioration.
Some signs of good adjustment in personal relationships. Probably
capable of unpredictable and violent reactions if under pressure,
but not normally likely to depart from socially acceptable behaviour.

F.13

Personal details. Age 40. Married and on fairly good terms with
his wife, who is violently anti-Semitic, a rather bitter and querulous
woman of 32. No children. Occupation: owns a small shop.
Politics: Labour. Spare time activity: Boy Scout work. Some
rather vague religious beliefs ("I hold in with religion"). Health is
fairly good but he has had some illness recently. Has never been
unemployed.

Social and institutional contacts. The only organisation he belongs to
is the Boy Scouts Association. He spends a good deal of his time

in this work. Stresses the fact that he could go anywhere in the world and be accepted at once. Also emphasises the public service aspect of the work—says a lot of people believe Scouters are paid and can't believe that anyone would do all this voluntarily. Doesn't believe in trade unions. Says they are fine in principle but don't support their members enough when in trouble. Supports this with a story about his brother who was wrongfully dismissed from a job.

Ethical views. Very emphatic about the virtues of tolerance and a policy of "live and let live". Stresses the importance of co-operation, says people can do anything if they work together. Would like to see a coalition between the Conservative and Labour parties— "With their money and our brains we could go a long way."

Competence of self and membership groups. Clearly believes that many things are in his power and are worth attempting. Has a number of economic worries including some debts, but has arranged these in order of priority and is working them off systematically. Somewhat conflicting views about groups. Everything is fine, given co-operation, but this is hard to achieve. Distinctly more sure of himself than of other people. Says you can make yourself felt politically and can get support against officialdom by putting pressure on your M.P. Feels he has been successful in this respect.

Attitudes to parents and authorities. Says little about his parents. Maintains contact with his mother who is very old. Says that in principle he believes in fairly strict discipline but in practice finds it pleasanter to be easy going. Likes working on his own, making his own conditions and not taking orders.

Jewish stereotype. Says Jews are hard workers and very co-operative. Knows they are unpopular, thinks this is due to ignorance and jealousy. Has some Jewish friends and knows the factual answers to several typical anti-Semitic accusations, including a real knowledge of the work of the Jewish Board of Guardians.

Future outlook. His own expectations are quite favourable. He expects to have his debts settled and his business in order in the near future. Thinks the country will be safe economically because of the strength of the Labour party. Expects that eventually there will be another war which will be "a terrible affair". Mentions Biblical prophecies in connection with this.

Reaction to interview. Seemed genuinely friendly and co-operative. After first interview checked up on interviewer's story by telephoning New Zealand House (told interviewer about this several weeks later), but thereafter showed no signs of distrust. Six interviews including two visits to interviewer's home.

Rorschach. A rather anxious personality with considerable repression, but also signs of good social adjustment. Personality is well controlled but not rigid. Probably above average intelligence but too inhibited to make full use of it.

G.5

Personal details. Age 41. Married and on very affectionate terms with his wife. Four children (eldest 14) and has adopted an orphan nephew. Occupation: truck driver. Politics: Labour. Spare time activity: gardening and furniture making—has made most of the furniture in the house. No religious beliefs. Has had a good deal of unemployment including two periods of nearly six months (these were before and shortly after marriage), but says "When I was laid off I fiddled a bit here and there, did odd jobs of polishing, and picked up any job I could find. I got along all right." Health good at present, but had what he describes as a slight stroke before the war but recovered well enough to go abroad in the army. Two of the children are in poor health and were in a convalescent home at the time of the first interview.

Social and institutional contacts. No clubs, but has a number of close friends. He and his wife do more joint visiting and going to parties than is usual in Bethnal Green, including visiting friends on the opposite side of London. (This is very rare.) Belongs to a union but is not keen and doesn't attend meetings.

Ethical views. Says very little on this point. Remarked as an aside that he thinks gambling (by which he apparently means betting on horses and dogs) is a disease. Is a pools enthusiast. His chief reason for disapproving of betting seems to be that people grumble when they lose. "I like cheerful people—can't stand grumblers. I don't go to the pub much now because the people there are always grumbling. If everything else is all right they have lost some money on the dogs. Well, if that's the case its their own fault and there's no use grumbling about it."

Competence of self and membership groups. Seems to have much more confidence in himself than in most others. His remark on his unemployment experience is typical of his feelings about himself,—he can get along all right. As far as groups are concerned he is more uncertain, inclined to complain that people don't stick together and support each other enough. He is also very critical of the taxation policy of the government, saying he didn't think it was in the best interests of the working class.

Attitudes to parents and to authority. His father died when he was small. He speaks very affectionately of his mother. He and his wife had a discussion on their respective upbringings during one of the interviews. She told stories about unpredictable behaviour on the part of her parents who quarrelled a lot. One of her brothers ran away from home for fear of the father. He says that the great thing about his mother was that she always meant what she said. She could be quite strict but "you always knew where you were with her". He is not much bothered by discipline—says he found the army all right—the discipline was easier than he expected. He is very easygoing with his own children. When he talks about them it is in terms of their health, happiness and educational progress. (He is very proud of his eldest daughter who has won a grammar school place.) Speaks favourably of his employer and of employers generally. His main complaints about authority are directed at the government.

Jewish stereotype. Jews are good and bad the same as anyone else. "People say they are crafty and beat the Englishmen at business. In that case the Englishman should wake up and run his business a bit better. You always get better service in a Jewish shop." His wife doesn't like Jews: "she doesn't even like me working for one. I've nearly always worked for Jewish governors and they have all been decent blokes. Of course they like to see the work being done and the money rolling in but that applies to everyone. If you are running a business there is no use in running it at a loss." Says you can always tell a Jew by his looks. Jewish women have very lovely hair, long and jet black, just like his wife. One of his sisters married a Jew to the great distress of all her relatives except G.5 who likes his brother-in-law. He told a story about an Englishman offering black market petrol to a Jew who refused to have anything to do with it.

Future outlook. Seems happy about his own prospects and talks chiefly about his plans for improving the house. He has just had electricity installed with money saved by putting aside threepenny bits. His next aim is to instal a bath. He doesn't know whether to expect another war or not. He doesn't think there will be another slump, especially because of the amount of work involved in the housing programme. "Even a door knocker has to be made by someone."

Reaction to interview. Very friendly. Invited interviewer inside at second interview and got his wife to make tea. She was very uneasy and suspicious until interviewer had produced his credentials. She says he is too easy going and happy-go-lucky. Five interviews including a visit with his wife to the interviewer's home.

Rorschach. Mildly obsessional character. Slow to adjust to new situations but adaptable if given time. Probably not an easy mixer at first but capable of good social adjustment. Some indications of depressive tendencies.

H.3

Personal details. Age 40. Married and has a good relationship with his wife. Two children (boys aged 5 and 2). Occupation: electrician. Politics: Labour. Spare time activity: gardening, and does private work for extra income. Some vague religious beliefs. Health good. Has had little unemployment but encountered difficulties when he tried to run his own electrical business before the war, though he did not actually go bankrupt.

Social and institutional contacts. No clubs but has a number of close friends including a farming family with whom he and his family spend their holidays. Belongs to a trade union and is in favour of it but thinks unions should take less part in politics. He is particularly upset by union support for Communists. Would like to have more social contacts and go to evening classes. Thinks this will be possible when the children are older.

Ethical views. Seems little concerned with moral questions. Says he used to be a "wide boy" before he was married, when he was a fairground attendant. Is very emphatic about the virtues of tolerance, says there is a Communist at work who is always jeering at anyone with religious beliefs. "I'm not a churchgoing man but if someone goes to church he should be respected for it. I don't like people scoffing at religion. It's the same with these race hatreds and things like that." Says he "wants to do more for my children than was done for me". Is very emphatic on matters concerned with his wife and children that their happiness was what counted—"the home must always come first".

Competence of self and membership groups. Has considerable faith in his own ability. Even if he lost his job he would get on all right. He could take up truck driving and he has some experience as a carpenter. "I would be prepared to take any of these jobs, or go road sweeping to keep some income flowing. It doesn't pay to be proud about your work." He has two disabilities that worry him— he wasn't well educated and he is very short. He would get on better if he had more education—he feels this is chiefly why his business failed. Also people take more notice of a tall person. Feels secure because he works for a well-established and prosperous firm. Working men are better off to-day than before the war and this is largely due to unions.

Attitudes to parents and authority. Says he had rather a hard time when young because his parents were so poor. He lost a good deal of his schooling through having to help on his father's stall in the market. He regrets this now but at the time he enjoyed it. He thought his parents were very good—he never remembers being beaten—but when they said something you could be certain they meant it. He is mildly critical of his employer. Is very indulgent to his children, saying that strict discipline is all very well in its way but he prefers to be free and easy. He would like to work on his own but feels he owes it to his family to have a secure job.

Jewish stereotype. "Like everyone else they are good and bad. Some have long noses, and some, especially the older ones, have foreign accents, and some you can't tell from anyone else."

Future outlook. Feels that he himself is well established and will continue to do well. Says he is happier now than at any other period in his life. Expects things to be quite good in future especially when the housing problem has been overcome. He doesn't expect another depression but fears there may be another war if present trends continue.

Attitude to interview. Seemed willing to help by answering questions but doubtful of his being much use. Became easier as interviewer seemed glad to get his opinions. By the end of the second interview was very friendly. Three interviews, inviting the interviewer in for tea at the last one and introducing his wife.

Rorschach. Slightly below average intelligence. A rather unusual record that is difficult to fit into the usual psychiatric categories. Perhaps a mild psychopath, and some depressive traits. Definite feelings of inferiority.

H.7

Personal details. Age 58. Married. Four children aged 18 to 28. Occupation: labourer. Politics: Labour. No particular spare time interests except football pools. No religious beliefs. Health good. Has had long stretches of unemployment, especially during the early twenties when he was first married.

Social and institutional contacts. No clubs, but some close friends whom he visits occasionally with his wife and family. Belongs to a trade union and attends meetings.

Ethical views. Says he doesn't like swearing. He finds it difficult to work with men who are always grumbling and swearing. He expressly objects to having rigid rules of conduct for people. "I don't mind a man who has a drink but I don't like a man who has a drink and then becomes noisy and quarrelsome and upsets his neighbours." Emphasises the need for tolerance. "I have no time for race hatred. If you are going to try and build communities you have got to get rid of that. If you hate one person you will probably hate others and then there is not getting on with people at all." He says the main political problem of to-day is providing enough food for the world.

Competence of self and membership groups. He is the only subject rated more than one point lower for his confidence in himself than in his group: practically all his feeling of strength seems to come from his sense of group solidarity and competence. Alone he can do very little, but as a member of a group (the working classes) he is safe. He carries this to its logical conclusion and assumes that because prospects are bright for the working class they are bright for him, in spite of his personal weakness. The working class constitute a majority in the country, he says; so as long as they vote solidly together the Labour party will win and their interests will be protected.

Attitudes to parents and authority. He said very little about his parents. Says he doesn't think family life in Bethnal Green has changed much since he was a child. People there have always been fairly free and easy with their children. "I know my parents did their best for me but I still feel I have only been dragged up and not brought up to live properly and get the best out of life. In the same way I haven't been able to do the best for my children in spite of wanting to." He is moderately anti-authoritarian. He dislikes the rich and says the working class have always had to fight for their rights, and will have to continue to do this, but he distinguishes between good and bad employers and is emphatic about doing things constitutionally. He is very egalitarian in his views—says everyone has the same brains and going to University is purely a matter of opportunity. His sons could have gone if he had been able to send them. This is the main type of social reform he would like to see in the future.

Jewish stereotype. Jews are like other people except in appearance. He has had a number of Jewish workmates and always got on well with them. Jews are easy to pick out in the street, "as easy as Negroes". Regards himself as exceptional in the neighbourhood in not being anti-Semitic. "If you had gone to any other house in the street, and *if* they had answered the door, and *if* they had been prepared to talk, they would have been up in arms as soon as you had mentioned the Jews." Jews were even more unpopular when he was young.

Future outlook. This all depends on working class solidarity, but on the whole he thinks it will be all right. There is a good chance of continued peace.

Reaction to interview. Very friendly and co-operative at the first meeting. The second visit was made at his suggestion but by the time interviewer arrived he seemed to have regretted it and was much more reserved on the second occasion. Would not do the Rorschach test.

K.1

Personal details. Age 30. Married. Two children (boys aged 4 and 9): Occupation: railway porter. Politics: Labour. Sparetime activities: football pools and dog racing, but can't afford to go to the dogs often. Would like to have a garden. No religious beliefs. Health good. Had a good deal of unemployment before getting his present job, which he likes, in spite of the low pay, because it is "regular and certain".

Social and institutional contacts. No clubs, no close friends. A keen trade unionist and attends meetings regularly. Says his union is trying to get a closed shop and he doesn't approve of this and is opposing it. Doesn't see much of his siblings who are scattered all over London but sees a lot of his father who lives nearby.

Ethical views. His objection to the closed shop was largely on ethical grounds. He says it is equivalent to making people pay for the right to work, and forcing them to obey, and he doesn't think this is right. He doesn't believe in having more rules and regulations than are absolutely necessary.

Competence of self and membership groups. Thinks unions do a lot for their members—they can usually get what the members want in terms of hours and conditions of work. At the same time it is easy to put forward your point of view in the union. Meetings are frequent and it is easy to express your opinion.

Attitudes to parents and authority. Expresses admiration and affection for his father. In spite of his 80 years he still travels about and goes away for holidays. He is a man who has always managed to enjoy life. Is very proud of his own children. Says very little about authority though his remarks on trade unions seem to imply that he is prepared to accept authority and have all his dealings with it through constitutional means.

Jewish stereotype. Jews have a distinctive physical appearance, but are otherwise much like everyone else. They have some different customs and different ways of cooking. One good thing about them is that they support each other and always live together in groups.

Future outlook. He thinks the chances of maintaining peace are good. Prosperity is also fairly safe. Even if there were another depression he would be all right now he has a permanent job.

Reaction to interview. Not an easy man to interview as he was rather brief and vague in his answers. Was friendly but seemed not particularly interested. Would not do the Rorschach test. Two interviews.

N.1

Personal details. Age 35. Married and on very good terms with his wife. Four children, age 14 to 3. Occupation: carrier—owns his own truck. Politics: Liberal. Spare time activities: social drinking, visiting friends and relatives. Religious beliefs: was brought up a Roman Catholic—says he doesn't go to church now but has retained most of his beliefs. Health good. Has never been unemployed —inherited his business from his father and has never been in serious difficulties.

Social and institutional contacts. No clubs but has numerous close friends and acquaintances in the neighbourhood. He spends a good deal of time with his friends either in the pub or exchanging visits. His mother and seven siblings live in two adjacent streets and he sees them all frequently. Does not belong to a trade union but is not opposed to them.

Ethical views. No very strict moral beliefs. Seems to be prepared to accept any behaviour which is not against the law and which does not cause inconvenience to other people. Frequently stresses the importance of understanding other people's point of view. Says he doesn't want his children to be hooligans and is rather anxious because there are a number of these in the area and he thinks they might pick up bad habits. Otherwise seems unconcerned by his children's behaviour and is certainly very indulgent to them.

Competence of self and membership groups. Says that if business should get bad he will have to look round and use his initiative in doing something extra on the side. "You can always get somewhere if you try hard enough." Also says you can always get your way if you set about it properly. He illustrates this with stories of his dealings with various local government officials. "The main thing is never to let people say 'No' to you, and if someone does manage it, look around for someone who will say 'Yes'."

Attitudes to parents and authority. Speaks casually but not disrespectfully of his father who is dead. Is on very affectionately free and easy terms with his mother. Says discipline is a good thing in the army as it is the thing that pulls you through in a tight spot, but in other circumstances other methods are better. Believes in keeping a watchful eye on the local M.P. and L.C.C. member to make sure they are looking after local interests. Gets very angry about doctors who are slow in answering calls or who prescribe medicine without making a proper examination. Can be quite critical of groups to which he belongs: e.g. the behaviour of the British Army in Italy. Regards class distinctions as inevitable and is inclined to boast that his brother is friendly with a peer who was his company commander in the army. Likes being his own boss and thus not having to bother conforming to other people's ideas.

Jewish stereotype. Like other people they vary. The ones he knows in Bethnal Green are very helpful. Praises their tolerance and says they never objected to clergymen taking services in shelters when they were present during the war.

Future outlook. Thinks there isn't likely to be another war. Prosperity is more doubtful but he is sure there won't be any bad slumps.

Reaction to interview. Very friendly and co-operative. The easiest man in the whole group to interview. After doing the Rorschach test he offered to find more people to do it if this would help the interviewer. Took interviewer to the pub and introduced him to his friends and relatives. Five interviews.

Rorschach. This is quite an exceptionally healthy record, from a man of slightly above average intelligence. Good control but no rigidity. Good social adjustment.

Here again it is possible to follow certain patterns right through these summaries.

(1) An implied expectation that there will be no necessary deterioration of circumstances in the future is observable in these cases. This is brought out by the repeated ambition to "give my children a good start in life", by E.8's devotion to the cause of political reform and E.13's plans to settle his business problems. The implication in all these cases seems to be that the future is to some extent controllable—it is worth making an effort to achieve one's ambitions. Even where there is no assertion that progress and good conditions are automatic (for example, A.2 was not convinced that further slumps could be avoided) the implication is that the individual and the group can plan and work to overcome, or at least to reduce, these difficulties.

(2) There is a reluctance to refer to people in terms of large groups. This is shown chiefly by the lack of stereotypes for Jews. They are described as "good and bad like everyone else", or "you can tell most Jews by their appearance, but not all of them".

(3) These tolerant individuals seem also to be tolerant in their views of what constitutes moral behaviour. Some of them express almost amoral attitudes. When they do express their views on moral issues they are usually couched in rather general terms and refer to such things as tolerance, loyalty to friends, workmates and fellow-citizens. Only passing references are made to specific types of action such as drinking, smoking, and swearing, as a test of morality. C.2 objected to heavy, solitary drinking and N.1 expressed some disapproval of the swearing of boys in the neighbourhood, linking this with a variety of other acts such as breaking windows and street lamps, and making a noise late at night, but in neither case was there any suggestion that these acts in themselves constituted a test of morality.

(4) The attitude to authority can best be described as not going to extremes. Even E.8, whose extreme left-wing views made him

highly critical of employers, was prepared to extend a due meed of praise to those among this group who seemed to him to deserve it. It is interesting to note that not one of the tolerant group falls into either of the extreme classes in respect to attitude to authority, and only one (N.1) has conflicting and obviously ambivalent attitudes. All the other individuals are rated either 2 or 4. H.3's statements about his employer are typical of this group. "Governors are easier with their men than they used to be. Some men try to take advantage of this, but I don't think this is right. I believe in doing a fair day's work for my money. My Governor at present was a major and runs the business army-style. It's all right in its way but if he was a bit more friendly it would make things easier. If he has a complaint he never makes it to you himself but does it through the foreman and the chargehand. If you've got to take a wigging it comes easier from the man at the top than from the one just above you—especially if you don't get on well with the chargehand." There seems to be an absence of strong feeling about the father's authority. Some of these men (A.2 is the most outstanding example) are able to discuss their parents with a considerable degree of objectivity. Even C.2, whose affection for his father is heightened by the latter's illness, is able to compare his own and his father's disciplinary methods without any sign of anxiety.

(5) There is a tendency for the members of this group to have a rather high degree of contact with individuals and groups outside the immediate family. Most of them are in close and frequent contact with relatives, and belong to a variety of social and political groups apart from trade unions.

The table set out on p. 142 (Table 16) shows the individual ratings for all members of this group for the variables listed in Table 9. (A rating of x indicates that insufficient data were available for rating the individual on the variable concerned.) Several factors emerge from this table. In the first place there is very little difference between feelings relating to the self and to the group as far as control over the environment is concerned. Most ratings are identical and numbers showing differences are almost equally balanced in each direction. The optimism ratings, however, reflect the general tendency for personal ratings to be higher than group ratings. A third point, the absence of extreme ratings with respect to authority, has already been noted. The most notable feature of the table is the set of ratings for unemployment. The correspondence

TABLE 16

RATINGS OF THE TOLERANT MEN

| | Variables | | | | | | | | | | | | | | | | | |
---	A.2	A.13	B.13	C.2	E.8	F.1	F.11	F.13	G.5	H.3	H.7	L.5	K.1	L.9	N.1	N.7	P.11	T.10
Control of individual over environment	4	5	4	5	5	3	X	4	4	4	2	2	4	2	4	3	5	X
Control of group over environment	5	4	5	5	5	4	4	3	3	4	4	2	5	2	4	X	5	5
Pessimism-optimism for self	4	X	4	5	5	4	X	4	5	4	4	2	5	2	4	2	5	X
Pessimism-optimism for group	4	3	4	4	5	4	4	3	4	3	4	2	5	3	4	2	4	3
Attitude to authority—leaders	2	1	1	1	4	1	1	2	1	2	1	1	1	1	3	X	2	1
Attitude to authority—followers	1	4	2	2	1	4	X	1	2	1	4	4	X	4	1	1	1	2
Isolation	5	X	X	4	5	X	4	4	4	4	4	5	3	X	5	X	4	4
Age	5	2	3	5	4	3	4	3	3	3	2	4	4	2	4	3	3	2
Unemployment	5	4	5	5	5	3	X	5	2	4	1	5	3	1	5	5	5	4

between unemployment and anti-Semitism ratings is obviously very much higher than when the whole group of 103 individuals is concerned. A detailed study of the ratings for the whole group reveals an interesting situation. The majority of people rated 5 for unemployment (i.e. those who have never been unemployed) are rated either 4 or 5 for anti-Semitism. Again nearly all those rated 5 for anti-Semitism are rated either 4 or 5 for unemployment. Apart from this, however, the ratings are scattered at random over both scales. The situation seems to be that while it is, on the whole, rather unlikely that a person who has experienced a great deal of unemployment will be tolerant there is no direct connection between *amount* of unemployment and *degree* of anti-Semitism. Some unemployment is rather likely to be associated with some degree of anti-Semitism, but the relationship cannot be stated more exactly than this. A relatively slight experience of unemployment may be associated with a great deal of anti-Semitism, and vice versa. This relationship is illustrated in the following table.

TABLE 17

DISTRIBUTION OF ANTI-SEMITISM IN RELATION
TO EXPERIENCE OF UNEMPLOYMENT

	Anti-Sem. 4 and 5	Anti-Sem. 1, 2, and 3
Unemployment 4 and 5 .	41	19
Unemployment 1, 2, and 3 .	13	16

These figures give $X^2 = 4 \cdot 5$. $P < 0 \cdot 05$ indicating that the relationship is significant.

It would therefore appear that unemployment can become a factor in the causation of anti-Semitism only in conjunction with other factors.

Finally there is the question of the number of anxiety-creating situations appearing in the lives of these individuals. Once again, only those who were interviewed at least twice are described. A.2, H.3, H.7, K.1, show no evidence of any important source of anxiety. E.8 and N.1 live in very bad housing conditions but are otherwise free of major troubles. C.2's father is seriously ill, F.13 has business difficulties and debts, G.5 still has some of the after-effects of a slight stroke and two of his children suffer from poor health. Thus, of this group, only three members have serious objective anxieties. Two others have anxieties of a lesser degree. This proportion is markedly lower than is the case with the extreme anti-Semites, all of whom have some cause for anxiety.

TABLE 18

DISTRIBUTION OF ANTI-SEMITISM IN RELATION TO ANXIETY-CREATING SITUATIONS

	Obvious cause for anxiety	No obvious cause for anxiety
Anti-Semites .	7	1
Tolerant .	3	6

These figures give the value of X^2 as 5·13. P < 0·03.

CHAPTER VIII

The Prejudiced Personality

THE results of the interviews and tests having been thus detailed, the next task is to state these results in a general form in order to show more briefly and clearly the difference between the characteristics displayed by the tolerant and anti-Semitic individuals. This chapter is intended to be chiefly a summary of the data presented in more detail in the last three chapters; the significance and implications of the data will be discussed and dealt with subsequently.

As the Rorschach records revealed some clear differences between the two groups, a classification based on these provides a starting point for comparison. On the whole it is obvious that the general level of mental health is higher in the tolerant group. It is true that there is a good deal of overlap, as all of the records show some signs of maladjustment, but whereas the two most markedly healthy records (A.2 and N.1) are from tolerant individuals, all of those showing clear-cut psychotic trends (B.6, C.7, and F.14) are from the prejudiced group. The most severely disturbed of the tolerant group is C.2, who appears from the Rorschach record to have a personality of a markedly depressive type. His interview material is consistent with this diagnosis though here the indications are less marked. Of the remaining prejudiced records three (S.11, Q.7, and G.2) are remarkable chiefly for the degree of repression indicated. The other prejudiced record (O.2) shows a high degree of neurotic disturbance, a diagnosis borne out by his interview record. F.13 is the only tolerant record showing marked signs of repression. The remaining tolerant records (E.8, G.5, H.3) do not fall into any obvious group. They all show various signs of disturbance but none of a severe character.

So much for the bare clinical classification. Much more important are the more detailed personality traits obtained from the interviews. A considerable beginning can be made by studying the correlations given in Chapter VI. Anti-Semites tend to be rather pessimistic about the future, as they feel that there are difficult times in store both for themselves individually and also for the groups upon whose welfare they depend. Because of their lack of confidence in their own ability and power as well as that of the groups to which they belong and from which they might expect support and protection, they cannot hold out much hope of overcoming these difficulties. One outstanding trait of these individuals is that they manage to imply both strength and weakness at the same time. They are strong, good, intelligent, hard-working and altogether worthy, and the people like themselves, the people with whom they identify, are similarly outstanding. But at the same time circumstances are too much for them. Fate, traitors, outsiders, the forces of events, are against them and somehow just cannot be overcome. They know how to get things done, how to oppose the boss and win disputes, but the trade union leaders are in the bosses' pay and will not move, and they can "rig" elections so that honest men cannot unseat them. The British people can produce plenty of goods to sell in order to keep up the national income; they are capable, hard-working people with ample ability to make the best, but people overseas will mismanage themselves into a slump and be unable to buy these goods, so that all the Britons' work will have gone for nothing. F.14's boast, "I am one of the true breed of Englishmen. I would starve before I licked the boots of any governor, and so would any true Englishman," is preceded by the statement that there are very few true Englishmen left now and the country is rotten to the core, and is followed later by the complaint that the competition of foreign workers is so strong that it is always necessary for the worker to do what the employer wishes, whether he likes it or not, because the alternative is to be replaced immediately; as there are few jobs available, a quarrel with an employer means almost certain unemployment.

The general picture is of an individual constricted, thwarted and shut in by external forces and by other people. He has little hope or self-confidence, but this is always due not to his defects but to the overwhelming difficulties of a hostile environment. His stereotypes of the Jew are largely in terms of political and economic power.

The anti-Semite who is in a central or leading position, who has some feeling of being an authority of sorts himself, is extremely anti-authoritarian in his attitude. He prides himself on his ability to stand up for himself, he assails his employer, the government and authority in general. He is, in his own estimation at least, a rebel. To what extent these attitudes are carried over into practice is a matter of some doubt. One suspects that, on the whole, they are not. The behaviour of G.2, Q.7, and S.11 in the interview situation and the inconsistencies in the statements made by F.14 and O.2 about their relations with employers suggest that these anti-authoritarian attitudes are largely a façade, a picture which they like to believe is true but which, in fact, is not painted from life. The anti-Semite who is in a follower situation is very different in his attitude—he is markedly submissive. For him obedience is almost always better than disobedience, though veiled and implied criticisms suggest that unadmitted rebellion smoulders beneath the obedient surface. The real situation seems to be that the anti-Semitic individual feels highly resentful of authority but is unable to express this in open rebellion of even the mildest type. Those anti-Semites who themselves qualify as leaders get as far as expressing rebellious sentiments in private but are probably as meek as the followers when actually facing their superiors. Even when questioned directly they say less about their employers than the tolerant individuals. This is understandable if the only statements they find it possible to make on the subject are in some sense untrue. It is probably significant that the only anti-Semite who talks freely about his employer is F.14—the most nearly psychotic member of the group, and therefore the least concerned about the degree to which his statements correspond to reality.

The relatively low correlation between anti-Semitism and submissiveness on the part of followers (see Table 9) seems to be due to (a) the very submissive attitude of most of the mildly anti-Semitic followers (the majority of those rated 4 for anti-Semitism are rated 2 for attitude to authority), and (b) the consistently moderate attitude of the tolerant group. The poor correlation is not reflected when the ratings for individuals with anti-Semitic scores of 1 and 2 are studied. Of the 15 followers in these categories only one is rated as moderately anti-authoritarian; all the others are rated 1, 2, or 3.

There is, however, one type of authority which the anti-Semites do not oppose. Throughout the records there is hardly a breath of criticism about their parents. Occasionally they refuse to talk about them, but usually they praise them highly even for those actions which bring discomfort to their children. Punishments, for example, are always just, even when severe. They in their turn are very much aware of their own duties as parents. The future well-being, both material and moral, of their children is their responsibility, and they feel its weight. O.2 is probably the most extreme example of this kind of attitude. He gives an account of his parents, which, if true (and he obviously accepts it as such) shows his father to be a pretty poor character, irresponsible and careless of the welfare of his wife and children. O.2's parents have separated, and he has a very high regard for his mother, but in spite of this, and in spite of the obvious implication of his statements about his father, he contrives to support both sides, does not draw the logical conclusions about his father's qualities as a husband and parent, but praises his ability as a craftsman. At the same time he is anxious and distressed about his responsibilities for the moral welfare of his own two sons.

This concern with moral responsibilities is often associated with some kind of rather rigid notion of right and wrong, usually in connection with some particular topic, which varies a great deal. Within this area the anti-Semite will pride himself on his conspicuous virtue. The implication is not that this particular piece of behaviour is more sensible or useful—the connotation is strongly moralistic.

The anti-Semites are not sociable beings, even among themselves. They keep within their own families, go for solitary walks, read a great deal, and go to the cinema for relaxation. With the exception of S.11 not one of the extreme group belongs to any organisation having a social purpose. They do not even, as a rule, have a great deal to do with their relatives. This absence of social contacts and activities is not openly described as a disadvantage; in fact the subject may assert that is his own wish ("I prefer to keep myself to myself", was a common remark), but other statements invariably carried the implication that it *was* a disadvantage: it was no use trying to be friendly with the neighbours, because they would use the opportunity to pry into one's affairs; clubs used to be quite good and worth joining, but nowadays the wrong people were in charge and it was not worth bothering about; if you tried to do the right thing by your relatives they just turned their backs on you as soon as they had got what they wanted. In one sense this lack of social contacts is just another example of the way in which anti-Semites feel themselves to be constricted and constrained by outside people and forces. It is interesting to note the correspondence between the distribution of FC responses on the Rorschach record (these responses are normally associated with good social adjustment), and the rating for social isolation. These responses are rare among the anti-Semites, three of them having one such response each. The correlation found between anti-Semitism and social isolation for the whole group of subjects supports the view that the distribution of FC responses would probably be significant in a larger group.

On the question of anxiety the picture is less clear. In a sense they can all be classified as anxious; their pessimism, lack of confidence, and general neuroticism all testify to this. To take these as an index of anxiety is merely to be repetitive, for these terms have already been used to describe the anti-Semitic subjects. If anxiety is to be a useful and meaningful category for a separate measurement it must be used to refer to something other than that implied by these terms. The anxiety lying behind these other indications is not directly expressed but has to be inferred. It is revealed in the form of neurotic symptoms and in other ways. In the present context anxiety must be more directly expressed. As far as the Rorschach test is concerned, only S.11 gives a clear indication of the presence of free-floating anxiety, while from the interview material only C.7 could definitely be classified as showing anxiety in this form. There are equally few direct expressions of anxiety relating to specific topics. In the Rorschach records O.2 and S.11 exhibit clear signs of anxiety relating to sex, while O.2's anxiety seems to be particularly associated with homosexual drives. This also came out (though less directly) in the interview material. It would appear that the anti-Semites cannot be described as readily and directly expressing anxiety, but they do express it in considerable measure by oblique means such as neurotic symptoms and expressions of pessimism and powerlessness in the face of environmental pressures. These are not verbalised as anxieties—usually they are cast in the form of matter-of-fact statements.

There are three other points which are not actually dimensions of personality but which should be mentioned here. The first is that anti-Semites tend to be older than the tolerant individuals. This tendency is marked enough to be statistically significant. The mean age for the extreme anti-Semites is 56·1, while that for the tolerant group is 41·8. Secondly, there is a significant tendency for anti-Semites to be affected by realistic anxiety-creating situations. It should be noticed, however, that in the majority of cases the individuals did not themselves directly express their anxiety over these matters. Very often even the existence of the situation was referred to only obliquely, while matters which were of less importance were emphasised. Thus, while the extreme anti-Semites lived in much better houses than did the tolerant group, they complained much more about the housing situation. In this context it is worth noting that when these men were asked who they thought should be given priority in new housing areas the anti-Semites nearly always named a group which would include themselves (the most obvious case was I.4 who said that priority should be given to old people without children) while the more tolerant men nearly always said, regardless of their own circumstances, "People with young children", or "the people who are in the worst houses now". The third point is that the relation between the occurrence in the past of a given type of anxiety-creating situation, i.e. unemployment, and the existence of anti-Semitic traits, was of comparatively slight significance.

Turning now to the tolerant individuals we find a very different picture. In the case of most of the traits studied by means of correlations for the whole group, the tolerant men display characteristics which are the opposite of those shown by the anti-Semites. They are optimistic both for themselves and the groups to which they belong. In the situations which they have to face alone they are prepared at least to give a good account of themselves, and in general they expect to succeed. Where they depend on the functioning of a group they again feel that the prospects are good. They have confidence that they themselves and the people who represent them are capable of coping with the problems set up by the external environment. They see their fellow men and other nations and groups not as sinister powers, incapable fools and rogues, but rather as relatively co-operative beings without sinister intentions. Fate is seen in a kindlier light and economic forces viewed with less gloom. They do not, as a general rule, expect wars and slumps in the immediate future, and they feel that if they occur they can be dealt with—wars will be won, and slumps will not be as severe as in the past. Their ideas are expansive, they do not feel shut in and controlled, they can make their own decisions and rely on themselves to carry them out. Mention of weaknesses tends to consist of realistic discussions of difficulties which have to be allowed for, rather than complaints about frustrating circumstances.

The tolerant individuals have much less to say about the ability of themselves and their groups to control the environment. The anti-Semites tend to be either completely pessimistic, or else very boastful with an admission that insuperable difficulties set their abilities at naught. In either case they talk about it a great deal. The tolerant people take the situation much more for granted. Their statements imply, rather than express directly, a feeling that something can be done about difficulties. They give an impression of something like quiet confidence as against the active disquiet of the anti-Semites. Tolerant people nearly always had to be asked direct questions on these topics, while anti-Semites talked about them spontaneously.

The idea of deterioration which is so constant a feature of the anti-Semitic attitude is missing from the tolerant people. This is one aspect of the tendencies towards optimism that show up so clearly in Tables 15 and 16.[1]

In the case of attitudes to authority, the contrast between the tolerant individuals and the anti-Semites is of a different kind. The tolerant men have no extreme attitudes on the subject; they do not produce a single authority rating of either 1 or 5 and the distribution of 2, 3, and 4 ratings does not show any really significant difference between the two groups of leaders and followers. All that can be said is that tolerant individuals tend to take a moderate and tolerant attitude to authorities. They may have an inclination to acceptance or opposition, but this is tempered by considerations reflecting the situation in which they find themselves. Thus, E.8, whose ideological leanings were very definitely in the direction of anti-authoritarianism, is prepared to make a realistic assessment of any given employer, and "give the devil his due". His attitudes, though undoubtedly inclined in one direction, are flexibile rather than rigid. The impression is gained that, unlike the anti-Semites, the tolerant men are expressing something approximating to their real feelings on the subject.

[1] An interesting sidelight on the way in which anti-Semites tend to be obsessed with ideas of deterioration can be seen in the speeches of the Fascists, and the articles in their paper *Union*. There one finds the constantly reiterated assertion that Fascism will come to power when the country is faced by some overwhelming disaster. Some of these speeches and articles almost give the impression of being a prayer for the rapid arrival of such a disaster.

The same kind of situation applies to attitudes to parental authority. Tolerant individuals are much more critical of their parents than anti-Semites, though they are not necessarily less attached to them. Thus we find A.2 discussing whether his father's death had a good or bad effect on his development, and stating that his father had been much too severe in his punishments. E.8 paints a picture of his parents which is critical but affectionate, while H.3 and N.1 describe their fathers in terms which one feels to be accurate and realistic, but which at the same time imply considerable respect and affection. Their chief concern with regard to their children is to provide for their general health, happiness, and future welfare. They tend to say that they *want* to do this rather than they feel they *ought* to do it. H.3 says "I want to give my children the things I haven't been able to have." A.2 talks of the plans he has made to see that his children will have a good chance educationally. This is not to suggest that they are not concerned with the moral aspects of their children's upbringing; in fact A.2, G.5, and N.1 all express some anxiety because of the difficulties which the environment provides in this respect; but they lack the rigid, obsessive interest in the matter displayed by the anti-Semites.

They also lack the rigidly moralistic attitude of the intolerant group. E.8 goes so far as to say that only the fear of prison keeps him from crime. None of the others show this degree of contempt for the conventions though H.3 cheerfully admits that he has been on the fringe of illegal activities in his days as a fairground attendant. In most cases the attitude is one of flexibility, of dealing with circumstances on their merits, rather than one of opposition to existing codes, and in viewing morality as applying to behaviour and attitudes in general rather than with reference to a particular kind of action such as drinking or smoking. The tolerant people seem to be able to accept that they will not be virtuous all the time, but the intolerant cannot do this, so equate virtue with some specific type of behaviour, and by strictly observing this "virtue" are able to assure themselves that they are virtuous people.

Social activities are much more prominent among the tolerant than the intolerant. Membership of organisations providing social contacts is the rule rather than the exception, and only in one case is there given a rating lower than 4 on the isolation scale. Contacts with friends and relatives are frequent and friendly, and include exchange of visits, parties, and other functions. Only two of this group do not score at least one FC response on the Rorschach test. Here again the approach of the tolerant people is an expansive one.

The indications of free-floating anxiety in the Rorschach records are only slightly greater in the case of the tolerant individuals than with the anti-Semites, and the difference is certainly not significant. Only two individuals can confidently be classified as displaying free-floating anxiety on the basis of this test. As far as the interview records are concerned only G.5 and F.13 can be characterised in this way. (F.13 is also one of the two who show this reaction in the Rorschach test.) It would therefore appear that indications of free-floating anxiety are not reliably diagnostic between these two groups. When direct expressions of anxiety on specific subjects are concerned the differences become greater. Four Rorschach records show a reaction of this kind—three in relation to sex, and one in relation to death. The tolerant subjects verbalise their anxieties on specific topics much more directly and freely than is the case with anti-Semites. Thus, in considering a move to Canada, A.2 expressed his fear of being discriminated against as a stranger when he settled there; C.2 expressed fears over his father's health; F.13 had a variety of economic and health troubles, and so on. It is not so much the existence of these difficulties (the anti-Semitic group had more difficulties—and more serious ones—to face) that is important, but the readiness with which they are faced and verbalised. Expressions of the kind "I an worried about . . ." or "I am afraid of . . ." were much more common in the tolerant records. In the anti-Semitic records it is possible to locate these areas of anxiety, but the tolerant people were inclined to point them out and talk about them, instead of leaving it to the interviewer to infer them from indirect indications.

It would therefore appear that the existence of anxiety-creating situations, and the direct verbalisation of the anxiety created, are both diagnostic between these groups but in opposite senses—i.e. while the intolerant group is affected more by these situations, the tolerant men talk more directly about the smaller number with which they are faced. This conclusion is consistent with the findings of Adorno and his associates (1950, pp. 412–13).

Summing up the position as far as the hypotheses put forward in Chapter II are concerned we can say that the results set out in the preceding four chapters have supported the majority of these hypotheses. A.(3), dealing with the correlation between free-floating anxiety and anti-Semitism, must be regarded as being opposed by the data obtained and should be abandoned and replaced by that set out in the preceding paragraph, namely that anti-Semitism is negatively correlated with a willingness to verbalise anxieties directly. A.(1) (a) on the relation between paranoid tendencies and anti-Semitism has been little affected by the data produced. The only subject clearly displaying these characteristics was strongly anti-Semitic and to this extent the hypothesis is supported, but such evidence is certainly not sufficient for it to be regarded as established. It remains, however, worthy of further testing. The remaining hypotheses are all supported by the results recorded and can be accepted as true for the population under study. The extent to which they can be generalised to other populations is discussed in the next chapter.

The failure to produce any worthwhile evidence on the association between paranoid tendencies and anti-Semitism is perhaps a little surprising in view of the frequency with which they are associated in the literature (cf. Lowy, 1948, p. 100, and Rose, 1948, p. 296). It seems probable that this emphasis has been at least partly due to a very loose use of the term paranoid. In its correct usage paranoia is a "psychosis presenting delusions of persecution of a pretty clearly defined type, well supported and defended by the patient, in other words, systematised", while "paranoid", "paranoic", and "paranoiac" are adjectival forms of this term, the last being normally used to refer to milder forms of the disorder. Thus "paranoiac character" is defined as "the character traits of the individual prior to the time that he develops the full-fledged paranoic syndrome. The projection mechanism is foremost in that the individual constantly blames the environment for his difficulties". (These definitions are all taken from Hinsie and Shatsky, 1940.) There seems to be a tendency on the part of many writers to equate projection with paranoia and to speak of any projective reaction as "paranoid". Such usage is unwarranted and confusing and in this book the term has been restricted to reactions which are clearly delusional and psychotic in character. Projective mechanisms of various kinds are found in many conditions apart from paranoia and to equate "projective" with "paranoid" can only result in confusion.

CHAPTER IX

A Theory of Anti-Semitism

I N the preceding chapters several kinds of data have been presented, principally the results of the theoretical speculations and observations of other students of anti-Semitism, the results of a general study of the whole Bethnal Green community, and finally the results of a study of a number of specific members of this community. An attempt will now be made, on the basis of this material, to produce a general theory of the origins and causes of anti-Semitism as exhibited in individuals. There are certain necessary limitations to such an attempt which need to be carefully noted.

The first of these is the problem of generalising from the data collected in a single area. There is no definite rule to be followed here, apart from the necessity of noting that this is, in fact, being done. To generalise from a particular instance is perfectly legitimate provided that the resultant generalisation is recognised as an hypothesis and not put forward as a definite statement of fact. The hypothesis, if properly formulated, can then be the basis for further research. Moreover, such an hypothesis can be a useful basis for an action programme, e.g. a programme designed to reduce racial prejudice in a community, even when the community concerned is not the one in which the research was carried out, since action based on such an hypothesis is, as a general rule, more likely to be successful than one based on mere guesswork and intuition.

Where other research on the same subject has been carried out in other types of communities the conclusions based on the combined results are much more trustworthy than those based on a single piece of research. This is particularly true in cases where the results obtained in the various communities deal with the same aspects of the problem and are in close agreement. In the present instance there are other studies whose results overlap to a considerable degree with those presented here, and as a consequence it is possible to put forward propositions having a fairly high degree of probability. As far as previously expounded theories are concerned, the results of a single study of this kind can, at the most, give some support to an hypothesis; they cannot prove it to be correct. They can, however, throw such serious doubt on a theory as virtually to disprove it. With these reservations in mind it is possible to proceed with the development of a theory based on the results presented earlier.

One point which seems to have been established with considerable certainty is that the personality characteristics of anti-Semites and tolerant individuals are very different. The studies of Hartley, Bettelheim and Janowitz, Eysenck, Adorno and associates, and the present research all reach this same conclusion: indeed there appears to have been no case in which a study on these lines was attempted with negative results. We thus have, in very general and imprecise terms, an answer to the question, "Who becomes anti-Semitic?"—namely, individuals whose personality type predisposes them to this kind of reaction. Such an answer does little more than open the way to a whole series of more specific questions: are there several personality types which constitute predisposition, or do they fall into a single category? Does the existence of a personality type of this kind necessarily imply an anti-Semitic attitude or is it necessary to activate and canalise the predisposition? If this latter alternative is correct, what situations and events are effective in converting the predisposition into an actuality? Under what circumstances does the predisposed personality develop?

As a beginning to providing an answer to these questions we can set up an hypothetical account of the way in which an anti-Semite develops in Bethnal Green, ignoring for a moment the wider aspects of the problem, and then examine this picture in the light of the results of other researches and of general social science theory.

According to the account given in Chapter III the typical individual in Bethnal Green reaches adulthood holding a somewhat precarious balance between his affectional needs and the love, support, and friendship provided by his environment, and with little expectation that the environment will prove to be stable and supportive. On logical grounds one can immediately indicate two possible types of deviants (there may, of course, be others as well).

One type of deviation from this norm would occur when the individual, in childhood, did not experience the deprivations described. The possibility of a healthy and integrated personality developing would then be increased, and variations from this norm would in any case be different from the typical character structure described earlier. The second type of deviant consists of those whose early experiences were similar to those of the typical group but whose degree of balance or integration is less than the Bethnal Green model type. This group can conveniently be divided into those who did not ever succeed in achieving the normal precarious balance, and those who having at some time achieved it were forced off balance by some later experience. The balance, it must be recalled, is between felt needs and felt satisfaction of those needs, or felt expectation that the satisfaction will be forthcoming. The loss of balance is represented by a reduction in the amount of satisfaction that is felt to be experienced, or in the expectation that the satisfaction will be forthcoming.

A Bethnal Green child who has experienced the familiar rejection and has then failed to achieve (for whatever reason) an accepted and acceptable position in some other group could be expected not merely to have no firm expectation of support from the social environment but to develop a definite expectation that this environment would be hostile or deprivative. In the same way one could expect that the rather uneasily balanced typical personality could have his latent fears aroused and his relatively meagre expectations seriously reduced by further experience of rejection, such as desertion by his wife, or loss of a job which was emotionally of great importance to him, or rejection by a friendship group on which he depended for affectional support. Such a person would fit well into the pattern of feelings of powerlessness, pessimism, and isolation found to exist among the Bethnal Green anti-Semites.[1] This expectation would also be consistent with the observation that anti-Semites had been more often affected by anxiety-creating situations than had the tolerant individuals.

A person who experiences a disaster of any kind faces, among other things, the problem of attributing the responsibility for this experience. The blame can be placed on himself, on some other members of one of his in-groups, or on the members of an out-group. The first alternative, the depressive reaction, is not the most

[1] For an analysis of the effects of this type of past experience on future expectations see Lewin (1948), pp. 103–124, especially pp. 105–109.

commonly accepted for the rather obvious reason that it involves abandoning any supporting ideas of his own worth. The second possibility implies an ending of ties with the in-group or groups chosen for blame; to a Bethnal Green man who values his group membership so highly this would be an extremely serious step. With his group ties reduced in number and lowered in strength he clings all the more grimly to those he has and therefore he cannot face the consequences of turning his blame on to them. An indication of this is seen in the refusal of all the anti-Semites to express any criticism of their parents, even when it was clear that they remembered situations which could easily have served as the basis for critical comment. This leaves only the third alternative, the attachment of blame or in other words the turning of the aggression resulting from the frustrating experience of rejection) on to some out-group.[1] When the group chosen to be the target of this aggression is "the Jews" the individual is said to be anti-Semitic.

Such blame will not normally be directly related to the experience of rejection; it will not, that is, take the form of "The Jews stole my wife", or "The Jews had me thrown out of the darts club", and this is not surprising when it is remembered that the most fundamentally important thing is not the concrete event but the individual's feeling of weakness and incapacity. In view of the usual nature of this incapacity—the inability to achieve satisfactory integration with one's primary groups—it is interesting to notice that the chief accusation levelled at Jews by Bethnal Green anti-Semites is that they are unusually successful in doing just this. The almost invariable reply to the question, "What are Jews like?" was, "They're a clannish lot." Group solidarity is not an unusual feature of the Jewish stereotype, and has some basis in reality, but in Bethnal Green it exceeds every other quality in the frequency with which it is used and the amount of affect accompanying the reference.

The question which immediately suggest itself is why Jews are chosen as the objects of this projection. It may occasionally happen that the choice results from some unfortunate experience of the individual in question, in which a Jew was concerned. Allport and Kramer (1946) report that their anti-Semitic subjects recalled more such experiences than did the tolerant ones, but they go on to point

---

[1] Cf. Dollard (1938), p. 41. This is the well-known phenomenon (viewed here from the standpoint of individual experience) of the function of aggression against out-groups as a means of strengthening the in-group integration. For a detailed description of these mechanisms from the point of view of the group see Shils and Janowitz (1948).

out that there is no guarantee that these recollections, even if true, are not the result rather than the cause of anti-Semitic attitudes. The data obtained in the present study show quite clearly that, in Bethnal Green at least, there is no connection at all between attitude towards Jews and actual contact or lack of contact with them in varying situations. As has already been pointed out this does not mean that the contact factor is not operative. A recent study (Watson, 1950) suggests that movement from a community with few or no Jewish members to New York City, where there is a large Jewish population, can sometimes result in, or be associated with, the development or strengthening of anti-Semitic attitudes. So in the case of Bethnal Green anti-Semitism it is probably not unimportant that there is a Jewish community in the borough and in the surrounding districts; but once this general, communal, contact exists the amount of individual contact seems to be quite unimportant in any particular case.

The characteristics of a suitable "scapegoat" group are well known. They are "visibility", and absence of retributive power. It is not particularly easy for a group to have the first characteristic when none of its members are physically present in or near the community.[1] Thus, in general, the presence of some members of the group to be attacked would seem to be a necessary pre-condition of their being chosen, but it cannot be regarded as a *cause* in the usual sense of the word. The Jews of Bethnal Green, as of most other communities, fulfil these conditions. There is the long history of the use of Jews as scapegoats, and the example of other neighbouring communities. In view of these social and historical facts it is not surprising that, when a man of Bethnal Green seeks an out-group towards which his aggressive impulses are to be turned, he should choose his Jewish neighbours. There would be cause for surprise only if Jews were the *sole* group chosen when others were also available; as we have seen, this is not the case, and Welsh and Irish, whose suitability for scapegoating is noticeably less than that of Jews, are also frequently chosen in this way.

The processes just described can best be illustrated by a consideration of two actual cases. Neither of these individuals was included

[1] There seems to be relatively little expression of colour prejudice in Bethnal Green. The coloured population of the borough is minute and coloured visitors even from the neighbouring borough of Stepney are rare. On the other hand, Welsh and Irish are comparatively common and fairly visible, and there is a good deal of prejudice expressed against these groups, sometimes even exceeding anti-Semitism in intensity.

in the sample of interviewees; they were men met by the author during the general study of the community and he had exceptional opportunities for becoming acquainted with them. Each of them was interviewed for a total of several hours and additional data on each man were obtainable from other sources. In the case of the younger man it was possible to interview people who remembered him as a child and who had known his parents.

The first of these men, Bob,[1] was a fifty-five year-old mechanic. His early upbringing appears to have followed the usual pattern; he was an intermediate member of a large family, the son of a stablehand. His mother went out to work. He left school at the age of twelve, worked with his father for some time and then joined the army. He spent most of his peace-time service life in India and the Middle East in a transport unit, where he worked at first with horses and later learnt the trade of motor mechanic. Still in the army when war broke out, he served on the western front. During the war he married. His marriage has been a happy one and he and his wife are still living together. At the end of the war he left the army (with the rank of corporal) to settle down to family life and obtained work as a mechanic in the firm in which his father (by now deceased) had been employed. He remained with this firm for fifteen years, by which time he was a senior foreman, claims to have been on friendly terms with the management, and was obviously very satisfied with his position. Not only was he economically successful; he appears to have identified very closely with the firm, still speaks of its accomplishments with pride and refers to the managing director in terms reminiscent of those applied by the old family retainer of fiction to a beloved master. In many ways there is an identification with his father, for example in his constant reference to it as his father's firm and his obvious feeling that some of its virtue stems from this association.

Bob had just completed fifteen years' service when he quarrelled with another senior foreman about the way in which some of the work was organised. The origins and the rights and wrongs of this difference are obscure, and in any case unimportant, but it soon reached the stage of seriously disrupting work. Bob, sure of his position, appealed to the management and was dismissed. He was given a good reference and had another similar position within

---

[1] To preserve anonymity, names and a few other details have been changed. No significant alterations have been made.

three weeks; this he has retained ever since. Objectively viewed his career seems to have been characterised by security and stability. In actual fact he has never recovered from the shock of his dismissal, and given the opportunity will talk about it at great length. It is notice-able, however, that he never complains about the firm from which he was dismissed. No matter how mournful and bitter he becomes about his experience, they remain above criticism. The bitterness, in fact, is never directed against anyone (except to a slight degree against the rival foreman), but remains in the form of vague expressions and a tone of voice, until, as he talks on, the subject matter drifts over to "those Yids"; then the bitterness and aggression become explicit. "Yids" can do almost anything, it seems. In particular they can drive "Englishmen" out of their livelihood. Bob talks at length about the way in which the local English stall-keepers have been driven out of business by Jews and he laments for them because of what they must have suffered in losing the business which they had built up. It is not at all difficult to see that what Bob is in fact mourning is his own loss of security and affection, the real target for his aggression being not the Jews but his rejectors, originally his parents and more recently his employers, who in this case were fairly obvious parent-surrogates.

Next Bob turns to another aspect of Jewish behaviour as it appears to him. The Jews have manoeuvred themselves into the position of being able to get the best of everything, particularly food. Kosher rites, he maintains, are merely ways of seeing that the best English meats go on to Jewish tables, while the likes of Bob must be content with imported frozen stuff. He and his fellows are powerless before the machinations of the Jewish clans, just as he is powerless (though naturally he himself does not draw the parallel) against the decisions of his parents and employers to reject him.

Ted has a different story to tell. A thirty-year-old unskilled labourer, he is the youngest of a family of three and an only son. He has never married. His father died shortly after Ted was born, and as a consequence his mother had to work to support the family. He was born with a rather obvious deformity which did not affect his physical strength or efficiency but made him, from his earliest schooldays, a figure of fun. In view of this it is not surprising that he developed an aggressive, cheeky, pseudo-hearty manner, and never succeeded in becoming integrated in any friendship group. At the same time he was eager for all the group life he could manage to get. He followed groups about, and was tolerated up to a point, but always with a good deal of banter and no sign of real affection. Unlike most boys and young men of the district who are strongly attached to a single group Ted has always had peripheral contacts with a variety of groups. Any sign of apparent interest in him is seized upon and dwelt on lovingly: the woman who sells him his daily newspaper, and the assistant in the tobacconist's shop which he patronises are, on the strength of friendly greetings and occasional inquiries about his doings, magnified into staunch friends with a deep interest in his activities. He is the easiest of men to interview, for any appearance of interest in what he has to say will encourage him to say it at great length.

Ted is still in much the same situation. He attaches himself to two or three darts clubs and is accepted as a member to the extent of being allowed to pay the membership fee and attend meetings. No one, however, will join him in a game and he is a very poor player. He is not even very good at keeping the score. He assiduously cultivates contacts at work and chance acquaintances. He boasts about his success as a ladies' man, but it soon becomes clear that this is based on a few contacts with prostitutes.

He lives with his mother and an unmarried sister who give him the freedom and the domestic service that is regarded as the working man's due, but he gets no real companionship from them. They share none of his interests and join in none of his pastimes. In return he speaks of them with the deepest affection and respect and frequently makes them gifts; even when he is trying hard, as he often does, to impress his listeners with his hard-boiled and dissolute character he always refers to his mother with reverence. Ted is also anti-Semitic, his chief complaint being that Jews are clannish. They keep to themselves and make contact with the non-Jew only for commercial purposes, for what they can get out of him. This of course is what Ted's acquaintances and relatives do to him, though he does not dare to say so because he depends so greatly on them for such small amounts of support and affection as he is able to get, and any display of open criticism on his part would instantly change the mildly irritable tolerance which he is shown into a decisive rejection.

Bob and Ted have had very different experiences in many ways and are now very different types of men, but they are alike in two respects: they are both anti-Semitic and both have felt more rejected than accepted, more deprived than gratified, in the most fundamentally important spheres of their lives. It seems that these two similarities are not unconnected. In the light of this one might expect that men who had suffered no early experience of deprivation would develop an expectation of a supportive environment, and that, provided good group contacts were then made, they would be in a position to face a certain amount of deprivation without feeling that their worst fears were being realised. The ratings given to the tolerant men in the group interviewed are consistent with this picture of relatively well-adjusted and confident people.

On the basis of these accounts of personal development we can suggest some hypotheses concerning the way in which anti-Semitism develops in individual members of a community. These hypotheses are certainly not new or original, but stating them may clarify the position reached so far in this discussion.

Hypothesis I. A predisposition to open hostility towards outgroups is formed when early childhood, and later social, experiences combine to produce an expectation of affection and security insufficient to meet the needs of the personality.

Hypothesis II. This hostility will be directed towards Jewish groups (*a*) when such groups are observable within the individual's social field, and (*b*) when such hostility does not result in punishment by groups or individuals whose support is important to the person showing hostility. Where these conditions do not apply, some other group will be chosen, and even where hostility is expressed towards Jews other suitable groups may also be treated in the same way.

Hypothesis III. The characteristics attributed to the Jewish group under these circumstances are likely to reflect some of the needs and repressed wishes of the hostile individual.

The terms of the discussion so far have been highly specific to Bethnal Green. The next problem is to see whether this specific account can be combined with the others surveyed in Chapter II, in order to provide something that may reasonably be called a general theory, based on actual research in a variety of situations. The first task is to compare the types of personality structure and other factors which the various writers have described as typical of anti-Semitic individuals in order to see to what extent it is possible to generalise on the matter.

Dealing first with sociological factors we find that, by and large, the results are conflicting. Correlations between anti-Semitism and such variables as socio-economic status, educational level, political affiliation and religious beliefs have been variously found to be negative, positive, or zero. The difficulties of assessing these results are increased by the variety of ways in which the results are expressed. Percentages, critical ratios, correlation coefficients and simple statements that differences were, or were not, significant have all been used. It is therefore impossible to do more than inspect the results and draw an impressionistic conclusion from them. The only really safe inference is that no connection between social, economic, political, and religious conditions and beliefs and anti-Semitic attitudes has yet been conclusively shown to exist. There is, for example, not the slightest justification for such a sweeping statement as, "It is universally found that education tends to work against anti-Semitism."[1]

Relationships between anti-Semitism and religious affiliation give similarly confused results, varying from the findings of Allport and Kramer that religious belief is positively correlated with intolerance, through that of Campbell who maintains there is no correlation, to that of Bettelheim and Janowitz that there is a positive correlation between religious belief and tolerance. The only possible course in the face of such confusion is to await further investigations. Of all the correlations under discussion the one which seems to have the most support is that between anti-Semitism and political belief, or rather between anti-Semitism and conservatism; even this, however, remains unproven and at the moment must be regarded merely as a rather likely hypothesis.[2] This divergence of results is all the more striking when one remembers that the variables being considered are fairly objective and capable of being easily and accurately recorded, so that the discovery of these discrepancies throws very

[1] Eysenck (1948, p. 279.) Campbell (1947, p. 520) gives results almost diametrically opposed to those of Eysenck.

[2] It seems desirable that research should be carried out to discover what the labels conservative, liberal, radical, etc., really mean when used in relation to the personality, and in particular how far they are related to Conservative, Liberal, and Socialist political affiliation, especially in relation to social background. It is conceivable that a man brought up in a working-class area, descendent of a long line of trade unionists, might vote Labour from sheer social conformity and might, within the left-wing groups, display the most extreme rigidity and opposition to change in practice and ideology. Some classification seems desirable which would list such a man as Socialist and conservative. Surely it is possible to be, in one sense, conservative even in one's methods of advocating revolution? Until some of these conceptual and semantic difficulties are cleared up there seems little likelihood of making much progress in the study of political, and other, attitudes. At the moment confusion would appear to reign supreme.

serious doubt on the value of any of these results for purposes of generalisation.

When we turn to factors more directly associated with the personality we find that the amount of disagreement is very much less. As already stated, every one of these investigators has reported significant differences between the characteristics displayed by the tolerant and intolerant individuals. Agreement extends, however, a good deal further than this, as can be seen from the following points.

As far as the clinical diagnosis of the subjects is concerned there seems to be general agreement on finding that a variety of clinical types occur among anti-Semites, but there is reason to expect that depressive types will not usually be found. The material available is not sufficient, however, to enable any firm conclusion to be drawn on this point. On the other hand the results of this investigation do not bear out the suggestion put forward by Ackerman and Jahoda that anti-Semitism may often be associated with homosexuality, as one of the three cases of latent homosexuality appearing in these records was a markedly tolerant individual. This is not to say that the two factors might not be associated on some occasions, but that there is no indication of a simple or invariable relationship.

If we combine the findings of the various studies that have been made we get a personality description which includes a considerable degree of detail. This composite picture is based on the results of the eight reports summarised in Chapter II, together with the results of the present research. Nothing is included unless it is supported by at least two pieces of research and opposed by none. Most statements in this picture are supported by at least three workers, some by as many as seven or eight. In view of this it can be regarded as having a high degree of reliability. Actual disagreement is practically non-existent and the variations in the number of workers in agreement is due merely to failure to cover the same ground.

People displaying marked anti-Semitic attitudes tend to have the following characteristics. They have narrow, constricted, poorly organised personalities which are frequently displayed as clear-cut neurotic and even psychotic symptoms, with paranoid tendencies appearing in some of the worst cases. They display a marked degree of pessimism and lack of confidence in themselves and in the groups to which they belong, but the weaknesses implied in these attitudes are not expressed and the attitudes are justified by reference to the power of external forces. These forces are sometimes located in other groups (e.g. the Jews) but even more frequently are seen as impersonal and vague, e.g. the action of fate. The world as a whole is seen as threatening and bad—this is part of the generally pessimistic outlook—with the attitude "If everything is so evil, what can I do against it?" As little contact is maintained with other people anti-Semites tend to be socially isolated persons, while the personal contacts they have tend to be poor ones. Personal relationships are nearly always seen in terms of dominance—submission. There is a rather poor contact with reality, situations being assessed in terms of the individual's general outlook rather than in terms of the actual position, thus demonstrating a rigid approach to life which may be carried over even into intellectual fields (Rokeach 1948). They usually display very little insight into their own mental processes.

There is a general concern with themes of punishment, again associated with external powers and groups, and supported by the view that punishments should be severe, while eligibility for punishment is assessed on the basis of a rigidly moralistic interpretation of conventional codes. The anti-Semites themselves tend to show a high degree of conformity, particularly in relation to parental authority. Parents are very frequently idealised and almost never criticised.

At the same time it is found that parent-child relationships in childhood were rarely good, and that the child experienced a considerable degree of frustration, usually in the form of rejection on the part of one parent or both. The latter are seen simultaneously as providers of material advantages and as capricious arbiters of punishment. When analytic or projective techniques are used to get below the surface of the personality it is discovered that there is a highly ambivalent attitude towards authority in general and the parents in particular. It seems likely that the particular aspect of the ambivalence toward authority that is expressed directly will depend on a variety of social and cultural factors, including whether or not the individual is himself in a position of authority. Aggressive impulses are also strongly expressed in a similar way, while there is considerable evidence that repression is strong and reaction formation is frequently an important factor in the formation of the personality. There is general agreement that the aggressive and other impulses are also dealt with by being projected on to out-groups and the external world in general. Projection also seems to be an extremely important function of these personalities. In addition they are highly egocentric and narcissistic, tending to relate everything to themselves and their own feelings. Underlying the whole personality is a high degree of anxiety and uncertainty.

One point that deserves mention is the expression of anxiety; concerning this there is some variation in opinion. At least part of the trouble arises here on the question of definition, and the establishment of suitable indices. The difficulties which arose in the present research on the question of locating evidence of free-floating anxiety have already been discussed. The problem is not made easier by the absence, in literature, of clear definitions of the concept.[1] Although its value in descriptive and therapeutic work is unmistakeable it is a difficult concept to handle in a research context. A study of the material reported on in the research work under review suggests that, in this particular case at least, the most useful distinction would be between anxiety which is overtly expressed (i.e. directly verbalised) and that which is expressed only indirectly (e.g. through symptoms or unrecognised inhibitions). It seems to be clear from the evidence that the mere existence in the personality of a marked degree of some form of anxiety is not of itself a discriminating index of anti-Semitism. There is definitely not a very high correlation between "normal" or "healthy" personalities and tolerance, for while it seems that most mentally healthy persons are probably tolerant the opposite relationship does not hold, and markedly neurotic individuals may be characterised by tolerance. As the neurotic condition necessarily implies the existence of anxiety in some form it is clear that this cannot be a particularly good indicator of anti-Semitism even though its absence may be strongly indicative of tolerance. There does appear to be, however, a useful distinction in the extent to which the anxiety is directly expressed, this trait being much more common among tolerant individuals than among the anti-Semitic. It would appear to correspond well with the view that anti-Semites are lacking in insight. Tolerant persons seem to be not so much lacking in conflicts as more aware of the nature of the conflicts, even though they may be little more successful in dealing with them (Frenkel-Brunswik, 1948, and Adorno, *et al.*, 1950, pp. 963–4).

[1] Almost any text on psychiatry or abnormal psychology has numerous references to the subject. For detailed or specialised references cf. Freud (1936), Fenichel (1945), Horney (1937), Sullivan (1940, pp. 9–10), and (1948, pp. 1–14).

So far in this chapter we have considered the way in which anti-Semites appear to develop in Bethnal Green and the extent to which investigators, studying subjects drawn from a variety of social backgrounds in two different countries, have agreed in their descriptions of the personality types normally associated with anti-Semitic attitudes. Is it possible, in the light of material presented earlier, to put forward a more generalised view of the development of such a personality type which is consistent with the results of these various pieces of research and with generally accepted social psychological theory? Such a project should be perfectly feasible provided that certain cautions referred to earlier are kept in mind. The types of personality described in this chapter have been observed by more than one worker, and the accuracy of the description is probably fairly high. The way in which this personality type is formed has not been observed with the same degree of detail, and the account of this process is derived largely (though not entirely) from a consideration of its end-result (the adult personality) in the light of psychological theory on personality development. In other words we are combining a probably correct description with a possibly correct theory, and the resultant conclusions must be regarded as hypotheses and not as statements of fact; at the same time it may be claimed that these hypotheses, having a fair amount of supporting data, are well worthy of further investigation, and are not to be lightly swept aside.

The first step in the formation of a prejudiced personality seems to be the establishment of a poor relationship with the parents in infancy and childhood, probably through the medium of some form of rejection of the child by the parents, usually associated with erratic discipline, thus laying the foundations for a belief that the world is an unfriendly, unpredictable place. There are, of course, no grounds for supposing that any poor relationship between parent and child will inevitably produce a prejudiced person. It is also necessary to remember that not every type of depriving or frustrating situation will be equally effective in producing the unhappy outlook described. Frenkel-Brunswik's (1948, p. 305) suggestion that severe discipline is the determing factor seems an over-simplification. It seems more likely that inconsistent treatment tends to produce the uncertain attitudes. Some of the tolerant men from Bethnal Green reported severe discipline in childhood, but most of them also described a home life that was consistently supportive. C.2 for example spontaneously remarked that although he had been strictly disciplined he felt that on the whole he had been better off than most of the neighbouring children because he had never been turned out into the streets to look after himself, but had always been able to use his home as the centre of his activities. E.8, H.3, and G.5 also reported strict discipline plus a consistently warm relationship with the parents and siblings. It seems fairly certain that to produce a general attitude of pessimism and uncertainty the child must experience not merely frustration or deprivation, but a frustration that is felt to be a real threat to the personality (Maslow, 1941). Such an experience gives rise to anxiety which is usually dealt with by means of some kind of neurotic defence mechanism. If the anxiety is handled in certain ways, e.g. by being turned against the self and revealed in the form of marked guilt feelings, the result will be a personality of a depressive type, and prejudiced characteristics are unlikely to appear.

The production of this tendency towards seeing the world as an unfriendly place may go no further if circumstances arise which enable the individual to make a satisfactory adjustment to his environment. In exceptionally helpful circumstances the tendency may even be reversed. In very unfavourable conditions it may have reached an advanced stage of development early in life and remain as a chronic condition. Should a temporary or partial re-adjustment be made, it may be upset by later experiences which re-activate the anxiety, i.e. by further experiences of rejection or deprivation.[1] It is probable that it is these feelings of anxiety over the insecurity and uncertainty of the environment which form the facet of the personality reflected in the high correlations obtained for pessimism and lack of confidence. The fact that a single general attitude underlies these would account for the high intercorrelations (0·54 to 0·77) which exist between the four variables concerned.

The projective material obtained from the subjects in some of the researches indicated that a good deal of aggression underlies the personality. It is reasonable to assume that this aggression is directed in the first instance against the sources of the insecurity, the authors of the rejections. But as these people are also the representatives of

---

[1] It is interesting to note that a study of individuals who had undergone in concentration camps, experiences of deprivation sufficiently intense to overwhelm all but the most unusually well-adjusted personalities, revealed that they displayed, generally in an exaggerated form, most of the characteristics of the Bethnal Green extreme anti-Semites. In the case of the ex-prisoners the deprivation had been so severe that the degree of predisposition appeared to be important chiefly in deciding how quickly maladjustment would occur. In more normal circumstances only the pre-disposed would be affected (cf. Grygier, 1954).

the in-groups, the sources of such support as the individual does experience, the direct release of aggression would be dangerous. One solution, adopted by the depressive, is to turn this inwards. The solution which concerns us in our study of prejudice is the direction of aggression outwards, in another direction. Thus a crucial difference between the tolerant and the prejudiced personality seems to be the choice between internalisation and displacement as a mechanism for dealing with feelings of aggression. The usual corollary to such displacement is to bring into action the further mechanism of projection. If one is to show aggression against a person or group it is usually necessary to provide a reason, and this can be done by projecting on the group or individual chosen one's own aggressive, anti-social drives, so that one can then see in this outsider cause for attack (cf. Fenichel, 1946, and Bettelheim, 1947).

The choice of drives, impulses, and characteristics to be projected on to the out-group will be in part determined by the wishes of one's own in-group. Because the in-group is so important to him the individual feels an intense need to do and to be the things that the in-group approves. Hence the conformity so clearly shown in the anti-Semitic personality and the need to get rid of some parts of oneself on to the scapegoat. As is so characteristic of a neurotic solution, there is considerable anxiety lest the attempt should fail, so that the anti-Semite does not merely conform—he makes a great virtue of doing so, and displays the strongly moralistic approach to this type of action. This drive for conformity will also make the individual concerned very ready to take over any prejudices and stereotypes commonly found among the members of his in-group. The way in which "scapegoating" practices are tied to cultural attitudes and to the local social structure and traditions can be seen by a comparison of the description of anti-Semitism given here, with that of witchcraft and witch-hunting among the Navaho Indians given by Kluckhohn and Leighton (1946, pp. 159–181, especially pp. 176–7).

Although so desirous of support and affection the anti-Semite is basically rather afraid of other people; they are part, a major part, of that unfriendly world which started the whole of his train of difficulties. Because he tends to attach himself to people, and to assume relationships, chiefly for what he can get out of them and not merely because he really likes the people and enjoys the relationship, it is not surprising that his social contacts should be found to be so poor in quality and so few in number. It is probably from this situation that anti-Semitic organisations derive so much of their appeal. They offer friendship for the friendless, a group for the ungroupable; a group, moreover, based on aggression. The appeal of such a group to its members is that it provides an open outlet for aggression without demanding too much of the kind of sociability that they find so difficult. Anti-Semitic street-corner speakers make a great deal of use of this kind of appeal.

One marked feature of Bethnal Green at the present time (and probably other districts as well) is the apparent divorce between anti-Semitism and Fascism. Few anti-Semites express even qualified support for the movement and most of them reject it vigorously— a situation which seems to differ markedly from pre-war days. It is probable that this is due to the very strong public disfavour in which Fascism is held at the present time. The only people for whom an open association with Fascism would have much appeal would be those who had virtually no contacts with other groups and so for whom membership of such a party was almost the only possible escape from a complete and intolerable isolation. For anyone who had retained some normal group contacts such an association would be too sharp a break with the conventions to be tolerated.

These are some of the ways in which social forces seem to affect the development of anti-Semitism, but there are doubtless other, more indirect ways as well. Reference has already been made to the effects on the once rejected personality of the experience of further rejections later in life. Here again social forces are of great importance and perhaps here also we have the key to the wide variation in the reports of the kind of social conditions associated with anti-Semitism. Situations which are felt as deprivations are likely to vary not only from person to person, but from country to country, class to class, and also, within the same milieu, from one time to another. Thus a decline in income or social status will probably be felt more if experienced during a time of general upward mobility, and will probably vary in significance from one social class to another. The fact that the historical and social movements which have been found to be associated with anti-Semitism are only partial in their effects has a dual explanation: in the first place they will affect the predisposed personalities only, and secondly the same events will appear in a different light to different individuals according to the social, economic and other influences affecting them at the time. It is easy to see here the reason for the inadequacies of such theories as those which would make various social and economic forces, the existence of class rivalries, of economic exploitation, of poor trade union membership or the experience of unemployment, a sufficient explanation for the spread of anti-Semitism. Indeed it is important to note that in many cases the unhappy experience which is the precipitating factor may have no connection with the social or economic situation in which the anti-Semite is living. A deserting wife, an ungrateful child, or dismissal from a friendship group, may just as easily be the point of strain, though such factors do not operate on such a large scale as the major social and economic forces. In the same way the mere existence of Jews in a community is certainly not a sufficient explanation for the fact that individuals with a need to find a scapegoat should normally make Jews their first choice. An understanding of many details of the social structure, and the place of the Jewish community in this structure both now and in the past, is necessary for an adequate explanation of this fact.

There remains the problem of the transmission of anti-Semitism through the family or other primary group institutions by a process of simple imitation of adults by children. While the theory that this is a basic cause of the transmission of anti-Semitism is rarely advanced in writing, it is frequently put forward in discussion, even by social scientists. It has the great twin charms of plausibility and ultra-simplicity. Unfortunately it will not square with the facts known about anti-Semitism, quite apart from implying a rather too simple view of the process of learning (cf. Miller and Dollard, 1945). Ackerman and Jahoda (1950, p. 84) point out that in about half their cases the parents were not anti-Semitic and some of them were actively pro-Jewish, while cases where tolerant individuals have had anti-Semitic parents are comparatively common. Parental influence, therefore, is certainly not the important factor that it is often believed to be—that is, in the sense of providing a set of attitudes which are simply copied by the children. That such influences do have some effect is to be expected and, in the absence of evidence to the contrary, a person with an unprejudiced type of personality might continue to accept anti-Semitic views which he had gained from his parents. Opportunities for obtaining evidence to the contrary are not hard to obtain and there is no reason to suppose that many individuals hold strongly anti-Semitic views merely because of ignorance. Previous lack of information does not explain the tenacity with which most anti-Semites hold to their views in spite of evidence to the contrary (cf. S.11's rejection of official statistics).

If we assume that the parents' attitudes are retained only in those cases in which the personality needs of the children are similar, most of these difficulties disappear. Parents, whether anti-Semitic or tolerant, whose characters are such that they tend to produce children of similar personality types, are likely to pass on their attitudes relatively unchanged, whereas those parents whose behaviour results in the development of children with significantly different characteristics from themselves will find that their attitudes to minority groups (and many other features of the environment) are unacceptable to their children. Though this explanation is more complicated than the imitation hypothesis it has the advantage of covering all cases, whereas imitation covers only two out of the possible four combinations of parents and children, and a separate explanation has to be invoked for each of the other two situations. This view does not deny the possible importance of imitation but merely defines more narrowly the conditions under which it is likely to take place (cf. Ackerman and Jahoda, 1950, pp. 84–5).

To sum up we can say that anti-Semitism is part of a complex form of reaction to experiences of deprivation extending from infancy into adult life. This reaction, though a result of psychological processes within the personality, is activated by social events and is canalised and modified by social forces. It is to be found in an environment which at one point in the individual's life-space produces expectations and attitudes which are markedly inconsistent with a flexible and balanced reaction to environmental pressures at some other points in the life-space. Anti-Semitism is a unique phenomenon, qualitatively different from other forms of prejudice, only insofar as historical and other forces have combined to produce a unique social situation, e.g. the widespread distribution of Jewish people and their frequent availability in the past for use as scapegoats. Other forms of prejudice such as anti-Negroism also have their own particular unique aspects. Neither psychological nor sociological concepts alone can explain the phenomenon adequately, as both types of determinants are closely interwoven and are constantly interacting in the process of the formation of prejudice.

The conclusion that anti-Semitism is a particular manifestation of prejudice rather than a unique situation is sharply at variance with many of the theories summarised in Chapter II but is supported by the results of practically all the experimental and field work described in the same chapter. It is probably true to say that the most general and most fundamental defect of those theoretical approaches is their efforts to consider anti-Semitism as something which is almost unique. Situations, motives and stimuli are dealt with as independent elements, and inadequate attempts made to see common features in varying circumstances. In general terms, the level of abstraction is too low.

Samuel (1940) is probably the most explicit and strenuous exponent of the uniqueness of anti-Semitism, but he is far from being the only one. It seems that it is very difficult to maintain both that anti-Semitism is completely unique and that Jews are fundamentally like other human beings. If the reactions of anti-Semites are always and necessarily different in nature and cause from those of xenophobes in general, then it would seem unlikely that the reasons for this could lie outside the Jewish people; to assert this uniqueness appears to be getting dangerously close to playing the anti-Semites' own game. Quite apart from the wisdom of this course it remains true that the factual evidence is almost entirely against it. One may take, for example, Samuel's quotations of fantastic statements by Hitler about Jews, which he regards as evidence in favour of his theory of uniqueness. Equally fantastic statements about Negroes and other groups are plentiful and the Law of Parsimony would appear to require that the likelihood of similar causes for these similar results be given far more careful consideration than Samuel is prepared to allow.

CHAPTER X

Problems for the Future

DURING the last decade research workers in all the sciences have come increasingly to realise that their work could not be divorced, except in an artificial and arbitrary way, from the practical application of the findings which resulted from it. This is particularly the case in the social sciences, both on account of their close and direct association with the values of living people, and because of the fact that, unlike the natural sciences, there does not yet exist a body of social technicians and engineers trained to deal with the practical problems by putting into effect the theoretical formulations of the research worker, and by acting as an intermediary between that worker and the people affected by his research. It is doubtful if the physical scientist of twenty years ago would have felt called upon to add to a research report any consideration of the social consequences of his findings. To-day he is much more likely to do so, while the social scientist would find it difficult to avoid the obligation should he wish to do so.

During the past decade also, anti-Semitism (in fact race relations in general) has become a topic for serious scientific research. This is not to say that the problem had previously escaped attention, or had not attracted interest. On the contrary, it has caused no little concern on the part of both Jews and Gentiles for at least the last century, but it would be true to say that until fairly recently the emphasis was almost entirely on doing something about the problem, and hardly at all on finding out what could be done. Methods of improving Jewish-Gentile relationships were freely expounded and often tried out. On the whole these schemes fell into two categories, environmental manipulation, and education. The fact that was common to both types was that only rarely was any attempt made to check the results of these schemes in a systematic manner. Some supposedly alleviatory action would be put into effect, and the changes, if any, observed in an impressionistic, rule of thumb manner. By the usual *post hoc ergo propter hoc* form of reasoning it was assumed that the observed (or even imagined) changes were the result of the action taken. Sometimes the assessment of change was so cursory as to be virtually non-existent.

A considerable variety of activities can be classed under the heading of "environmental manipulation". Any legislation including that enabling Jews to hold various public offices, schemes to raise the standard of living of either Jews or anti-Semites, plans for making illegal any form of anti-Semitic propaganda, efforts to segregate Jews, or to provide increasing opportunities for them to mix with Gentiles—all such activities fall under this heading.

Educational activities are equally various. Lectures, discussions, films, the printing of books and pamphlets, the holding of open-air meetings, debates between Jews and anti-Semites, letters to editors, the approach to children and young people in classrooms and youth clubs, are among the varied methods which have been, and are being used. Almost always the aim has been to prove that Jews are not as black as the anti-Semites have claimed. It is possible that many of these activities of both kinds may have been very successful; it is fairly certain that in many cases they were almost completely unsuccessful. What is really important, however, is that as a general rule the initiators of these activities did not really know to what extent they had succeeded or failed, and when they did know, they rarely understood why the particular results had been achieved. The reason for this ignorance is twofold: first a lack of any adequate "before and after" measurements,[1] and secondly, a failure to make any attempt to allow for, or assess the effect of, simultaneous and unexpected events which might have influenced the results of the action taken. As a consequence of this neglect to carry out any systematic check on influences and results we are able to produce, in spite of the large amount of effort put into attempts to reduce anti-Semitism, very little worthwhile evidence as to the types of action which are most effective under varying circumstances. It should be noted that experiments along these lines, conducted by social scientists, and intended for research purposes, are frequently

---

[1] It is, of course, true that methods for making such measurements with any great degree of accuracy are a comparatively recent development. It is also true that in nearly every case the methods used were much inferior to those available.

open to the same criticisms as those initiated by non-scientists with no research aim in view.

It is not necessary to review here the experimental work that has been carried out; this has been done elsewhere (Rose and Rose, 1948, pp. 282–3, and Williams, 1947, pp. 7–35) with conclusions that completely support the contention that little is known from the results of this work. In view of the slight amount of assistance which can be gained from a study of previous attempts to reduce prejudice it seems worthwhile to try to assess, on the basis of what is known about anti-Semites, the likely results of some of the more commonly used, or proposed, methods of lessening anti-Semitism.

A study of reports and articles in contemporary books and periodicals gives the impression that three suggestions are most frequently put forward for reducing anti-Semitism. These are (1) legislative action to make anti-Semitic utterances and activities punishable at law; (2) legislative and other action to reduce poverty and other social evils in the belief that people who have fewer frustrations will be less likely to become anti-Semitic (a particular variant of this is the Marxist view that by abolishing economic class distinctions the need for anti-Semitism will disappear); and (3) educational and other action in order to make it known that Jews are very much like other people and can reasonably be treated as such. It is proposed to take each of these approaches in turn and consider its probable effectiveness in the light of the theory of anti-Semitism put forward in the last chapter (cf. Krech and Crutchfield, 1948, pp. 499–530).

The proposal to outlaw anti-Semitism can be studied from two points of view. There is first the question of technical practicability—could appropriate laws be framed and administered? Consideration of this question is a matter for experts on the subject and has been dealt with elsewhere (Committee on the Law of Defamation, 1948, p. 11); as a practical proposition it seems open to serious doubt. Secondly, it may be asked, "If such laws could be passed and enforced, what effect would this have on the amount of anti-Semitism?" It would of course prevent open publication and speech-making; but if one judges by the situation in Bethnal Green the amount of this is small and the public reached minute, at any rate in normal times. It may be that, given circumstances in which anti-Semitism could become a popular movement, legislation might considerably slow down the speed of its spread, and the knowledge that such legislation had been enacted might increase the sense of security of some members of the Jewish community. Would it have any other effects? It is well known that in most circumstances people's opinions and attitudes are activated and changed far more effectively by personal contact with someone holding definite views than by speeches and written material (Lazarfeld *et al.*, 1948, pp. 49–51 and 150–8), and that informal discussions have a far greater effect in this respect than more formal approaches (Lewin, 1947); so that individuals predisposed to anti-Semitism would be unlikely to escape exposure to it. Only a secret police system far more efficient and ruthless than that of Hitler could exercise even a moderate control over these methods of dissemination.

The same thing is even true to some extent of publicly spoken and published material. Communication is a complex process, and language, the chief means by which communication is carried on, is a highly flexible tool. The extent to which anti-Semitic propagandists, even under the present law, make use of symbolism and innuendo to assail their victims is an indication of what could be done in this direction if the necessity arose, and here again legal control could be obtained only at the expense of freedom of speech. This discussion can be summed up by saying that legislative action, under any conditions likely to be acceptable in a democracy, could do no more than officially remove certain forms of anti-Semitism from the public gaze, and reduce some of its more obvious manifestations. The experiences of Soviet Russia where legal action, backed (in most cases) by the support of a totalitarian state, has been unable to eradicate anti-Semitism, further reduce the hope that such action would be effective (Steinberg, 1944, pp. 23–8; Pinson, 1947; Anon. 1949).

The alleged success of anti-discriminatory legislation in the United States is frequently put forward as an argument in favour of the legislative approach. From detailed reports it appears that these laws have been very successful in reducing some of the grosser manifestations of racial intolerance, but have had no effect on, and indeed have not been aimed at, such activities as making anti-Semitic speeches or remarks and the publication of anti-Semitic literature (Burma, 1951). In view of the finding that anti-Semites are highly conformist in their attitudes it is possible that the passing of anti-discriminatory legislation, *which could be enforced*, would help to make anti-Semitism, like Fascism, unpopular and unfashionable, but it would be unrealistic to assume that much could be accomplished in this way without running counter to public opinion on freedom of speech. It is worth noting that one authority has argued that an important reason why the Nazi anti-Jewish activities produced so crushing an effect on Jewish morale was precisely that too much reliance had been placed by German Jewry on the value of legal emancipation, which "is only a beginning, a programme that raises considerably more problems than it solves" (Reichmann, 1950, p. 22). In any case it is clear that legislation can do no more than reduce expressions of anti-Semitism. Legislation may reduce the symptoms, but leaves the disease unchecked.

The effort to reduce anti-Semitism by means of environmental adjustment to suit the needs of people likely to be affected by anti-Semitic propaganda has a more promising appearance in view of the theory put forward in the last chapter that environmental influences play an important and necessary part in the production of anti-Semitism. The primary difficulty of this approach to the problem is that of knowing what kinds of action will be most effective. Although poverty and unemployment are frequently suggested as important factors, the results of this and other studies (notably that of Bettelheim and Janowitz) suggest that the correlation between the personal experience of economic difficulties and anti-Semitism is rather low and that the attitude to its possibility is much more important. Moreover, it seems that experiences not connected with economic difficulties, or having only slight connections with them, can be serious precipitating factors in the production of extreme anti-Semitism.

While the association of anti-Semitism with social and economic upheavals is too well attested for its importance to be denied, the connection is obviously neither simple nor direct, and there would seem to be little hope, short of the establishment of a Utopia, of doing more than somewhat reducing the strength of anti-Semitism by this method. Certainty of employment, better housing, and other social reforms can probably do something to lower the incidence of anti-Semitism by avoiding the activation of the prejudice potential in individuals whose personalities are inclined towards this reaction. These reforms, therefore, desirable for their own sakes, can probably be relied on to assist in the reduction of all forms of prejudice. Considering how difficult it is to achieve these desirable states even when motivations far stronger than the wish to lessen anti-Semitism are present, it does not seem advisable to place too much hope in social reform as a primary, short-term attack on prejudice. It is quite certain that the quick and simple cure of the "abolish capitalism" type is neither quick nor simple and is only tinkering with one facet of a much wider problem.

The overall conclusions on these two rather impersonal mass attacks on prejudice is that while they cannot be dismissed out of hand as useless, they are subject to many serious limitations, will be partial in their effects, and, in the case of the legal approach at least, are likely to conceal rather than remove the expression of anti-Semitism. The greatest danger inherent in these methods is that they might induce an unwarranted complacency or arouse hopes which are certain to be disappointed. They have a place in the war on prejudice but their limits need to be clearly understood.

When one considers what can, for the moment, be broadly called the educational approach to reduction of prejudice, two basic facts must be kept clearly in mind, namely, that active prejudice is rarely due to ignorance, and that anti-Semitism is not a unique, simple, isolated, phenomenon but is closely associated in a variety of ways with other attitudes, with certain personality characteristics and with certain types of social experiences. Both of these essential facts are usually ignored.

There is no generally accepted theory of anti-Semitism based on the view that prejudice is a function of ignorance. All the theories and all the evidence provided by research suggest that in anti-Semitism the irrational elements are the most important, that prejudice is not a negative thing, an absence of knowledge, but rather something positive, the fulfilment of a need. Yet the fact remains that the vast majority of educational programmes aimed at the reduction of prejudice appear to be based on the assumption (usually unstated) that ignorance is the important point. Ignorance is, of course, associated with anti-Semitism, and some people can be won over by a convincing argument, but as a general rule the positive element enters in, and must be dealt with before the educational process can be effective.

Furthermore, though the evidence is equally in favour of the view that anti-Semitism is one of a group of related attitudes, a symptom of underlying tensions, most programmes for combating it appear to be aimed specifically at this one attitude in isolation. It is only a slight exaggeration to suggest that some campaigns against anti-Semitism are rather like an effort to "cure" a case of measles by painting over the spots. Unfortunately anti-Semitism is a more chronic condition than measles and a spontaneous recovery is unlikely to take place during the painting process. This is not to suggest that every manifestation of prejudice needs to be tackled simultaneously in every case. Under many conditions anti-Semitism (or colour prejudice, or some other specific attitude) may have an importance sufficiently greater than the other possible expressions of inter-group hostility to warrant special attention. What is suggested is that when a single type of prejudice is aimed at, this should be a result of deliberate policy based on a proper assessment of the situation and not on an ill founded assumption that this is the only approach possible. It suggests that whatever symptoms, or group of symptoms, be the centre of interest, careful attention should always be paid to the less obvious but more basic aspects of the problem.

Any purely educational programme faces two difficulties which will inevitably reduce its success. The first is that information and propaganda are normally absorbed and used chiefly by the people who have the least need (from the propagandist's point of view) for it (Lazarfeld et al., 1948, pp. 73–93; Cooper and Jahoda, 1947). The prejudiced are likely to avoid the information either by keeping away from situations where they might be presented with it or by misinterpreting it in some way. The merely ignorant are presumably both less likely than the prejudiced to take positive steps to avoid being influenced by the information provided and less inclined than the tolerant to take steps to come into contact with it. The chief recipients of such information, unless a special effort is made to ensure otherwise, will always be the already converted. The second difficulty is that even if the educationalist succeeds in making contact with a prejudiced person (as contrasted with one who is merely misinformed) he is faced with the problem of removing the prejudice before the proffered information will be accepted. Anyone who has tried lecturing, or leading discussion groups, on race relations, or any other emotionally charged topic, cannot fail to be aware of the way in which prejudiced individuals can avoid being reached and held by logical argument, and how easy they find it to throw doubt on the accuracy of the information offered. The necessity, in other words, is for re-education rather than for education, and this is a much more complex matter involving many special difficulties (Lewin, 1948, pp. 56–68, Zilboorg, 1943, pp. 3–71, and Weltfish and Lippitt, 1945).

These considerations suggest that educational work should be supplemented by activities of a more or less therapeutic kind designed to relieve the needs for prejudice. An approach along these lines could probably best be attempted by working with the individuals concerned either singly or in groups, and making use of such techniques as have already been tried with some success in the field of child guidance, marriage welfare and industrial relations (Bowlby, 1949; Jaques, 1948; Coch and French, 1948; Kelnar, 1947; Wilson, 1949). The chief difficulty in the way of such an approach is the necessity for using workers who have undergone a considerable amount of training. This means that with few people available for the task it becomes slow and expensive. On the other hand it promises to be much more successful than many other, not inexpensive, programmes. There is, of course, no suggestion that this approach would involve anything in the nature of intensive or long term therapy. It would have the strictly limited goal of reducing the need for expressions of hostility against out-groups to an extent which would permit more orthodox educational methods to take effect.

These conclusions need to be qualified in several respects. Perhaps most important is the question of who should be the main focus of attention in the effort to reduce prejudice. So far in this discussion, and usually in campaigns to combat anti-Semitism, the general population is regarded as being divided into two groups, the prejudiced and the tolerant, and all activities tend to be directed indiscriminately at the former. One thing that has been made very clear by a number of research projects is that the intensity of prejudice varies very considerably from one person to another and it is probable that the most effective approaches would show an equal degree of variation according to the audience selected.

On the basis of the results of the Bethnal Green investigation it would seem that the most seriously prejudiced individuals (groups 1 and 2) would usually be well beyond the reach of any educational, or simple, short-term, therapeutic technique. It is probable, however, that this need not be regarded as a major set-back. There is reason to suppose, as already pointed out, that the proportion of these extreme cases is higher in Bethnal Green than in the country as a whole, and from what is known of these men it appears that these extremists are, because of their relatively restricted social contacts, less likely than more tolerant individuals to have an important influence on their fellows. In terms of an anti-prejudice campaign, which aimed to use its resources most effectively, these extreme cases can probably be safely ignored.

It is at this point that a large gap in our knowledge becomes important. Up to the present time most attention has been paid in research to the more extreme cases, while mildly prejudiced individuals, similar to the group 4 men in the Bethnal Green sample, have received little attention. In terms of research programmes this has been a reasonable approach, but it is becoming urgently necessary that the less extreme anti-Semites should be studied in more detail. It is probable that such studies can most usefully be incorporated in action programmes designed to reduce prejudice. In the absence of more definite information it is probably reasonable to assume that people whose prejudice is based on misinformation rather than personality needs would be classed with this mildly prejudiced group, and insofar as purely educational and propagandist approaches can be successful they will be successful with these people.

A second reasonable assumption is that in general the mildly and moderately anti-Semitic have some positive drive towards the expression of prejudice, and given suitable circumstances, this may be increased in intensity so that they transfer to the more prejudiced end of the scale, to groups 1 and 2. The existence of the comparatively small number of highly prejudiced people, however regrettable, is unlikely to be dangerous unless there is a large group of potential converts to their cause. The group 3 and 4 members constitute, in a sense, a large reservoir of potential converts to either the prejudiced or the tolerant position. It would therefore seem to be good tactics to concentrate attention on these people (cf. Haimowitz and Haimowitz, 1950).

What cannot be stressed too strongly is that such efforts are likely to be completely wasted unless some attempt is made to control the conditions under which they are made, and to assess the results achieved. Only when this is done can ineffective methods be discovered and abandoned. Furthermore, careful investigation needs to be made to see that the facts available are directed at those people who are likely to respond to them, and not wasted on the already converted and the unconvertable.

There are two other classes of people on whom attention might suitably be concentrated. These are, first, certain key individuals who are in an especially favourable position for influencing others, those whom Lewin (1947a) referred to as "gatekeepers", and secondly, children. There are different reasons for the selection of each of these groups. The role of the "gatekeepers" is obvious. They are important for the influence which they have on others. They tend to be leaders of opinion and are likely to have a maximum influence on the more strongly conformist members of the prejudiced group. Even when such people are already tolerant themselves, a better understanding on their part of the nature and importance of prejudice, and of the methods of combating it, should increase their ability to assist in the reduction of prejudice. The use of various group discussion techniques with such people might well have repercussions far beyond the individuals actually taking part in the work of the group.

There is evidence to suggest (Frenkel-Brunswik, 1948; James and Tenen, 1951) that intolerance in children is much easier to overcome than is the case with adults. There is, unfortunately, little or no evidence to indicate how permanent these effects may be. It certainly seems, however, well worth exploring these possibilities further.

A note should perhaps be added on the need for considering not only the individuals at whom these efforts are to be directed, but also those whose task it will be to take part in such work. Bettelheim and Janowitz (1950, p. 146 n.) point out that some individuals who are enthusiastic "fighters for tolerance" can be extremely ineffective, and may even increase the intolerance of those with whom they come into contact, because it is clear from their manner that for them the campaign for tolerance is indeed a fight, an outlet for hostility. It is, in other words, serving for them a purpose similar to that which anti-Semitism serves for the intolerant. A moderate anti-Semite, involved in a discussion with such a person, will probably sense that he is not so much being reasoned with as attacked, and will be encouraged to respond in kind. It is probably necessary for campaigners for tolerance to examine their own motives as carefully as those whose views they are opposing.

It is interesting to note in this connection that the results of one investigation suggest that persons showing a slight amount of ethnic prejudice may make better psychotherapists than some of those who show an extremely friendly attitude. Many of the latter show strongly aggressive characteristics which they project on to the strongly prejudiced, Fascists and others, while showing little insight into their own aggressive feelings (Haimowitz and Haimowitz, 1950). This gives further warning against equating lack of prejudice with mental health.

If the theory put forward in the last chapter has any truth in it the conclusion would seem inescapable that in the long run the most effective attack on anti-Semitism and prejudice generally is along the lines of prevention, that is, in this case, by aiming at a reduction in the development of prejudiced personalities. The implication of the theory is that tolerance is closely related to personality development, and that efforts designed to promote the growth of well adjusted personalities offer one of the chief long-range hopes of producing a marked and lasting reduction in prejudice.[1] To say this is not to suggest either that more limited and short-term programmes should meanwhile be abandoned, or that such a solution is in any way simple; on the contrary, it appears at first glance to be far more complicated, difficult, and expensive than any of the solutions proposed earlier. It is quite possible, however, that the real choice is not between a simple and difficult method, or between a slow and speedy cure, but between activities which are relatively cheap, easily planned and carried out, but which produce practically no lasting effect whatever, and programmes which are slow and expensive but offer some hope of an eventual permanent improvement in the situation. The doubts which can be cast on the effectiveness of the more conventional approaches are sufficiently serious to make this suggestion worthy of careful consideration. It must inevitably be distasteful for people suffering the consequences of prejudice and discrimination to turn aside from immediate activities to long range planning which cannot possibly show an impressive amount of progress within the lifetime of the planners, but if there is one thing that is absolutely certain in the field of race relations it is that there can be no panacea, no quick and easy way out.

The most obvious fact that emerges from a study of programmes of reform is that we simply do not have the information necessary

---

[1] It should be noted that one implication of the analysis of the social situation in Bethnal Green contained in Chapter IV is that efforts to forward the cause of mental health will be, in part at least, limited by the extent to which social conditions (notably housing and security of employment) can be improved to a degree which makes a more satisfying way of life physically possible.

for making a really intelligent and satisfactory choice from among the various alternatives proposed, though certain of these seem to be much more promising than others. The primary need then is for more research so that the best methods can be adopted with confidence, and an end made of the waste of time, effort, and money on those approaches which are not fitted for the task to be performed.

With this in mind an attempt can now be made to describe some of the more crucial gaps in our knowledge and the kinds of research which would be needed to bridge them. For a report on research to end in this way is not a confession of failure. It is a truism that any piece of research which is not over-pretentious in its claims, or over-trivial in its subject matter, will raise more problems than it solves, and the first step towards further progress is to ascertain clearly those questions which most urgently need to be answered.

The first point which must be made is that sufficient progress has been achieved to make it unnecessary and undesirable for research to be undertaken on vague, undifferentiated lines. It is now possible to choose a definite part of the field, and to apply the resources available to the solution of some definite problem, or series of problems. It is also certain that there is no longer any excuse for, or value in, small questionnaire studies on some highly selected group, used merely because it happens to be available. Small scale, inadequately planned and financed projects are unlikely, at this stage, to add to our sum of knowledge and will consequently be merely a waste of time, money and effort.

No claim is made that the problems set out below constitute an exhaustive list of those needing to be solved. They are no more than a representative selection from the main areas of the field, and though some effort has been made to include most of the really important and urgent tasks, no guarantee is given that this has been achieved. Moreover, no attempt has been made to include problems from neighbouring areas of related disciplines. Doubtless, many important questions concerned with race prejudice are awaiting research in history, ethics, economics, and political science, but they are not considered here. There are again numerous psychological problems, not concerned specifically with the study of prejudice, but dealing with more fundamental topics (e.g. the mechanisms of personality development and the determination of the direction of aggressive drives) which will not be discussed, though their solution would throw much light both on problems of prejudice and on questions in many other fields as well. Many of these topics have been referred to in previous chapters.

Most of the problems to be discussed have already been raised either explicitly or by implication, as for example, the confusion which exists concerning both the sociological factors associated with anti-Semitism and the contradictory nature of the results so far achieved. In view of the fact that investigators who have differed so widely in their findings on sociological variables have agreed to such an extent on the psychological ones, it seems reasonable to suppose that there is no simple, invariable correspondence between these factors and anti-Semitism, and that if general propositions concerning this relationship are to be formulated, they will need to be on a higher level of abstraction than has hitherto been attempted. This means that efforts to measure correlations between social or economic class, or religious beliefs, or educational level, or experience of economic difficulties and anti-Semitism, are unlikely to produce any useful results.

It is probable that the apparently simple facts of religious affiliation, voting behaviour, and other similar factors are actually extremely complicated, and that their significance varies considerably from one social situation to another. In other words, the research workers who have used "simple" variables of the kind mentioned have been ignoring many complexities, including much that is known about the determinants of the perception of social situations. Many of the apparently contradictory correlations are probably largely spurious in the sense that one variable in the correlation (e.g. political party supported) consists in fact of a complexity of elements, the nature of which is not fully known and which have been rather fortuitously thrown together and provided with a deceptively simple label which may or may not have some real connection with the actual content of the variable in question. Several men interviewed in Bethnal Green made highly critical remarks about the Labour Government then in power. Often their arguments were those commonly used by Conservative supporters, but if they were then asked how they actually voted they would reply in surprised tones, "Labour, of course, how else would a working man vote?" To classify these men together with an ardent young middle class man for whom Socialism is a crusade involving a sharp break with the traditions of his family seems to involve some very large assumptions.

As another example we can take the nature of the association between religious belief and anti-Semitism, where investigators have reported every degree of correlation from significantly positive to significantly negative. It would seem desirable to approach the problem rather differently in the future, and instead of attempting simple correlations of this sort, to use a more refined method and seek for correlations of various kinds. Adorno and his associates have made a beginning in this direction and report that deep religious belief shows a positive correlation with tolerance while "conventional religiosity" correlates positively with prejudice. The findings of Allport and Kramer and the views of Loewenstein (1951) seem to be consistent with this conclusion, but further confirmation and considerably more detailed information is necessary. It would be desirable for an investigation on this topic to be undertaken with a sufficient number of subjects to allow for a good deal of subdivision for statistical purposes, while leaving groups large enough for significant results. It would be necessary to take into account a considerable range of variables, such as the relationship of the subject's beliefs to those of his parents; the particular sect to which he belonged; the strength of his beliefs as measured by various types of behaviour (other than frequency of attendance at religious services, which would not differentiate between various types of non-attenders); the kind of religious instruction received as a child; tendencies towards fundamentalism and liberalism in doctrines accepted; the social standing of the particular sect and congregation in the subject's community; the nature of pressures in the particular community for and against the holding and expressing of various types of religious belief; and it would be desirable to attempt a study of the connection between the unconscious and irrational aspects of each personality and the acceptance or rejection of religious beliefs. Until we have data approaching this order of complexity it is unlikely that any useful generalisations on this topic can be made, while in view of the diversity of results so far reported it will be necessary for the investigation to be carried out more than once in different areas for any degree of certainty to be possible.

Other types of sociological data may require a somewhat lesser degree of complexity, but here again the best approach seems an avoidance of simple correlations between situation and attitude. Probably a more fruitful attack would be to classify situations according to the subject's own evaluation, or at any rate, according to some system that enabled this to be taken into account, as the results of most research suggest that experiences are most relevant when seen *by the subject* as gratifications or deprivations. Such an evaluation would probably vary according to certain accompanying circumstances, such as the presence or absence of other sources of gratification carrying an equivalent degree of social approval; the extent to which the situation is condemned, excused, or approved by the community; the relation of the situation to the individual's most important goals, and particularly those goals which are highly valued by the community. It seems at least possible that the significance of a given type of situation will vary from class to class and from one cultural area to another. The role of the customs of the community concerned, in providing different scales of gratifications and deprivations for men and for women, needs careful study, particularly if it is found that in some communities, contrary to general experience, the women are more anti-Semitic than the men; while investigations in communities having few, or no, Jewish members are needed to throw further light on the relationship between anti-Semitism and amount of contact with Jews. Another possible example of cultural variation concerns the question of age. It is likely that in a community in which people acquired increased status as they grew older a positive correlation between age and prejudice would not be found.

It is undoubtedly of great importance that more precise data should be obtained as to the exact association of easily observable situations with anti-Semitism, since this seems to be the most likely method of predicting an increase, and so being able to take appropriate steps to combat it. The points made earlier in this chapter with respect to the need for research into the effectiveness of methods of reducing prejudice become relevant here.

Returning to the topic with which this book has been primarily concerned—the connection between personality and prejudice—we find a somewhat different situation. The amount of agreement so far achieved enables the research worker to accept certain basic propositions and to proceed to the elucidation of further details.

As has already been pointed out, very much more information is required about individuals who exhibit anti-Semitism in a comparatively mild degree. It is conceivable, for example, that while in most cases this mildness is associated with a relatively slight development of personality characteristics associated with the more extreme forms of prejudice, it may in some cases be due to the expression of aggressive feelings being inhibited by various types of social pressures. It would be desirable to know how effective this inhibition is, and under what circumstances it might break down and release the full strength of the aggressive drives. Investigation is also needed into the extent to which personalities of the type described as predisposed to prejudice can release their drives in other directions and avoid altogether the expression of racial prejudice. Mayo has described a group of political agitators whose personality characteristics appear to correspond roughly with those of the anti-Semites of Bethnal Green (Quoted by Urwick, 1950, pp. 21-2). It may well be that the other aggressive opinions and attitudes of these men had psychologically the same meaning as the anti-Semites' prejudice, in which case the two could be combined in some wider category; it then becomes important to study the forces which operate to determine the direction that the expression of prejudice is likely to take.

There is one further significant area of research which, while lying outside the limits imposed upon this book, is none the less of great importance. Any comprehensive study of anti-Semitism involves studying not only the attitudes and behaviour of Gentiles towards Jews, but also those of Jews towards Gentiles. The actions of anti-Semites do not merely affect Jews, they also produce reactions which are an important part of the situation; so far little attention has been paid to them apart from a certain amount of passing reference to the phenomenon of Jewish anti-Semitism. One of the few attempts to consider the psychology of the Jewish reaction to anti-Semitism is the set of hypotheses put forward by Bettelheim (1947) on the basis of his experiences in a concentration camp.

Stated very briefly this theory is that the activities of anti-Semites set up in many Jews anxieties which are dealt with by means of neurotic mechanisms rather similar to those which the anti-Semite uses in dealing with his anxieties, and consequently these Jews find it just as difficult to adjust themselves to the realities of a situation as do the anti-Semites. For this reason, according to Bettelheim, these Jews construct a stereotype of "the anti-Semite" which is almost as imperfect and unserviceable as the anti-Semitic stereotype of "the Jew", and they sometimes find it necessary, in order to justify their fear of "the anti-Semite", to depict him as much more dangerous than he really is. A similar reaction is probably observable in some of those Jews who, despite all evidence to the contrary, insist that anti-Semitism has no similarity with other forms of prejudice, thereby implying that Jews are in some undefined way a unique group (cf. Bettelheim, 1948). Another, not infrequent, Jewish reaction to anti-Semitism with possibly a basically similar motivation, is seen in vigorous objections to efforts to make a scientific study of the subject, or even to attempts to reduce prejudice by educational programmes. Bettelheim's views on these reactions may, or may not, be correct, but they are undoubtedly worth investigating. It is certain that Jews do react to anti-Semitic behaviour and that these reactions, forming an important part of the total situation, should be studied (cf. Saenger and Gordon, 1950).

Recent research has made it increasingly clear that when a situation exists which involves relatively chronic tensions between individuals, whatever the rights and wrongs of the situation, it is almost invariably found that the actions and reactions of all the parties concerned have an influence in maintaining the state of tension (Jaques, 1950; Trist and Bamforth, 1951). In attempting to understand such conditions in order to relieve the tensions, it is necessary to understand all aspects of the total situation and not merely the roles of those most obviously responsible.

The reason for the neglect of the problem of Jewish reactions up to the present is not difficult to imagine. Jewish investigators, not unnaturally, have felt that the most important part of anti-Semitism lay with the anti-Semitic Gentiles and it was there that any study should be pursued. The unprejudiced Gentiles, in their turn, have felt too guilty at the behaviour of members of their own group to put forward suggestions for research which might seem to be an echo of the accusations of the anti-Semites themselves. Such motives are understandable but need to be overcome if scientific research into the field of race relations is to be carried on successfully.

The most fundamental point to be borne in mind is that social science research is, even more than other types of scientific research, a slow, difficult and expensive affair. It not infrequently happens that a piece of psychological research involving a great deal of time and effort is equivalent, in its result, to a single set of observations on the part of, for example, a chemist. No well trained chemical research worker would be prepared to rely upon a single series of observations but would repeat his experiment until convinced that his results were correct. Social scientists (and more particularly those people who expect social scientists to help in the solution of their problems) must be prepared to devote the necessary resources of time and money to the repetition of complicated experiments and observations if they wish to obtain certain knowledge for use in planning future actions.

Bethnal Green: An Historical Sketch

THE casual passer-by does not regard Bethnal Green as a likely spot for historical investigation. The narrow, monotonous streets of shabby brick dwellings, the ugly overhead railway bridges with their inevitable clouds of smoke, and the obviously nineteenth century appearance of the churches and most other public buildings, all combine to suggest that Bethnal Green's history comprises a period of mushroom growth following the Industrial Revolution, and a subsequent period of virtual stagnation, at least so far as building is concerned, until, in more modern times, blocks of flats begin to make their appearance.

It is true that, compared with many parts of London, including some of the neighbouring boroughs, the known history of Bethnal Green is slight in quantity, but it extends back to Roman times and provides a considerable amount of material, both factual and legendary, the famous story of the Blind Beggar and his daughter being the chief example of the latter. It would be easy, but, for purposes of this study, unprofitable, to become immersed in such topics as the derivation of the district's name, its association with the Bishops of London, and with Samuel Pepys (Allgood, 1905). For the purpose in hand, the history of Bethnal Green was just beginning at the end of the seventeenth century. In this period two factors stand out prominently. The first is the extent to which Bethnal Green was peopled by foreign refugees, the second, the rapidity with which it changed from a country village to an overcrowded London Borough.

It is not surprising that East London has always included among its population a large number of persons of foreign birth or descent. Within the City the medieval guilds and their successors, often backed by the power of legal authority, maintained restrictions on manufacture, trade and employment generally, which made it virtually impossible for newcomers to establish themselves. Such people, if they wanted to set up business, found it necessary to do so outside the city walls. For a variety of reasons, chiefly connected with the availability of transport and markets, they chose the areas due east of the City (Smith, 1939). Many of these newcomers came from other parts of England, or were even inhabitants of the City seeking to escape from the restrictions of the Guilds, but from Elizabethan times they had included foreign refugees, chiefly Protestants from France and the Low Countries. The first influx followed the massacre of Saint Bartholomew in 1572, and resulted in the formation of a settlement just outside Bishopsgate which became known as Petty France. The sack of Antwerp in 1585 produced another migration. Like the earlier French refugees many of these people were silk weavers and they settled in the same area, spreading east to Spitalfields (Sabin, 1931, pp. 7–8).

It was, however, the revocation of the Edict of Nantes which resulted in the chief migration. Between 1685 and 1687 over a hundred thousand refugees arrived in this country, fifteen thousand of whom settled in the neighbourhood of London, chiefly in Spitalfields and the western areas of the present borough of Bethnal Green, thus producing the first spate of building in the district. Gascoyne's map of 1703 shows plainly that with the exception of the new buildings, Bethnal Green consisted chiefly of farmland, with just a few houses and gardens, many of them country residences of city merchants, in the neighbourhood of the present Bethnal Green Gardens, then the "Green" from which the hamlet took its name.

By 1743 the increase in population was such that the creation of a new parish was necessary and work was commenced on the new church, Saint Matthew's, in the same year (George, 1951, pp. 67 and 80). Rocque's map of 1746 shows that the church stood in the midst of open fields roughly halfway between the traditional centre of the hamlet and the new housing area in the west. At the time of the creation of the parish the population was estimated at 15,000, living in 1,800 houses, nearly all packed into a small area (*ibid.* p. 11). This rapid increase did not continue (George, 1951, p. 413). Strype, in his 1755 edition of Stow's "Survey of London", is able to report of Bethnal Green, "that this parish hath the face of a country, affording everything to render it pleasant, fields, pasturage, grounds for cattle, and formerly woods and marshes". Forty years later two-thirds of the district was still farmland (Vale, 1934, p. 20). In 1808 it was necessary to maintain a cattle pound to deal with straying animals in the area (*ibid.* p. 53); in 1813 the northern parts of the Cambridge Heath Road were so little built upon that St. Paul's could still be seen from there (*ibid.* p. 90), while two years later *The Times* carried an illustrated advertisement for a fishing pond known as the Wellington Fishery (*ibid.* p. 40), located near the now densely populated Wellington Row in the north-western part of the borough. At this time the country to the east of the Cambridge Heath Road was very thinly settled. A great deal of land in this area was broken up into small gardens and allotments which were worked, as a spare time occupation, by the weavers of the western districts and Spitalfields.

It was during the second quarter of the nineteenth century that the greatest changes in the district took place. By 1847 the population had multiplied by six, and reached the figure of 82,000—not very far short of the 129,680 that it was eventually to achieve in 1901; most of this growth, which seems to have taken place after the end of the eighteenth century, does not appear to have been associated with the prosperity of the inhabitants of the area (*ibid.* pp. 22-3). The weaving industry during this period was in a struggling condition, failing to maintain itself in the face of foreign competition, in spite of attempts by Parliament to protect it. John Wesley, who preached in the parish on a number of occasions, reports of the people in 1777 that "Many of them I found in such poverty as few can conceive without seeing it".

In 1848 Doctor Hector Gavin presented a report to the Health of Towns Association on the sanitary condition of Bethnal Green at that date (Gavin, 1848). He describes the district as "a populous parish, itself constituting no mean town", but goes on to describe people who "have their health injured, their lives sacrificed, their property squandered, their morals depraved", by the overcrowded, insanitary conditions in which they have to live. In the eastern areas and the neighbourhood of Victoria Park there had, at that time, been little building, but despite this the district to the east of the Cambridge Heath Road was not an attractive one.

The houses . . . are remarkable for their great deficiency of drainage and for their dirty streets, but there are, comparatively, few courts, and still fewer alleys; where they do exist, however, they are in no respect superior to the filthy hovels and wretched abodes common to the (other) districts. The gradual conversion of summer houses, cabins, and wooden-sheds into human habitation, is to be remarked . . . (The roads) are always very dirty, sometimes abominably filthy. (*Ibid*, p. 7.)

From this report, and from the maps and statistical tables attached, it appears that by this time the greater part of Bethnal Green was populated at almost its maximum density, later increases being largely in those districts in the east and north-east which until that time had not been built upon. With the exception of those areas which were cleared for the building of blocks of dwellings during the past 60 years, and those destroyed by bombs, Bethnal Green's houses at the present day are chiefly the same buildings seen by Dr. Gavin. Externally conditions have greatly improved; the open sewers, the cesspools, and the filth in the streets have disappeared; the water supply has improved (though frequently it has not improved beyond the stage of one tap per dwelling—even this, however, is vastly better than the outdoor tap supplying four houses, with the water turned on three times a week for two hours, at low pressure, as described by Dr. Gavin) but standards of housing are still deplorably low and overcrowding is the rule rather than the exception. Water supply was not the only utility that was inadequate. As late as 1900 a Bethnal Green correspondent was writing to a local paper to complain of the slow progress made in supplying gas to the borough (*East London Advertiser*, 6th January, 1900). In October, 1903, we find it reported that Bethnal Green was the only borough in North-East London not lighted by electricity. (*East London Advertiser*, 24th October, 1903.) During this period it is observable that most East London newspaper references to Bethnal Green combined to suggest that the area was regarded by the neighbouring districts as rather backward by comparison with their own conditions.

Those areas which at the time of Dr. Gavin's visit were still unpopulated were, in general, more fortunate than their western neighbours. When they were built upon, in the second half of the century, the houses were greatly superior in quality. The streets bordering Victoria Park, the Bonner Road and Approach Road areas, and some streets to the east of Regents Canal, were peopled largely by the middle class. Three and four storied houses with large rooms contrasted with the tiny, two storied, often only three roomed, cottages of the older areas. The streets were wider, straighter, and their layout much better planned.

To make matters worse for the greater part of the borough, weaving, the chief industry of the district, went into rapid decline. The commercial treaty of 1860 resulted in a flood of cheap French silks pouring into the country. The East End industry, already struggling, was quite unable to withstand the competition. In 1831 there were 17,000 looms in the Bethnal Green—Spitalfields area, employing more than 50,000 people. In 1931 eleven elderly persons provided the total manpower of Bethnal Green's weaving industry. This combination of population increase and economic decline comprises the greatest part of Bethnal Green's history for the second half of the nineteenth century, and the area which had so recently been fertile farmland became one of the worst slums in the city (Sabin, 1931, pp. 13–19).

This mournful period contained, however, the beginnings of better things. After the passage of the Public Health Act of 1848 Bethnal Green shared in the general improvement in living conditions, while philanthropic and public-spirited individuals began to take an interest in the work of social betterment. The district's first settlement, Oxford House, was founded in 1884, and by the end of the century a number of churches and other religious bodies were maintaining schools and other educational and social institutions of various kinds. In 1869 one of the worst areas in the borough was cleared to make room for the Columbia Road Market,[1] and in the closing years of the century the London County Council began work on clearing the most westerly section of the borough in order to erect blocks of dwellings. This district, now known as the Boundary Street Estate, was previously one of the poorest and most degraded parts of Bethnal Green.[2] One of the earliest districts to be settled by the Huguenot weavers, it had steadily deteriorated to become a centre of vice, poverty, and crime. Since that time the work of clearance and rehousing has proceeded steadily, the work

---

[1] Nova Scotia Gardens had been a district notorious as a centre of the body-snatching or "resurrection" industry, with its associated murders and other crimes (cf. Anon, 1832, pp. 68 and *passim*).

[2] Morrison, A., *A Child of the Jago* (London: Penguin Books, 1946). Whatever its value as a work of literature, this novel does appear to give a fairly accurate account of life in this area just before the clearances. That the district had long had an unsavoury reputation can be seen from the following quotation from a newspaper of 1862, "New Nichols Street, Half Nichols Street, Turville Street, comprising within the same area numerous blind courts and alleys, form a densely crowded district of Bethnal Green. . . . It abounds with the young Arabs of the streets, and its outward moral degradation is at once apparent to anyone who passes that way. Here the police are *certain* to be found, day and night, their presence being required to quell riots and preserve decency." Quoted in Thornbury, p. 14.

being shared among the L.C.C., the local Borough Council, and various private individuals and companies. The wholesale destruction of houses during the Second World War has considerably hastened this process, since most of these are being replaced by blocks of dwellings. No official figures are available, but an estimate based on a sample drawn from the electoral roll for the borough suggests that more than one-third of the people of Bethnal Green lived in these dwellings by 1949.

It was towards the end of last century that another change took place—and one of primary importance for this study—the arrival of the Jews. Almost from the first, after their readmission to England in the reign of Charles II, the Jewish population of England had tended to concentrate in the East End of London. To begin with they were mostly Portuguese Sephardic Jews living in the area north of the Tower of London and east of Bishopsgate (Adler, 1930, pp. 192–4). Their numbers were small and until the end of the seventeenth century did not include any great proportion of poor persons. The latter began to increase when 20,000 Jewish refugees (German and Polish) from the Thirty Years War reached England. Their settlements stretched eastwards from Aldgate along Whitechapel Road and it was probably at this period that Bethnal Green received its first Jewish inhabitants, in that part of the borough which touches on the Whitechapel Road, in the neighbourhood of Brady Street.

There was, for nearly two hundred years, no great increase in the numbers of English Jews. In 1858 they totalled only 30,000, nearly all of whom lived in London. Shortly after this date the effects of the Russian persecutions began to show themselves in an increased flow of Jewish refugees from eastern Europe. By the end of the century some 70,000 had arrived in this country. Again their chief settlements were in the eastern parts of London, particularly at Mile End (Modder, 1944, pp. 237–43). In the early days of this influx Bethnal Green's Jewish population must have remained small, except perhaps in the neighbourhood of Brady Street and in Brick Lane. In 1881 the total number of "persons of foreign birth and nationality" living in Bethnal Green was estimated at 925, compared with the total of nearly 16,000 in the districts which make up the modern borough of Stepney (Smith, 1902, p. 112). The reason for this is that the immigrants, landing in Stepney, poor and often without friends, at first crowded into the overpopulated riverside slums and only slowly, and as their fortunes and knowledge of the area improved, moved into new districts (Potter, 1902, pp. 184–6). Bethnal Green, being already overcrowded with local born folk, who were not prepared to make room for foreigners, was less hospitable to these people than Stepney, where their co-religionists formed a large part of the population.

The period from 1880 to 1900 is one of the most fully documented in the history of the East London Jews, and it would be possible to write a very lengthy account from the material available (Booth, 1902; Russell and Lewis, 1900). We can see how these destitute immigrants struggled to improve their condition, how they introduced to the East End the garment-making and boot and shoe trades in their modern mass-production forms, which to the present day are among the chief industries of the district. Throughout the whole period they spread outwards from Stepney into the surrounding boroughs. Sometimes they displaced existing tenants, paying higher rents and then overcoming this disadvantage by sub-letting, a practice which, while it provided homes for more of the newcomers, increased the already great overcrowding. Frequently, particularly in the case of Bethnal Green, the influx of Jews took place when tenement dwellings were erected to replace slum clearances (Russell and Lewis, 1900). The Boundary Street Estate already referred to is an example of this. Prior to the clearances the population was entirely non-Jewish, but Russell's map shows some of these streets as 50 per cent Jewish in 1899. In 1901 the foreign-born population of Bethnal Green was 4,634. Of these more than half came from Russia and Poland, and most of the remainder from Germany, Austria, and the Balkans; a few were Italians (*East London Advertiser*, 23rd August, 1902). This constituted 3·5 per cent of the total population. A schoolteacher who taught in the Boundary Street area in 1919 states that 90 per cent of the school children were Jewish at that date.

In this same period we can see the beginnings of the development of the furniture trade as an important Jewish industry, but here again Bethnal Green lagged behind her neighbours. Only 72 foreign-born persons were engaged in this trade in 1887 out of the total of 4,766 persons employed in it in Bethnal Green, whereas in Stepney the comparative figures are 239 and 1,804 (Aves, 1902, pp. 159 and 213). At this date Bethnal Green was already regarded as the centre of the East End furniture trade, a position it has maintained almost to the present day. Gossett Street was then the main centre for the trade, which seems during the previous forty to fifty years to have displaced weaving as the main occupation of the district. The reasons for the choice of woodworking as an alternative to silk weaving do not appear to be known.

So much for the material conditions of life for the Jews in Bethnal Green at the turn of the century. What of their social position? More particularly, what kind of relations did they enjoy with their Gentile neighbours? Here the picture is not so clear. Booth's work is, on the whole, silent on the point though we are able to gather from passing references that all was not well. One of the most obvious features of the Jewish community appears to have been the number of individuals who succeeded in rising from a position of abject poverty to a condition which, in the East End, was regarded as tolerably comfortable, and this success was resented by their Gentile neighbours. Other writers, notably Russell (1900, pp. 42-3) and Besant (1899, pp. 195-6) were chiefly concerned to show that unlike the countries from which the Jews came there was no anti-Semitism in East London, and hence they began by painting a suspiciously idyllic picture of conditions there; here again, however, passing references suggest that in reality conditions were less than perfect. This is confirmed by a review of the book by Russell and Lewis in the *East London Advertiser* of 12th January, 1901, when the reviewer asks, "Do the East Enders take so kindly to the foreign invasion as Mr. Russell makes out?" Russell for instance refers to an "outcry" which was raised about injuries to English working men by the unfair competition, and he devotes a good deal of space demonstrating that this fear is groundless (*op. cit.* pp. xi ff.). ter he refers to the feelings of hostility among the East Enders districts bordering on those where the Jews have taken over all accommodation (*ibid.* pp. 16-17), and he accepts the inevitability ostility towards the Jews as long as they "remain an isolated peculiar people, self-centred in their organisation and fundaally alien in their ideas and aims" (*ibid.* p. 8). Again he says, e Jews are always to remain separate they are likely also to a constant source of disquietude and offence" (*ibid.* p. 137). begins in the same way by saying that there is no Jew-baiting and but admits that Jews are not popular. He then goes on ss the reasons for this, concluding that it is due to their epared to go to any lengths short of actually breaking the ake a success of their business (*op. cit.*, pp. 195-6).

With the exception of two very short-lived periodicals which made their appearance during the 1860's, Bethnal Green has never had its own local newspaper and we have to rely for contemporary reports on newspapers published in Stepney and Hackney. Although both papers served Bethnal Green, both showed less interest in that borough than in other districts—so much so that during the early years of the century the Stepney paper, *The East London Advertiser*, did not even publish the results of parliamentary and local elections held in Bethnal Green. In spite of this, a study of the files of these two newspapers produces a quantity of material that can be used to give a rough picture of relations between Gentiles and Jews in the borough, provided that a number of qualifications are kept in mind.

The first difficulty to be solved is the extent to which it can be assumed that conditions in the neighbouring boroughs apply also to Bethnal Green. Even more uncertain is the extent to which the sentiments explicitly and implicitly expressed as the editorial policy of these papers are typical of the majority of the people of the districts concerned. In the following sections it has been assumed that only reports of actual events (including reported statements of local people) can give anything like a reliable picture of the situation. In the few cases where editorial or other outside opinion has been quoted, this has been clearly indicated. Also, only material relating directly to Bethnal Green has been used, except where it is definitely stated that the contrary is the case. It will, however, be seen that there is no reason for believing that anti-Jewish feeling was much weaker in Bethnal Green than in other parts of the East End.

There are three observations which can be extensively documented from editorial comment, from reports of speeches made by local members of Parliament and other public figures, and from the correspondence columns of the papers. The situation which had resulted from the influx of refugees from Europe (which at this date was still continuing) was causing general concern. Whether or not the refugees were blamed, whether or not the overcrowded and unsatisfactory conditions of life in the East End were associated with the fact that most of the newcomers were Jews, and whether or not a large influx of foreigners was regarded as desirable, the incontestable fact remained that conditions in the East End were highly unsatisfactory from the point of view of public health, the amount of unemployment and the incidence of crime. It is easy to see now that an intelligently planned immigration scheme to deal with the refugees immediately on arrival, coupled with adequate laws relating to the sub-letting of dwellings, could have largely eliminated these evil effects. Such actions would have been contrary to the whole spirit of the times, and in any case the development reached an acute stage so quickly that those in authority can hardly be blamed for not having anticipated it.

Whatever the rights and wrongs of the case the situation existed and called for attention, and it is here that the second generalisation can be made. Most speakers and writers who tried to influence public opinion on this subject took the line of blaming the new-comers for all the evils of the situation. The third generalisation is that almost without exception these propagandists made "the Jews" the specific object of their attacks. Nearly always they would begin by saying that this was not the case, that they referred only to the criminal, the diseased, and the degraded among the refugees, regardless of creed or nationality. These statements were often made from platforms on which sat Jewish leaders; sometimes they were even made by Jews; but with almost no exceptions it is impossible not to assume that these attacks were in fact being made upon Jews as such, or at any rate, East European Jews. For example, a description of the May Day procession of 1904 which begins as a diatribe against undesirable aliens continues as follows—

> The demonstration was a real triumph for the East End aliens. They swarmed to the West End in their thousands, carrying their little alien babies and bags of oranges, with the peel of which they strewed the park. From Hyde Park Corner to Marble Arch and across to the Serpentine the Park was full of Polish Jews, German Jews, Stepney and White-chapel Jews, talking all kinds of tongues except English. . . . Several thousand "Yids"—undersized, ill-fed, and dirty—gathered round a cart on which were seated a dozen of their fellow–tribesmen, with a little scrap of red muslin dangling from a stick in front of them with the words "Workers, prepare for the general strike" as the watchword of the group. . . . The impression left on many minds was that the procession had something to do with a Jewish festival. (*East London Advertiser*, 7th May, 1904.)

The difficulties which attended any attempt to prevent propaganda against the "undesirable alien" becoming anti-Semitic are well illustrated by a letter appearing in the *East London Advertiser* for

5th July, 1902. It is such an excellent illustration of this point that it is worth quoting in full.

Sir. My attention has been called to a leaflet headed "British Brothers League"[1] and signed by Messrs. A. T. Williams, L.C.C. and F. E. Eddis in the course of which it says "If you or any of your friends have suffered by the Alien Jews coming here, now is the time to say so."

As the organiser of the British Brothers League I should like to say that the first condition that I made on starting the movement was that the word "Jew" should never be mentioned and that as far as possible the agitation should be kept clear of racial or religious animosity.

If the above leaflet was issued by the British Brothers League then the League has departed from its original policy.

I am informed, however, by an official of the League that this leaflet was issued without the authority of the Executive Committee.

Presumably Mr. A. T. Williams L.C.C. consulted Major Gordon M.P. before the leaflet was drawn up. In which case these gentlemen would appear to have executed a change of front since issuing their leaflet in February last.

That leaflet which was printed in both English and Yiddish contained the following:

"Do not be deceived by people who are trying to make you believe that 'alien' means 'Jew'. It does not! 'Alien' means 'foreigner'. Religion has nothing to do with it!"

Your obedient servant,

William Stanley Shaw.

Founder and Ex-President of the British
Brothers League.

During the early years of the century there was no lack of anti-alien and anti-Jewish propaganda, spoken and printed, in the East End. The agitations which led to the setting up of the Royal Commission under Lord James in March, 1904, provided an opportunity which the anti-Semites were not slow to use. This situation continued until after the Aliens Bill (based on the report of the Commission and first brought before the House in 1905) was finally dropped by the newly-elected Liberal government in 1906.

[1] This league had been founded about six months earlier amid scenes of great enthusiasm at a mass meeting in the People's Palace, addressed by local leaders and well-known people (including Marie Corelli). Its aim was stated to be "England for the English". The meeting was reported at great length in the *East London Advertiser*, 18th January, 1902.

Examples of the type of propaganda can be found in almost any issue of the East London papers during this period. It is interesting to note that the anti-Semites aimed some of their most bitter vituperations at a young Liberal who took a prominent part in opposing the passage of the Aliens Bill—Winston Churchill. Also worthy of note is a Parliamentary candidate's advertisement of January, 1906, which says simply, "England for the English and Major Gordon for Stepney."

Given this general atmosphere of fairly successful anti-Semitic propaganda in the East End as a whole, what can be discovered about the situation in Bethnal Green as distinct from the general picture? With reference to the facts already given, it should be pointed out that the newspaper reports make it clear that many of the Bethnal Green civic and political representatives were concerned in the various anti-Semitic and anti-Alien campaigns equally with those in Stepney. On the other hand, however, the Bethnal Green members of Parliament, both before and after the 1906 election, were members of the Liberal party which was largely opposed to the Aliens Bill. It would certainly be very unsafe to assume from this that there was less anti-Semitism in Bethnal Green than in the more southerly borough. One of the fieldworker's Bethnal Green informants, who was a schoolboy at this time, has reported that he can remember great anti-Semitic feeling. When blocks of flats were being erected the story would go around that they were being financed by the Rothschilds and would be available for Jews only. It was common for Gentile schoolboys to collect outside Jewish schools (which closed later in the day than the Gentile schools) and stone the Jewish boys as they emerged.

Until the outbreak of war in 1914 only one definite account of open anti-Semitism in Bethnal Green found its way into print. On 16th September, 1911, the *Hackney Gazette* printed a report with the headlines "Barring Jewish Dairymen—Strong Action by Bethnal Green Guardians", and beginning with the statement "A feeling of anti-Semitism seems to have broken out amongst the Bethnal Green Guardians". It then goes on to state that when the Board met to consider the half-yearly contracts, one member moved that the milk contract should not be given to the lowest tender, on the grounds that it came from a Jewish firm. This was agreed to. An amendment that the matter should be referred to the Finance Committee because this decision would involve an increased cost to the ratepayers was defeated, one member saying "We won't have any Jews—we don't want them." The report goes on—

> Miss Mary James, the chairman of the Board of Guardians, who presided, said, "Seeing that there is apparently some feeling over this milk contract, although I did not personally vote, I must admit I would not vote to give a contract for milk to a Jew—they would not deal with us for food." (Loud cheers and a cry from Mr. Dan Jones (a local milkman), "Good luck to you, and bravo! Miss James.")
>
> When the poultry contract was reached there were only two tenders, both at the same price, the contractors being Mr. Nathan, a local Jew, the present contractor, and a Mr. Rowles, also a local poulterer.
>
> Dr. Style. "I move Rowles. No Jews!"
>
> This was duly seconded and carried.

The following week a report was printed that Miss James had stated that the failure to give the contract to the lowest tender was a mistake which had been rectified. She denied that there had been a Jewish boycott.

After the outbreak of war Bethnal Green received even less attention in the East End press, and it is impossible to judge the situation. Anti-Semitism was not a frequent topic in any context and I am unable to find any direct reference to the subject until 18th August, 1919, when the *Hackney Gazette* published a letter from a resident of Clapton complaining that Jews were buying houses in the area and converting them into factories. However, during and immediately after the war, there were indications of some anti-alien feeling in the East End and it is not difficult to imagine that some of this was expressed as anti-Semitism, particularly as two of the complaints, sweating, and "doing Englishmen out of jobs" have frequently been associated with anti-Semitism in more recent times. From this time silence again descends except for occasional vague remarks about Englishmen being kept out of work by "outsiders", (e.g. *Hackney Gazette*, 18th August, 1924, Leading Article) until 1926 when on 23rd January, the *East London Advertiser* refers editorially to the fact that the presence of a "Jewish element" on the local Council was an important factor in the process, observable in Stepney, of "secularising Sunday".

Here again one has no guarantee that this reflects popular opinion in Bethnal Green. About all that can be inferred is that the silence of the papers during this period suggests that anti-Semitism was less of a force than it had been prior to the war. It is certain, at least, that it was not being used as a public issue. This impression is supported by two reports appearing in the *East London Advertiser* on 13th March, 1926, and early in 1930 respectively. The first relates that at a meeting of a literary and debating society in Bethnal Green, a motion that foreigners should be allowed to settle in England had been debated and carried, while the latter is a lengthy précis of an address given by a local Gentile doctor on Jewish achievements in medicine. On 4th July, 1934, however, we again find the *Hackney Gazette* featuring a complaint about the conversion of houses to factories, and the Jewish practice of keeping shops open on Sundays, while on the 18th of the same month it is reported that the member of Parliament for Hackney Central entertained in his home staff and students from a Jewish college, and during his speech of welcome took the opportunity to deny rumours that he was associated with the Fascist Party. The only previous local newspaper reference to this party was a report of a debate on economic policy, held in Stepney in 1926 under the auspices of an association of unemployed, between a member of the Labour Party and a member of "the British Fascisti".

From this time onwards reports on the Fascists and on anti-Semitism increase rapidly. The *Gazette* twice complains editorially (25th July, and 29th August, 1934) of the damage that a Jewish boycott of German goods is doing to British trade with Germany, and consequently to the level of unemployment in Britain. This, it was asserted, "is playing into the hands of the Fascists". On 29th October, however, the formation of an Anti-Fascist Association, supported by all Hackney Members of Parliament, was given a one-and-a-half column report, while two days later a Fascist meeting addressed by Mosley in the Albert Hall covered a bare half column. From the middle of 1934 occasional letters written by members of the British Union of Fascists appear, followed in due course by replies from various people, while commencing from 17th July, 1935, we find reports of disturbances at meetings held in Bethnal Green by both the British Union of Fascists and the Communist Party, resulting in the appearance of people in court on charges of assault, obstruction, and so on.

During the next five years these reports, and the letters supporting and attacking Fascism, increased in frequency, but on the basis of the newspaper reports it is quite impossible to say more than that Bethnal Green included a considerable number of people who responded favourably to the anti-Semitic opinions expressed by the Fascists, and a considerable number who opposed these opinions —a conclusion which can easily be reached without having recourse to the lengthy procedure of the content analysis of newspaper reports. The majority of the reports carried by both newspapers do not relate to Bethnal Green, and a study of the addresses of persons arrested at Fascist and Communist meetings shows that they cover most parts of London and are never restricted to the area in which the meeting was held. The view that events at meetings in a particular district can be taken as indicating the state of public opinion in that district is clearly untenable. It is certain that reported clashes were in fact largely a series of skirmishes between the mobile forces of two opposing factions. Observations at Fascist and anti-Fascist meetings from 1947 onwards, when the same familiar faces could be seen in audiences at meetings all over London, suggest that the same pattern was being repeated at this later date.

The only data of a more precise nature available are the results of voting in local elections. The first appearance of Fascist candidates at elections occurred in March, 1937, when the party contested South West Bethnal Green and Shoreditch at the L.C.C. elections. All four candidates were defeated, but in Bethnal Green the two Fascists each polled just over 3,000 votes against the 7,700 of the Labour candidates and the 2,200 of the Liberals. In the neighbouring borough of Shoreditch the Fascists (one of whom was William Joyce) obtained over 2,400 votes.

Later in the same year the Fascists put up a number of candidates at the borough elections. In Bethnal Green some seats were contested in each ward. The results for each ward were as follows:

North Ward. Six seats. Four Fascist candidates. Highest vote (Labour) 2,272. Highest Fascist vote 731. Highest Liberal vote 630.

South Ward. Nine seats. Two Fascist candidates. Highest vote (Labour) 2,588. Highest Liberal vote, 1,208. Highest Fascist vote, 854.

East Ward. Nine seats. Eight Fascist candidates. Highest vote (Labour) 4,474. Highest Fascist vote, 1,805. Highest Liberal vote, 1,603.

West Ward. Six seats. Two Fascist candidates. Highest vote (Labour) 2,095. Highest Liberal vote, 1,122. Highest Fascist vote, 480.

Some seats were also contested in neighbouring boroughs. In Hackney three candidates stood in one ward, the most successful securing 242 votes. In Shoreditch four wards were contested by a total of eleven candidates. The votes obtained ranged from 267 down to less than 100. In interpreting these figures for the present purpose it must be remembered that anti-Semitism and Fascism, though closely associated, were not identical. The figures for anti-Semitic attitudes would certainly have been much higher.

The only further source of detailed information on Bethnal Green during the inter-war period is to be found in the *New Survey of London Life and Labour* (Smith, 1931, Vols. II and III) based on investigations carried out chiefly in 1928. In many respects the position had changed relatively little as compared with that described in Booth's survey. The furniture and wood-working trades were still the most important, followed by the manufacture of boots and shoes, clothing trades, distributive industries, and road transport. The amount of poverty was considerable, Bethnal Green ranking third among the boroughs of London for percentage of persons living in poverty (17·8 per cent). Comparatively little information is available concerning the Jewish members of the community. It was reported that "Jews are not so numerous as in Stepney but their numbers are said to be increasing" (*ibid.*, Vol. III, pp. 345–6). In other contexts Jews are referred to for the whole of London or for some other large area and it is impossible to give any accurate figures for Bethnal Green. It is stated, however, that the number of Jews engaged in the woodworking and furniture trades is increasing (*ibid.*, Vol. II, p. 219) while the fact that they are engaged in large numbers in both the clothing and the bootmaking trades is also noted (*ibid.*, Vol. II, pp. 269–271 and 373–5). Apart from such isolated scraps of information there is no material on which to base any account of the situation in Bethnal Green as far as the position of Jews was concerned at this particular time. One set of figures relating to Bethnal Green has an indirect bearing on this point. These state the proportion of foreign-born residents in the population 1881, 1911, and 1921. The percentages for these three years are 1·1, 6·7, and 6·0. There is no means of knowing how many of these foreign-born residents are Jewish though it is certain that the majority would be. The fall in the figure for 1921 means little, as the decrease in immigrants would be offset by the increasing number of locally born Jews. There are, however, no figures on this point, and those quoted do no more than help confirm the impression that the Jewish population in Bethnal Green was increasing up to the outbreak of the Second World War.

Information covering the war years is again sketchy, attention being concentrated on other topics. From accounts given by people living in the borough during this period, and from occasional newspaper comments, it would appear that anti-Semitism, while no longer expressed openly at public meetings, remained at a high level. It is reported, for example, that Jews (and more rarely Fascists) were widely blamed for a panic which occurred on 3rd March, 1943, in a crowd entering the local Underground Station in order to shelter from an air raid. The panic resulted in the deaths of 173 people. Evidence at an official inquiry made it clear that there was no factual basis whatever for this accusation (Dunne, 1945). That these rumours were taken seriously can be seen from the fact that though the report on this inquiry was not published until after the war, this particular finding was announced in the House of Commons by the Home Secretary shortly after the disaster. The sub-heading "Not Caused by Jewish Panic" appears over one local newspaper's report of Mr. Morrison's statement, which was the main front page news item that day (*Hackney Gazette*, 9th April, 1943).

How much have we been able to learn about the nature and causes of anti-Semitism in Bethnal Green from this historical survey? Not very much, it must be admitted, but a few points can be noted. In the first place it is evident that a tradition of influxes of religious refugees from the Continent had little or no effect in checking the development of prejudice as each group appeared, and secondly, it is clear that anti-Semitic feelings can be exploited for political purposes. Neither of these conclusions is surprising or in any way new. The most important lessons that can be learnt from the material presented in this chapter relate to the limited value of newspaper files, official statistics, and the results of the traditional type of social survey for studies of this kind. On the basis of the material presented above, for example, it would appear that anti-Semitism was moderately strong before 1900, flared up violently after 1902, died down again to a considerable degree after 1906, and was almost non-existent until 1934 when it flared up again with greatly increased violence.

There is little reason to believe that this is the true picture. That some anti-Semites were particularly active and noisy during the periods 1902–1906 and 1934–9 and that during these periods they received a great deal of publicity in the press is certain, but of the other years all we really know is that the situation was not described in print. It may well be that in 1922 (for example) anti-Semitism was at its highest point in the history of Bethnal Green (in the sense that at that time there were in the borough more people holding strongly prejudiced views than at any other time) but that as it was not organised, and hence not publicly expressed in speeches and demonstrations, we know nothing about it. Research such as this gives no indication of the actual distribution of attitudes but only of the distribution of certain kinds of expression of those attitudes. We know that anti-Semitism in Bethnal Green is not a new thing but has a history going back at least into the last century, and that at two different periods this anti-Semitism has been stimulated and organised for political purposes. Such conclusions add little to our knowledge.

APPENDIX B

The Rorschach Test Results

ACH extreme anti-Semite or tolerant person who was interviewed on a second occasion was asked to do the Rorschach
test. Only two refused (both tolerant people) with the result
that fourteen of these records were obtained, seven for each group.
These groups are admittedly too small for reliable results, but their
value is enhanced by the fact that they are the extreme cases from a
random sample, and the results have value as supporting evidence.

The use of a test of this kind for research purposes raised various
methodological difficulties. The problem of actually persuading the
subject to attempt the test has been described in Chapter V; the
remaining difficulties are concerned chiefly with the question of
assessing the significance of the results obtained.

The data provided by a Rorschach test consist of a largely
qualitative evaluation of the personality in terms which are partly
quantatitive but partly qualitative. The problem is therefore a
special instance of the general difficulty—discussed in an earlier
chapter—of quantifying qualitative material. In the case of the
Rorschach, two special difficulties arise. The first is the method of
comparing two individuals who show the same trait in different
degrees. It is not difficult to state which records indicate extreme
maladjustment of some sort, while those which indicate a good
adjustment are equally obvious; but how to classify the intermediate
records is a serious problem.

In the second case the difficulty arises from the fact that, unlike
an intelligence test, the Rorschach test does not reveal any single
item; nor does it describe a set of relatively distinct categories as
does a test like the Bernreuter Personality Inventory or the Minnesota
Multi-Phasic Personality Inventory. It displays an overall picture
of the main aspects of the personality, a kind of interlocking pattern,

and it becomes difficult to break this up into sections for comparative purposes.

When attempting to use the Thematic Apperception Test for a similar purpose, researchers were faced with this same difficulty (Frenkel-Brunswik, 1948a). In this case it was found possible to abstract the main themes which appeared in the responses, and having grouped them into classes, to count the number of instances of each class in any record. Such a procedure is less simple in the case of the Rorschach test, as separate "themes" are less easily distinguished; but it is possible to indicate certain aspects of personality as they are revealed by the test. Thus the presence of anxiety, a tendency to be affected more strongly by either internal or external factors, or the presence of strong repressing forces, will be revealed when they are a part of the personality under study, and the number of instances of such cases can be counted. Here again the primary difficulty is that of deciding when an indication becomes sufficiently marked to be regarded as warranting inclusion as an instance— where, in other words, does one draw the line between significant and insignificant indications? The choice which is made is bound to be somewhat arbitrary.

In one study of anti-Semitism the Rorschach test was given to thirty subjects, after which the number of instances of each type of response in the anti-Semitic records was compared with the same score for the tolerant records, by means of the test for significance of differences between means (Reichard, 1948; Frenkel-Brunswik and Sanford, 1945). It is reported that only one significant difference appeared—the tolerant group had a higher score for M. These investigators then selected the six types of responses which showed the greatest degree of discrimination, and combined them to produce a set of six signs which they suggested might prove to be diagnostic for anti-Semitism. They attempted to relate the various signs showing the greatest differences to definite personality traits, a procedure which would probably be regarded with some doubt by most Rorschach workers, as it is normally maintained that the use of a single type of response is rarely significant in itself and becomes significant only because of its position in a pattern, just as a flushed face is a sign of ill health when associated with a normally pale complexion, a high temperature, and an irregular pulse-rate, whereas in other circumstances it may be a sign of embarrassment, recent strenuous exercise, or over-indulgence in alcohol. While there are a few signs that are nearly always associated with either relatively healthy or relatively disturbed personalities the precise significance of any sign can be stated only when its position in the whole set of responses is considered (Klopfer and Kelley, 1946, pp. 16–20; Mons, 1947, p. 56).

A recent review of the application of statistical methods to Rorschach results (Cronbach, 1949) has pointed out that the techniques of the type used by Reichard are not applicable to results of this kind, and it must therefore be assumed that her results prove nothing. Unfortunately, insufficient details are given in her article to enable the data to be re-calculated by more reliable methods. This is regrettable, as under the circumstances her conclusions are of little value for comparative purposes. The fact, for example, that her six signs have no significance in distinguishing between the tolerant and intolerant persons in the present record proves nothing either way.

In view of these considerations a detailed statistical study of the various kinds of responses obtained from the subjects of the present research was attempted without much expectation of significant findings. The greater part of this appendix will be devoted to a brief account of the personality of each subject as shown by the test record. An attempt will then be made to assess the extent to which these results supply evidence relating to the hypotheses under study. Some use will be made of statistical procedures in this connection.

THE ANTI-SEMITIC GROUP

B.6

R = 34. 6 M (1 additional); 6 FM; (2 additional K); 22 F; (1 additional C'); F = 65 per cent. A = 45 per cent. P = 6. O = 3. M : ΣC = 6 : 0. Last three cards = 41 per cent. W : M = 6 : 6. W = 17 per cent. D = 53 per cent. d = 17 per cent. Dd = 13 per cent.

Succession is orderly.

There is a tendency to perserveration (13 responses are human or animal faces); the frequency of small and rare detail is high (exceptionally high for this group); the quality of the responses throughout is low; the quality of F is very variable; W per cent is low and the quality of W is poor; there are frequent remarks about the cards, most of these refer to the intentions of the makers and tend to impute a rather malevolent outlook ("that's put in to trap you", "that's to throw you off the scent"—at the limit stage he said "I didn't take no notice of the colour. I thought they had put it in as a trap to try and fool you so I left it alone"—he studied the back of card II and commented critically on the foreign language); 8 responses refer to humans or animals that are "distorted", "grotesque", or "caricatured"; one human and two animal responses are "prehistoric"; M is high (very high for this group) but the quality is low (3 of the M responses are pseudo-human, one is a d and one a dd response, while the sixth has poor form). All this suggests schizophrenic trends with some paranoid reactions. There are, however, no markedly confabulatory, contaminated or Po responses (one response is a near Po) and the succession is orderly. There is, therefore, no reason to expect acute psychotic episodes.

There are numerous references to aggressive, attacking and violent male figures—two charging bulls, a bull's head, a bear, a man dressed as an ape, "a heavy animal—prehistoric type". Nearly all the other animal responses are dogs. There are only three references that can be interpreted as having any female associations, a woman's leg (card V where he missed the usual P), a woman's profile, and a peahen (he is very insistent that it is not a peacock). He seems to be, on the one hand obsessed with relationships to powerful masculine figures, and at the same time quite unable to deal with them. He either disguises them in some way or flies to consideration of some small part of the blot. In card III where he sees the usual men he calls them "caricatures of a couple of dudes", and then proceeds to break them up, seeing parts of their bodies as bull's heads, fishes, and trees.

C.7

R = 10. 1 M (1 additional); 2 FM (2 additional); 1 FK; 3 F (2 additional); 2 Fc; (1 additional c); (2 additional C'); 1 FC (1 additional).

F = 30 per cent. A = 30 per cent. P = 2. O = 4. M : ΣC = 1 : 0·5. Last 3 cards = 30 per cent. W : M = 9 : 1. W = 90 per cent. S = 10 per cent.

He displays a considerable flight from reality. Seven responses have definite confabulatory elements. This seems to be chiefly a consequence of a desperate striving for W responses and a determination to take the blots literally. This is best seen in Card VIII where he starts with the bottom orange Ds as sweet pea flowers, tries to bring the side Ds in as insects that are crawling on the flowers, but says they look like mice and finally leaves it undecided, then takes the rest of the blot as a pine tree that is grown as shelter for the sweet peas. In another blot (Card I) he contrives to see a building simultaneously from inside and outside.

In two cases (Cards III and VII) he produces a response chiefly by filling up the white space with the details of an imaginary face, a human face in Card III, apparently stimulated by the bow tie, a cat's face in Card VII, where the top Ds suggested the ears.

His only M ("two females side by side" in Card II) is poor. The figures are not clearly seen and are women only because they are wearing fur coats. He quickly turns this into FM with all the red removed.

This is obviously a very disturbed record. It is probable that the appearance of disturbance is somewhat exaggerated by low intelligence but even so, marked schizophrenic traits are clearly indicated.

Form level is low. There are several self references. The two non-existent faces which are said to be looking at him suggest paranoid trends but this is not conclusive. Several signs of castration anxiety.

*F.*14

R = 10; 2 m; 4 FM (3 additional); (1 additional Km); (2 additional F); 1 Fc (1 additional); (1 additional FC′); (1 additional C′F); 3 CF (1 additional); (1 additional C). F = 0 per cent. A = 60 per cent. P = 3. O = 2. M : ΣC = 2 : 3. Last 3 cards = 30 per cent. W : M = 9 : 2. W = 90 per cent. D = 10 per cent.

The most obvious feature of this record is the absence of F except in the form of additionals. This, combined with the comparatively uncontrolled colour responses and the behaviour of the subject in the test situation (he walked about the room, waved the cards and gesticulated), the rapid response rate (58 seconds is the average response rate) all suggest hypomania. In addition schizophrenia is suggested by his two confabulatory responses, several bizarre responses (e.g. in Card X "a canary with a weasel in its beak" with both the canary and the weasel having colour as the main determinants); frequent personal references including boasts that a man with his experience would do this better than average; the varied form level. He has a marked striving after W (e.g. Card III "Two waiters with a butterfly flying between").

The general impression is of an uncontrolled, excitable man with a strong desire to impress, but no ability to concentrate, and with marked schizophrenic tendencies. The possibility of his deteriorating cannot be ruled out. Low average intelligence.

G.2

R = 23. 3 M; 9 FM (1 additional); 2 m; (2 additional K); 1 FK; 8 F (2 additional); (1 additional Fc); (1 additional C′). F = 32 per cent. A = 65 per cent. P = 5. O = 3. M : ΣC = 3 : 0. Last 3 cards = 36 per cent. W : M = 9 : 3. W = 36 per cent. D = 59 per cent. Dd = 5 per cent. Succession orderly.

With the exception of two additionals, all responses are on the left hand side of the graph indicating a failure to accept and utilise his emotions. He criticised the cards continually, complained about their inaccuracies and deficiencies and the difficulties of seeing things in them, though he claimed to be able to see things much better in the regular patterns on wallpaper. He also tended to frame his responses as questions as if unable to make up his mind definitely. There are some indications of psychotic tendencies (1) two bizarre responses, (2) a near Po response, (3) some degree of stereotype, (4) frequent responses referring to faces looking out of the blots. He turned one of the cards over and studied the back. His criticisms and desires for perfection and regularity suggest an obsessional character, in spite of the rather low F per cent. The psychotic signs are not conclusive and are perhaps best regarded as indications of confusion and of the strong projective, or near-paranoid, traits commonly found in obsessionals. His intelligence is probably at least average but his personality difficulties would prevent him from making full use of it. The level of repression is fairly high.

O.2

R = 6. 1 M; 1 FM (1 additional); (1 additional K); 1 FK; 3 F; (1 additional CF); Cards III, IV, VI, and VII rejected. F = 50 per cent. A = 33 per cent. P = 3. O = 1. M : ΣC = 1 : 0. Last 3 cards = 50 per cent. W : M = 5 : 1. W = 83 per cent. D = 17 per cent.

Obviously a very disturbed record with the rejections as its most conspicuous feature. The responses are too few in number to analyse in much detail.

Very great disturbance over male sexuality, especially homosexuality, is strongly indicated. Nearly all the usually phallic symbols are indicated with the remark that they are to be "obliterated" or are "gruesome". The first rejection is Card III with the usual response of two men. Even when pointed out to him he could see these only with great difficulty. Card IV with its phallic symbol is rejected—later, with help from the tester he saw it as a fur skin. Card VI (again a phallic symbol) is rejected as is Card VII. Card VI was seen at the limit stage as a skin. Card VII remained unacceptable —he could not see the usual figures. In Card V he missed the usual popular (when it was pointed out at the limit stage he suggested a tropical butterfly—"because of the two tails"). In the original response to Card V he saw the usual wings as a boy and a girl lying head to head with folded arms and with something, he didn't know what (the usual body of the bat) between them. Card X is a near rejection, the response being "drawings out of an imaginative mind —gruesome". His main reference in the inquiry is to the top black D which he describes as gruesome. It is "doodling such as a child might do". He cannot see the usual Ps even when pointed out.

Q.7

R = 36. 1 M; 20 FM; 4 Fm; (1 additional K); 10 F; (1 additional C'). F = 31 per cent. A = 70 per cent. P = 9. O = 4. M : ΣC = 1 : 0. Last 3 cards = 31 per cent. W : M = 11 : 1. W = 31 per cent. D = 61 per cent. d = 6 per cent. S = 2 per cent. Succession is orderly.

An extremely introversive character with a high degree of repression. No expression of any emotional reaction to his environment. The record is full of symbols of anxiety at mysterious and cruel powers in the form of various birds and animals of prey (eagles, tigers, lions, bears), an explosion, a bomber, a soldier (his only M), a volcano and a dragon. He shows very marked colour shock. There are signs of homosexual tendencies, and indications of paranoid trends, but these are not conclusive. On the whole the indications are for a very anxious, and rather obsessional man, with the latent homosexual and paranoid tendencies often associated with obsessional characters. Intelligence slightly below average.

S.11

R = 24. 2 M; 7 FM; 2 m; 2 k; (3 additional K); 9 F; (1 additional Fc); 1 FC'; (1 additional C'); 1 FC. F = 37 per cent. A = 50 per cent. P = 7. O = 1. M : ΣC = 2 : 0·5. Last 3 cards = 33 per cent.

W : M = 7 : 2. W = 29 per cent. D = 67 per cent. d = 4 per cent.
Succession is orderly.

Throughout the record he makes frequent comments and qualifications to indicate that he does not regard the blots as perfect pictures. He describes his responses in great detail, and debates with himself about the species of animals seen. While not completely incapable of emotional response the record is markedly introversive, and indicates a good deal of repression and anxiety. The anxiety is associated chiefly with human relationships (both his M's are cartoon characters and he sees the usual men in Card III as cartoons of birds) and to a lesser extent with sex and vague dangers. His intelligence is slightly above average. An anxious and rather obsessional man.

A.2   THE TOLERANT GROUP

R = 24. 2 M; 5 FM (1 additional); (1 additional M); (1 additional K); (3 additional FK); 7 F (1 additional); 3 Fc; 1 C'; 5 FC (1 additional); 1 CF (2 additional); (1 additional C). F = 30 per cent. A = 42 per cent. P = 5. O = 4. M : ΣC = 2 : 2·5. Last 3 cards = 38 per cent. W : M = 18 : 2. W = 75 per cent. D = 25 per cent. Succession is orderly.

On the whole a healthy normal record. There are indications of a personality which is fairly well controlled but not unduly constricted. Also signs of insight and tact, though also indications of immaturity in the high FM and low M. On the other hand the F level is generally high, form is well seen and clearly described. Some indications (notably the additional pure colour response, and some difficulties with the last three cards, especially Card IX), are present to suggest that emotional reactions to external stimuli are not always under complete control. There are definite signs of latent homosexuality and this appears to be the chief source of difficulty, but he shows signs of being able to make a good recovery, e.g. after difficulties with Card III (including the additional C response) he produced two good W's for card IV—there are similar recoveries in Cards VII and X. There are signs of ambition in his striving after W. Intelligence rather above average.

C.2

R = 17. 7 FM; 9 F; 1 Fc (1 additional). F = 47 per cent. A = 89 per cent. P = 2. O = 3. M : ΣC = 0 : 0. Last 3 cards = 41 per cent. W : M = 0 : 0. D = 76 per cent. d = 18 per cent. Dd = 6 per cent.

A depressive record. The small number of responses, high A per cent, the absence of W, of M, and of colour responses all indicate this. The number of FM and the Fc responses and the marked shading shock indicate a neurotic rather than a psychotic depression. Form level is very variable but mainly good. The content includes no sign of psychotic reactions. It is interesting that apart from this, most of the content of his record is similar to B.6. He shows the same preoccupation with aggressive masculine figures in the shape of wild animals but his handling of the problem is obviously very different—he tends to avoid close human relationships. Also these animals are much more clearly seen and described than in the case of B.6. The constricted nature of the record makes it difficult to assess in detail. Intelligence is probably average, but his emotional difficulties prevent it being fully used.

*E.*8

R = 19. 3 M; 7 FM; 1 K; (3 additional K); 1 FK (1 additional); 3 F; (3 additional Fc); 1 FC′; 1 FC; 2 CF (1 additional). F = 16 per cent. A = 48 per cent. P = 6. O = 2. M : ΣC = 3 : 2·5. Last 3 cards = 42 per cent. W : M = 12 : 3. W = 64 per cent. D = 26 per cent. S = 10 per cent.

The graph shows a fairly strong, relatively uncontrolled personality who is deeply influenced by environmental factors and reacts strongly to them. On the other hand there are signs of personal insight and ability to make tactful and sympathetic contact with other people, and some indications of good social adjustment, though this is rather overshadowed by the signs of strong reaction to the environment. The content suggests a higher degree of control than the graph—most of his responses are well seen and carefully described, though he has difficulty with Cards VI and IX. The position would seem to be that under normal circumstances he can cope satisfactorily with his environment and his fellow-men, but that he could fairly easily be disturbed or provoked into a fairly violent action which might make him somewhat unpredictable in his social relationships. There are definite signs of anxiety not necessarily attached to any particular object and also of anxiety associated with sex. Intelligence appears to be average.

*F.*13

R = 15. 3 FM; 2 m (1 additional); 2 K; 5 F; 1 Fc (1 additional); 2 FC (1 additional); 1 CF. F = 33 per cent. A = 33 per cent. P = 5.

O $=$ 1. M : ΣC $=$ 0 : 2. Last 3 cards $=$ 27 per cent. W : M $=$ 14 : 0.
W $=$ 93 per cent. D $=$ 7 per cent.

A very difficult record to summarise briefly as there are a number of apparently conflicting signs. He is a very anxious man with a high degree of repression and considerable difficulties over human relationships. He seems to have an extremely ambivalent attitude towards women, alternating between admiration and aggression, which he shows by describing various articles of feminine adornment and then finding that they have serious imperfections. Ambivalence is one of his major characteristics, e.g.—Card II is seen first as two animals fighting and then as two animals dancing together. The phallic symbols of Cards IV, V, and VI are associated with a bear, a bird of prey and a torpedo, suggesting that he sees masculine sexuality as violent and aggressive.

He seems, at considerable cost in repression, to be maintaining a somewhat precarious balance internally. His external relationships, in view of this, are surprisingly good. Given a situation which is fairly predictable and where he has time for adjustment he can probably function quite well. He might easily break down under stress.

He finds it difficult to concentrate on details and tends to escape into a vaguely ambitious phantasy life. His intelligence is average but he is probably too inhibited to make full use of it.

G.5

R $=$ 12. 2 M; 4 FM; (1 additional Fm); (1 additional K); 5 F (2 additional); 1 Fc (2 additional); (1 additional for each of cF, FC′, F/C and CF). F $=$ 42 per cent. A $=$ 67 per cent. P $=$ 7. O $=$ 1. M : ΣC $=$ 2 : 0. Last 3 cards $=$ 50 per cent W : M $=$ 7 : 2. W $=$ 58 per cent. D $=$ 42 per cent.

A slightly unusual record in that the additional responses amount to nearly half the entire record and because of their number and position have to be taken into account more than is usually the case. From the main responses only we get a picture of a slightly rigid, or mildly obsessional personality, with a rather poor emotional life. He seems to show signs of repression or severe inhibition not so much through the use of m as through the transformation of some of the usual FM to F in the shape of insects in museums. He is definitely below average intelligence. There are signs of depressive trends in the content. He shows anxiety at a number of points, first at Card IV which he rejects though he gives a rather poor response (a patch of moss in a pool) at the inquiry. He shows considerable colour shock in Card VIII but recovers to give a poor response. The shock carries over to Card IX but by Card X he has recovered to give three populars and quite a good M. Some of the apparently poor responses may be due to low intelligence as well as to anxiety. The record suggests a rather anxious man who can adjust to circumstances though not very rapidly. Probably not an easy mixer but able to make good relationships if given time.

H.3

R = 11. 5 FM; (1 additional FK); 2 F; 2 Fc; (1 additional c); (1 additional C'); 1 FC; 1CF. F = 18 per cent. A = 72 per cent. P = 4. O = 2. M : ΣC = 0 : 1·5. Last 3 cards = 27 per cent. W : M = 8 : 0. W = 82 per cent. D = 18 per cent.

A very sparse record and not easy to assess. The F per cent, though low, is adequate, especially when supported by the Fc and additional FK responses. He obviously has difficulties with human relationships though the absence of M may be in part due to rather low intelligence. The high W suggests a rather over-ambitious approach; his comments during the test suggest this is combined with marked feelings of inferiority. There are signs of considerable anxiety associated with sex. He begins with a very anxious response with a castration theme but recovers with a good FM in Card II and thereafter shows no gross anxieties.

N.1

R = 27. 4 M; 7 FM; (1 additional M); 10 F; 2 Fc; 1 FC'; 3 FC (1 additional). F = 37 per cent. A = 30 per cent P = 8. O = 6. M : ΣC = 4 : 1·5. Last 3 cards = 37 per cent. W : M = 10 : 4. W = 37 per cent. D = 63 per cent.

With the possible exception of A.2 this is the most healthy record of the entire group. The F per cent is adequate for good control but avoids rigidity. The colour and texture responses suggest a good sensitive adjustment to the social environment. The M column is rather low in relation to the FM which is quite high but this appears to be normal for this group, and is probably a function of the intellectual level and educational background. His intelligence is above average. His poorest responses, including one F, appear in Cards IV and VI, suggesting some anxiety in connection with the sexual symbolism, but this is well within normal limits.

When these records are considered as a whole certain rather striking conclusions emerge. The first is that the anti-Semitic group does not contain a single individual who can be regarded as normal. Three of the records show clear psychotic tendencies, while four have various neurotic disturbances.

The tolerant group on the other hand includes no case with clear indications of psychotic trends and the neurotic signs are on the whole less frequent than in the intolerant records, though there is clearly not a simple division between the "normal" and the "neurotic" as far as the two groups are concerned. The most disturbed tolerant record is that of a case of depression.

The second conclusion is that when the scores for each group on individual scoring categories are compared we find that most of the differences are not significant. This statement needs some qualification, however. In the first place, as indicated earlier, single scoring categories have only a very limited value; certain signs are nearly always associated with good adjustment and mental health, others with the opposite, but the pattern of the responses is much more important, and therefore the fact that the individual scores do not show significant difference does not destroy the value of the results obtained.

In the second place it should be noted that some of the differences obtained are proportionately very large; for example, the tolerant group produced six times as many FC responses and more than three times as many Fc responses as the anti-Semitic group; these in turn produced nearly five times as many human responses, four times as many m responses, nearly three times as many F– responses and nearly twice as many small and rare detail responses as the tolerant subjects. It is therefore possible that the absence of significance in the case of some of these categories is due entirely to the small size of the groups and that, given larger samples, differences of the same order would be found and would achieve significance.

In general it is found that FC responses are associated with good social adjustment, Fc with sensitivity and tact, m with repression. The significance of small and rare detail responses varies considerably from one record to another according to the relationship with other scores, and the same is true of the H and F– responses, though the latter are always a sign of some kind of maladjustment or of low intelligence. One can therefore say that the results obtained from these records are consistent with the proposition that anti-Semitic individuals are less well adjusted socially, less sensitive and tactful in their human relationships, and more repressed than tolerant persons, but that pending further research with large samples it is not possible to do more than put this proposition forward as a hypothesis that is sufficiently strongly supported to warrant further testing.

When these signs showing the greatest differences between the two groups are tested according to the methods advocated by Cronbach (1949) two of them are found to be significant.[1] These are the scores for FC and for texture responses (Fc), both of which are significant at the 0·05 level ($X^2 = 3·8$ and 4·6 respectively). In spite of this significance the result must be accepted with caution because of the small size of the group.

[1] This method consists of pooling the two groups of scores, placing them in rank order, dividing the group at the median, placing the results in a 2 × 2 table and testing for significance by X^2.

Bibliography

ACKERMAN, NATHAN W., and JAHODA, MARIE. *Anti-Semitism and Emotional Disorder*. New York, Harper, 1950.

ADLER, E. N. *A History of the Jews in London*. Philadelphia, Jewish Publication Society of America, 1930.

ADORNO, T. W., FRENKEL-BRUNSWIK, ELSE, LEVINSON, D. J., and SANFORD, R. NEVITT. *The Authoritarian Personality*. New York, Harper, 1950.

ALLGOOD, HENRY G. C. *A History of Bethnal Green from the Earliest Times to 1680*. London, East London Advertiser, 1905.

ALLPORT, GORDON W., and KRAMER, BERNARD M. "Some Roots of Prejudice," *Journal of Psychology*, 22, 1946, 9–39.

ANON. *The History of the London Burkers*. London, Kelly, 1832.

ANON. "Anti-Semitism in the Soviet Union," *The Economist*, CLVII, 1949, 1011–1012.

AVES, ERNEST. "The Trades of East London Connected with Poverty," *Life and Labour in London*, edited by Charles Booth, First Series, Vol. IV. London, Macmillan, 1902.

AXLINE, VIRGINIA M. "Play Therapy and Race Conflict in Young Children," *Journal of Abnormal and Social Psychology*, 43, 1948, 300–310.

BEAGLEHOLE, ERNEST. "Character Structure," *Psychiatry*, 7, 1944, 145–162.

BEAGLEHOLE, ERNEST and PEARL. *Some Modern Maoris*. Wellington, New Zealand Council for Educational Research, 1946.

BESANT, WALTER. *East London*. London, Chatto and Windus, 1899.

BETTELHEIM, BRUNO. "The Dynamism of Anti-Semitism in Gentile and Jew," *Journal of Abnormal and Social Psychology*, 42, 1947, 153–168.

BETTELHEIM, BRUNO. "Review of *Essays on Anti-Semitism*, edited by K. S. Pinson," *American Journal of Sociology*, 54, 1948, 273–274.

BETTELHEIM, BRUNO, and JANOWITZ, MORRIS. *Dynamics of Prejudice*. New York, Harper, 1950.

BOGARDUS, EMORY S. *Immigration and Race Attitudes*. Boston, Heath, 1928.

BOOTH, CHARLES (ed.). *Life and Labour of the People of London*. London, Macmillan, 1902.

BOWLBY, JOHN. "The Study and Reduction of Group Tensions in the Family," *Human Relations*, II, 1949, 123–8.

BROWN, F. J. "The Origins of the Anti-Semitic Attitude," *Jews in a Gentile World*, edited by I. Graeber and S. H. Britt. New York, Macmillan, 1942.

BUREAU OF APPLIED SOCIAL RESEARCH. *Training Guide on Sampling*. Mimeographed, Columbia University, 1948.

BURMA, JOHN H. "Race Relations and Antidiscriminatory Legislation," *American Journal of Sociology*, 56, 1951, 416–423.

CAMPBELL, A. A. "Factors Associated with Attitudes towards Jews," in *Readings in Social Psychology*, edited by T. M. Newcomb and E. L. Hartley. New York, Holt, 1947.

COCH, LESTER, and FRENCH, JOHN R. P. "Overcoming Resistance to Change," *Human Relations*, I, 1948, 512–532.

COLLIS, ARTHUR T., and POOLE, VERA E. *These Our Children*. London, Gollancz, 1950.

COMMITTEE ON THE LAW OF DEFAMATION. *Report of the Committee on the Law of Defamation*. Cmnd. 7936. London, H.M.S.O., 1948.

COOK, C. T. "The Evangelical Attitude," *Gentile and Jew*, edited by Chaim Newman. London, Alliance Press, 1945.

COOPER, EUNICE, and JAHODA, MARIE. "The Evasion of Propaganda," *Journal of Psychology*, 23, 1947, 15–25.

COUNCIL OF THE METROPOLITAN BOROUGH OF BETHNAL GREEN. *Bethnal Green: The Official Handbook*. London, Burrow.

CRONBACH, LEE J. "Statistical Methods Applied to Rorschach Scores," *Psychological Bulletin*, 46, 1949, 393–429.

CURLE, ADAM, and TRIST, E. L. "Transitional Communities and Social Reconnection: A Follow-up Study of the Civil Resettlement of British Prisoners of War, II," *Human Relations*, I, 1947, 240–292.

DARKE, C. H. *The Communist Technique in Britain*. London, Penguin Books, 1952.

DOLLARD, JOHN. *Criteria for a Life History*. Newhaven, Yale University Press, 1935.

DOLLARD, JOHN. *Cast and Class in a Southern Town*. Newhaven, Yale University Press, 1937.

DOLLARD, JOHN. "Contribution to a Symposium on Culture and Personality," *American Journal of Orthopsychiatry*, 8, 1938, 41.

DOLLARD, JOHN, DOOB, L. W., MILLER, N. E., MOWRER, O. H., and SEARS, R. R. *Frustration and Aggression*. London, Routledge and Kegan Paul, 1946.

DUNNE, LAURENCE R. *Report on an Inquiry into the Accident at Bethnal Green Tube Station on 3rd March, 1943*. London, H.M.S.O., 1945.

EYSENCK, H. J. "Primary Social Attitudes: I. The Organisation and Measurement of Social Attitudes," *International Journal of Opinion and Attitude Research*, I, 1947, 49–84.

EYSENCK, H. J. "The Psychology of Anti-Semitism," *The Nineteenth Century and After*, 144, 1948, 277–284.

EYSENCK, H. J. and CROWN, S. "An Experimental Study in Opinion-Attitude Methodology," *International Journal of Opinion and Attitude Research*, 3, 1949, 47–86.

FENICHEL, OTTO. *The Psychoanalytic Theory of Neurosis*. New York, Norton, 1945.

FENICHEL, OTTO. "Elements of a Psychoanalytic Theory of Anti-Semitism," *Anti-Semitism: A Social Disease*, edited by Ernest Simmel. New York, International Universities Press, 1946.

FISHER, R. A. *Statistical Methods for Research Workers*. Edinburgh, Oliver and Boyd, 1943.

FISHER, R. A., and YATES, F. *Statistical Tables for Biological, Agricultural, and Medical Research*. Edinburgh, Oliver and Boyd, 1949.

FRANKLYN, JULIAN. *The Cockney*. London, Andre Deutsch, 1953.

FRENKEL-BRUNSWIK, ELSE. "A Study of Prejudice in Children," *Human Relations*, I, 3, 1948, 295–306.

FRENKEL-BRUNSWIK, ELSE. "Dynamic and Cognitive Categorisation of Qualitative Material," *Journal of Psychology*, 25, 1948, 253–277.

FRENKEL-BRUNSWIK, ELSE. "Interaction of Psychological and Sociological Factors in Political Behaviour," *American Political Science Review*, XLVI, 1952, 44–65.

FRENKEL-BRUNSWIK, ELSE, and SANFORD, R. NEVITT. "Some Personality Factors in Anti-Semitism," *Journal of Psychology*, 20, 1945, 271–291.

FREUD, SIGMUND. *Civilisation and Its Discontents*. London, Hogarth Press, 1934.

FREUD, SIGMUND. *Inhibitions, Symptoms, and Anxiety*. London, Hogarth Press, 1936.

FREUD, SIGMUND. *Moses and Monotheism*. London, Hogarth Press, 1939.

GAVIN, HECTOR. *Sanitary Ramblings*. London, Churchill, 1848.

GEORGE, DOROTHY. *London Life in the Eighteenth Century*. London, London School of Economics, 1951.

GLASS, RUTH. "Social Aspects of Town Planning." *Architectural Review*, 1945.

GLASS, RUTH, and FRENKEL, MAUREEN. *A Profile of Bethnal Green*. (Mimeographed), London, The Association for Planning and Regional Reconstruction, 1946.

GLOVER, EDWARD. *War, Sadism, and Pacificism*. London, Allen and Unwin, 1946.

GOLDING, LOUIS. *The Jewish Problem*. London, Penguin Books, 1938.

GORER, GEOFFREY. "Themes in Japanese Culture," *Transactions of the New York Academy of Sciences*, Series II, 5, 1943, 106–124.

GRYGIER, TADEUSZ. *Oppression*. London, Routledge and Kegan Paul, 1954.

HAIMOWITZ, MORRIS L. and NATALIE R. "Reducing Ethnic Hostility Through Psychotherapy," *Journal of Social Psychology*, 31, 1950, 231–242.

HARDING, K. R., and HOOPER, H. J. *Report of Survey of the Boundary Street L.C.C. Estate, Bethnal Green*. (Mimeographed.) The London Council of Social Services, 1948.

HARRIS, CONSTANCE. *The Use of Leisure in Bethnal Green*. London, Lindsey Press, 1927.

HARTLEY, E. L. *Problems in Prejudice*. New York, King's Crown Press, 1946.

HERSKOVITS, M. J. *Man and His Works*. New York, Knopf, 1948.

HERZOG, HERTA. *Training Guide on the Technique of Qualitative Interviews*. (Mimeographed.) Bureau of Applied Social Research, Columbia University, 1948.

HINSIE, L. E., and SHATSKY, J. *Psychiatric Dictionary*. New York, Oxford University Press, 1940.

HORNEY, KAREN. *The Neurotic Personality of Our Time*. London, Routledge and Kegan Paul, 1937.

JAMES, H. E. O., and TENEN, C. "Attitudes Towards Other Peoples," *International Social Science Bulletin*, 3, 1951, 553–560.

JAQUES, ELLIOT. "Interpretive Group Discussion as a Method of Facilitating Social Change," *Human Relations*, I, 4, 1948, 553–549.

JAQUES, ELLIOT. *The Changing Culture of a Factory*. London, Tavistock Publications, Ltd., 1950.

JEPHCOTT, PEARL. *Girls Growing Up*. London, Faber, 1945.

JEPHCOTT, PEARL. *Rising Twenty*. London, Faber, 1948.

KARDINER, A. *The Individual and His Society*. New York, Columbia University Press, 1939.

KARDINER, A. *The Psychological Frontiers of Society*. New York, Columbia University Press, 1945.

KELNAR, JOHN. "Treatment of Interpersonal Relations in Groups," *The Journal of Social Issues*, III, 1947, 29–34.

KINSEY, A. C., POMEROY, W. B., and MARTIN, C. E. *The Sexual Behaviour of the Human Male*. London, Saunders, 1948.

KLOPFER, B., and KELLEY, D. M. *The Rorschach Technique*. New York, World Book Company, 1946.

KLUCKHOHN, CLIVE, and LEIGHTON, DOROTHEA. *The Navaho*. Cambridge (Mass.), Harvard University Press, 1946.

KLUCKHOHN, CLIVE, and MOWRER, O. H. "Culture and Personality: A Conceptual Scheme," *American Anthropoligst*, 46, 1944, 1–29.

KLUCKHOHN, CLIVE, and MURRAY, H. A. (eds). *Personality in Nature, Society and Culture*. New York, Knopf, 1948.

KRECH, D., and CRUTCHFIELD, R. S. *Theory and Problems of Social Psychology*. New York, McGraw-Hill, 1948.

LASKER, BRUNO. *Race Attitudes in Children*. New York, Holt, 1929.

LAZARFELD, P. F., BERELSON, B., and GAUDET, H. *The People's Choice*. New York, Columbia University Press, 1948.

LEWIN, KURT. "Group Decision and Social Change," *Readings in Social Psychology*, edited by T. M. Newcomb and E. L. Hartley. New York, Holt, 1947.

LEWIN, KURT. "Frontiers in Group Dynamics, II," *Human Relations*, I, 2, 1947, 143–153.

LEWIN, KURT. *Resolving Social Conflicts*. New York, Harper, 1948.

LOEWENSTEIN, RUDOLPH M. *Christians and Jews*. New York, International Universities Press, 1951.

LOWY, SAMUEL. *Co-operation, Tolerance, and Prejudice*. London, Routledge and Kegan Paul, 1948.

LYND, ROBERT S. *Knowledge for What?* Princeton, Princeton University Press, 1946.

MANNHEIM, K. *Man and Society*. London, Routledge and Kegan Paul, 1940.

MARCUS, JACOB. "Defences Against Anti-Semitism," *Essays in Anti-Semitism*, edited by Koppel S. Pinson. New York, Conference on Jewish Relations, 1946.

MASLOW, A. H. "Deprivation, Threat, and Frustration," *Psychological Review*, 48, 1941, 364–6.

MERTON, ROBERT K. "The Self-Fulfilling Prophecy," *Social Theory and Social Structure*. Glencoe, Free Press, 1949, 179–195.

MERTON, ROBERT K., and KENDALL, PATRICIA L. "The Focused Interview," *American Journal of Sociology*, 51, 1946, 541–557.

MILLER, NEAL E., et al. "The Frustration-Aggression Hypothesis," *Psychological Review*, 48, 1941, 337–342.

MILLER, NEAL E., and DOLLARD, JOHN. *Social Learning and Imitation*. London, Routledge and Kegan Paul, 1945.

MODDER, MONTAGU F. *The Jew in the Literature of England*. Philadelphia, The Jewish Publication Society of America, 1944.

MONEY, JOHN. "Unanimity in the Social Sciences, with Reference to Epistemology, Ontology, and Scientific Method," *Psychiatry*, 12, 1949, 211–222.

MONS, W. *Principles and Practice of the Rorschach Personality Test*. London, Faber and Faber, 1947.

MORRISON, ARTHUR. *A Child of the Jago*. London, Penguin Books, 1946.

MYRDAL, GUNNAR. *An American Dilemma*. New York, Harper, 1944.

NEWCOMB, THEODORE M. "Autistic Hostility and Social Reality," *Human Relations*, I, 1, 1947, 69–86.

PANETH, MARIE. *Branch Street*. London, Allen and Unwin, 1947.

PARKES, JAMES. *An Enemy of the People*. London, Penguin Books, 1945.

PARKES, JAMES. *The Emergence of the Jewish Problem, 1878–1939*. London, Oxford University Press, 1946.

PARSONS, TALCOTT. "The Sociology of Modern Anti-Semitism," *Jews in a Gentile World*, edited by I. Graeber and S. H. Britt. New York, Macmillan, 1942.

PARSONS, TALCOTT. *The Social System*. London, Tavistock Publications, Ltd., 1952.

PINSON, KOPPEL S. (ed.). *Essays on Anti-Semitism*. New York, Conference on Jewish Relations, 1946.

PINSON, KOPPEL S. "Anti-Semitism," *Encyclopedia Britannica*, 1947, II, 78.

POTTER, BEATRICE. "The Jewish Community," *Life and Labour in London*, edited by Charles Booth, First Series, Vol. III. London, Macmillan, 1902.

REICHARD, SUZANNE. "Rorschach Study of Prejudiced Personality," *American Journal of Orthopsychiatry*, 18, 1948, 280–6.

REICHMANN, EVA G. *Hostages of Civilisation*. London, Gollancz, 1950.

RENNAP, I. *Anti-Semitism and the Jewish Question*. London, Lawrence and Wishart, 1942.

ROBB, J. H. "The Concept of National Character and Some Tentative Applications of this Concept to New Zealand," Unpublished thesis, Victoria University College Library, 1946.

ROBB, J. H. "The Contribution of Psychopathology to Sociology," *Sociological Review*, 44, 1952, 53–72.

ROETHLISBERGER, F. J., and DICKSON, W. J. *Management and the Worker*. Cambridge (Mass.), Harvard University Press, 1939.

ROKEACH, MILTON. "Generalised Mental Rigidity as a Factor in Ethnocentrism," *Journal of Abnormal and Social Psychology*, 43, 1948, 259–278.

ROSE, ARNOLD and CAROLINE. *America Divided*. New York, Knopf, 1948.

ROSE, LIONEL S. (ed). *Fascism in Britain*. Factual Survey No. 1. London, 1948.

ROSE, LIONEL S. (ed). *Survey of Open-Air Meetings Held by Pro-Fascist Organisations, April–October, 1947*. Factual Survey No. 2. London, 1948.

ROSE, LIONEL S. (ed). *Fascist and Anti-Semitic Activities and the Law*. Factual Survey No. 3. London, 1948.

RUSSELL, C., and LEWIS, H. S. *The Jew in London*. London, Unwin, 1900.

SABIN, A. K. *The Silk Weavers of Spitalfields and Bethnal Green*. London, Board of Education, 1931.

SAENGER, G., and GORDON, N. S. "The Influence of Discrimination on Minority Group Members in its Relation to Attempts to Combat Discrimination," *Journal of Social Psychology*, 31, 1950, 95–120.

SAMUEL, MAURICE. *The Great Hatred*. London, Gollancz, 1940.

SARTRE, JEAN-PAUL. *Portrait of the Anti-Semite*. Translated by Erik de Mauney. London, Secker and Warburg, 1948.

SELF, P. J. O. "Voluntary Organisations in Bethnal Green," *Voluntary Social Services*, edited by A. F. C. Bourdillon. London, Methuen, 1945.

SHEATSLEY, PAUL B. "Public Relations of the Polls," *International Journal of Opinion and Attitude Research*, 2, 1948, 461–465.

SHILS, EDWARD A. and JANOWITZ, MORRIS. "Cohesion and Disintegration in the Wehrmacht in World War II," *Public Opinion Quarterly*, 12, 1948, 280–315.

SLAWSON, JOHN. *Scientific Research on Anti-Semitism.* (Mimeographed) American Jewish Committee, 1944.

SMITH, H. LLEWELLYN. "Influx of Population (East London)," *Life and Labour in London,* edited by Charles Booth, First Series, Vol. III. London, Macmillan, 1902.

SMITH, H. LLEWELLYN. (ed.) *The New Survey of London Life and Labour.* London, King, 1931.

SMITH, H. LLEWELLYN. *A History of East London.* London, Methuen, 1939.

SPINLEY, B. M. *The Deprived and the Privileged.* London, Routledge and Kegan Paul, 1953.

SULLIVAN, H. S. "Basic Conceptions of Modern Psychiatry," *Psychiatry,* 3, 1940, 1–117.

SULLIVAN, H. S. "The Meaning of Anxiety in Psychiatry and Life," *Psychiatry,* 11, 1948, 1–14.

THORNBURY, WALTER. *Old and New London,* Vol. II. London, Cassell.

TRESSALL, ROBERT. "The Ragged-Trousered Philanthropists." London, Penguin Books, 1940.

TRIST, E. L. "Co-ordinated Social Researches in a Scottish Area: V. The Functional Penetration of a Social Field," *British Association for the Advancement of Science,* Blackpool Meeting (Section J), 1936.

TRIST, E. L., and BAMFORTH, K. W. "Some Social and Psychological Consequences of the Longwall Method of Coal-Getting," *Human Relations,* IV, 1, 1951, 1–38.

TRORY, ERNIE. *New Foundations,* Brighton, Crabtree Press, 1946.

URWICK, L. "Elton Mayo (1880–1949)," *British Management Review,* 8, 1950, 21–2.

VALE, GEORGE F. *Old Bethnal Green.* London, Blythenhale Press, 1934.

VALENTINE, HUGO. *Anti-Semitism Historically and Critically Examined,* Translated by A. G. Chater. London, Gollancz, 1936.

WALLIN, PAUL. "The Prediction of Individual Behaviour from Case Studies," *The Prediction of Personal Adjustment,* edited by Paul Horst. New York, Social Science Research Council, 1941.

WATSON, JEANNE. "Some Social and Psychological Situations Related to Change in Attitude," *Human Relations,* III, 1, 1950, 15–56.

WEINRYB, BERNARD D. "The Economic and Social Background of Modern Anti-Semitism," *Essays in Anti-Semitism,* edited by Koppel S. Pinson. New York, Conference on Jewish Relations, 1946.

WELTFISH, GENE, and LIPPITT, RONALD. "Further Remarks on the Re-education of Racial and Religious Prejudice," *Journal of Social Issues,* I, 1945, 49–54.

WILLIAMS, ROBIN M., Jr. *The Reduction of Intergroup Tensions.* New York, Social Science Research Council, 1947.

WILSON, A. T. M. "Some Reflections and Suggestions on the Prevention and Treatment of Marital Problems," *Human Relations,* II, 3, 1949, 233–252.

YATES, FRANK. *Sampling Methods for Censuses and Surveys.* London, Griffin, 1949.

YOUNG, PAULINE V. *Interviewing in Social Work.* New York, McGraw-Hill, 1935.

ZILBOORG, GREGORY. *Mind, Medicine, and Man.* New York, Harcourt Brace, 1943.

ZWEIG, F. *Labour, Life, and Poverty.* London, Gollancz, 1948.

ZWEIG, F. *The British Worker.* London, Penguin Books, 1952.

INDEX